Modern Fortran

Style and Usage

Fortran is one of the oldest high-level languages and remains the premier language for writing code for science and engineering applications. *Modern Fortran: Style and Usage* is a book for anyone who uses Fortran, from the novice learner to the advanced expert. It describes best practices for programmers, scientists, engineers, computer scientists, and researchers who want to apply good style and incorporate rigorous usage in their own Fortran code or to establish guidelines for a team project. The presentation concentrates primarily on the characteristics of Fortran 2003, while also describing methods in Fortran 90/95 and valuable new features in Fortran 2008.

The authors draw on more than a half century of experience writing production Fortran code to present clear succinct guidelines on formatting, naming, documenting, programming, and packaging conventions and various programming paradigms such as parallel processing (including OpenMP, MPI, and coarrays), OOP, generic programming, and C language interoperability. Programmers working with legacy code will especially appreciate the section on updating old programs.

Norman S. Clerman is currently a private consultant. He was formerly the Chief Computer Scientist at Opcon Design Associates, LLC, a small company engaged in lens design.

Walter Spector has been employed by Silicon Graphics International's Professional Services organization (formerly Cray Research Inc.) since 1984.

PRELIMINARY REPORT

Programming Research Group
Applied Science Division
International Business Machines Corporation

November 10, 1954

Specifications for

The IBM Mathematical FORmula TRANslating System,

FORTRAN

Modern Fortran

Style and Usage

Norman S. Clerman
Walter Spector

Silicon Graphics, Inc., Fremont, California

CAMBRIDGE
UNIVERSITY PRESS

CAMBRIDGE
UNIVERSITY PRESS

University Printing House, Cambridge CB2 8BS, United Kingdom

One Liberty Plaza, 20th Floor, New York, NY 10006, USA

477 Williamstown Road, Port Melbourne, VIC 3207, Australia

4843/24, 2nd Floor, Ansari Road, Daryaganj, Delhi - 110002, India

79 Anson Road, #06-04/06, Singapore 079906

Cambridge University Press is part of the University of Cambridge.

It furthers the University's mission by disseminating knowledge in the pursuit of education, learning and research at the highest international levels of excellence.

www.cambridge.org
Information on this title: www.cambridge.org/9780521730525

© Norman S. Clerman and Walter Spector 2012

First published 2012

A catalogue record for this publication is available from the British Library

Library of Congress Cataloging in Publication data
Clerman, Norman S., 1946–
Modern Fortran : style and usage / Norman S. Clerman, Walter Spector.
    p.   cm.
Includes bibliographical references and index.
ISBN 978-0-521-51453-8 (hardback)
1. FORTRAN (Computer program language)   I. Spector, Walter, 1956–   II. Title.
QA76.73.F25C56   2012
005.13'3 – dc23   2011026625

ISBN   978-0-521-51453-8   Hardback
ISBN   978-0-521-73052-5   Paperback

To Miriam for all her love and endless encouragement.
Norman S. Clerman

To Irene, Nyssa, Simon, and Sammy with love.
Walter Spector

Contents

Source Code Listings

Preface

Audience

We wrote this book for anyone who writes programs using Fortran. We think it will be useful for the following categories of programmers:

- Those who are learning Fortran from scratch and want to start on the right foot.
- Those who are familiar with pre-modern FORTRAN (up to FORTAN 77) and would like to learn some of the new concepts and techniques of modern Fortran (Fortran 90 to Fortran 2008).
- Those who have advanced knowledge of Fortran, have experimented with various styles, and are open to new ways to improve their programs.
- Those who have experience with other languages, who know the importance of good coding style and who want to apply it to their Fortran code.
- Those who want to create coding guidelines for teams of programmers, or establish a good style for a project.

General Considerations

The past four revisions of the Fortran Standard comprise alternating major and minor revisions, Fortran 90 and Fortran 2003 being the former, Fortran 95 and Fortran 2008 the latter. This book concentrates primarily on Fortran 2003. We present Fortran 90/95 methods and note where the techniques and methods of Fortran 2003 supercede them. Fortran 2008 capabilities are described, but to a lesser extent.

Each programmer will judge the importance of the new features of the language based on his or her experience and needs. The new C Interoperability may be very important to a programmer who often needs to build an application written in both languages. To another, the new object orientation may be more important, and for a third, the new parallel programming features in Fortran 2008 will be of great value.

This book is not a textbook, nor is it an exhaustive guide to the language. For those needs, in addition to the standard itself, we refer the reader to References [55] and [1], both with long publishing histories. This book is, instead, a book of guidelines, or rules, that a reader may want to adopt when writing code. We attempt to explain what we consider to be good coding techniques. Some of these are general – they apply to all languages – others are specific to Fortran. We concentrate on characteristics of the language, especially those of Fortran 2003, that we feel require careful and detailed explanation. Others we discuss only briefly or do not discuss at all. We have striven to write each guideline in a clear and succinct manner, brevity being a key goal. We advocate strict adherence to some of the rules. It serves no purpose, for example, not to include an **implicit none** statement in every program unit, and the advantages of doing so are enormous. Our approach to other rules, though, is more to suggest coding or style guidelines than to dictate them, and, in some instances, simply to offer alternatives. In each rule, we make frequent references to other rules, while at the same time trying to make each independent so the reader does not have to constantly jump from one to another. All the same, those guidelines that present new and somewhat complicated aspects of the language, by necessity, require more space. We have taken "typographical license" and somewhat violated our own formatting rules. For instance, we use more end-of-line comments than we recommend for your code.

The next section outlines the organization of the book, listing the subjects covered in each chapter. The earlier chapters cover basic topics that apply to all languages; the later chapters deal more specifically with Fortran. In the examples and the sample code, there is no natural progression from simple to more complex code. The assumption is that the reader is at least somewhat familiar with Fortran. The book contains code utilizing new language features that are explained later in the book. We believe that cross references to other sections and other rules will suffice to make these clear.

Organization

Chapter 1 defines the typographical conventions used throughout our book.

The next several chapters take a "top-down" approach to organizing and coding Fortran applications. Several design objectives that constitute goals for the writing of excellent code are presented in Chapter 2.

Chapter 3 discusses source form and layout. Chapter 4 is dedicated to the naming of various entities. Chapter 5 discusses comments and internal program documentation.

Chapter 6 begins to discuss specifics of using modules as a key to organizing code, the use of derived types, and organization of procedures and their argument lists. Chapter 7 discusses data in more detail, and control flow through procedures. Chapter 8 presents input/output (I/O). Chapter 9 provides more on the organization of modules and program units and their packaging in files. Its final section covers an important new Fortran 2008 feature for large programs – submodules. Submodules offer a solution to the well-known problem of "compilation cascades."

The remaining chapters are a potpourri of special topics.

Chapter 10 explains several techniques for writing generic code. Chapter 11 forms an introduction to object-oriented programming, a major feature of Fortran 2003.

Chapter 12 is an introduction to several forms of parallel processing that are commonly found in programs. Chapter 13 contains guidelines about the considerations the programmer must make when writing code that performs floating-point numerical operations. Chapter 14 is an introduction to C Interoperability.

The final chapter, Chapter 15, contains recommendations on updating programs that pre-date Fortran 90.

These serve as starting points for the interested programmer. Far more extensive and detailed references are available for most of the topics (References [1], [55], and [39]).

Appendix A contains the source code listing of programs Type_bound_demo and Unlimited_demo, two complete programs that are referenced from several different chapters in the book, and Appendix B collects all the rules in a list with the page reference to their location.

References to the Fortran Standard refer to Fortran 2003, unless otherwise specified (see Reference [39]).

1.

Introduction

1.1 Acknowledgments

The authors thank the Numerical Algorithms Group Ltd. (NAG) who provided us with copies of their excellent compiler with which we could test our code. In particular, thanks go to Mr. Malcolm Cohen, Mr. Rob Holmes, Mr. Ian Hounam, Mr. Rob Meyer, Mr. Mike Modica, and Mr. John Morrissey.

The Portland Group provided us with a copy of their compiler. Special thanks go to Ms. Laura Gibon for arranging that.

We thank Mr. Art Lazanoff for the use of his network server system for our CVS repository.

We thank Mr. Dan Nagle who offered vigorous criticism and some good suggestions.

The following persons read over the manuscript; to them we owe our gratitude: Dr. Greg Brown, Dr. Charles Crawford, Mr. Ryan O'Kuinghttons, and Dr. James Hlavka.

Thanks go to Ms. Stacy L. Castillo at the IBM Corporate Archives for arranging permission to use the material for the frontispiece.

It was a great pleasure to work with our editors at Cambridge University Press: Ms. Heather Bergman, Ms. Lauren Cowles and Mr. David Jou.

1.2 Typographical Conventions

The following typographical conventions are used in this book:

- medium-weight serif font – normal text
  This sentence is written in the font used for normal text.
- ***bold italicized serif font*** – rules
- medium-weight sans serif font – computer code
- **bold sans serif font** – Fortran keywords
  Examples are the words "**null**," "**associated**," and "**save**" in Rule 74. Note that the font for keywords and for names from the computer code is used in the body of the normal text, not just in the code segment.
- *medium-weight italicized serif font* – terms from the either the Fortran 2003 or the Fortran 2008 Standard, References [39] and [43]

In source code listings, points of ellipsis (...) are used to indicate missing code – nonessential code that is left out for brevity and clarity.

1.3 Source Code Listings

For the most part the code examples in the book are short sections of code. As such, they cannot be compiled. In some instances, however, complete programs are presented as numbered listings. In both cases, comments explaining the key points are embedded in the code and then referred to in the text. These are marked and numbered, in both places, by "*Cmnt-i:," where i is the comment number. Here, for example, is one such comment and the following two lines of code, and then the explanation referring to it in the text:

```
! *Cmnt-1: Check arguments for sanity
select case (direction)
case ('forward', 'FORWARD', 'reverse', 'REVERSE')
```

Using Rule 63, the first argument check (*Cmnt-1) can be entirely eliminated...

2.

General Principles

"The purpose of computing is not numbers. The purpose of computing is understanding."
– Hamming

1. *Write programs that are clear to both the reader and the compiler.*

The first and foremost general principle of programming is clarity. From clarity comes the ability to test, to reuse, and to audit. One simple test is whether you believe you will be able to understand the code if you come back to it a year later.

Of course, you write programs to have the computer calculate something for you. And you know that the computer must be told exactly what to compute. Your program must completely and correctly specify what is to be computed.

If you are making a numerical calculation, you likely have some consideration for the efficiency of your calculation. The best way to gain efficiency is to first choose an efficient algorithm and then to write simple, clear, and logical code to implement it. Compared with more complex code, it is easier to understand and easier for the compiler to optimize.

In addition to writing code for the computer, you are also writing code for humans, yourself included. The purpose of the calculations and the methods used to do so must be clear.

To achieve these goals, write code that is as simple as possible. Use white space to aid your eye in following the calculation specified by the source code. Comment what cannot be understood from the code itself. The rules in this book follow from these ideas. Using them will promote consistency of visual layout, documentation, programming logic, and the naming of program entities. This consistency, in turn, increases clarity; the program is clear to a programmer, whether he or she is familiar with it or not, or experienced or not. Moreover, for the programmer who is charged with learning and modifying it, a program written in a consistent manner reduces the time required to get "up to speed."

Ways to document a program are described in Chapter 5. The term "self-documenting" is often used to describe code that conveys its design without excessive commentary. The names of both variables and named constants should indicate what they represent. The algorithms used in the program should be familiar to anyone educated in the field for which the program has been written. We recommend the naming conventions in Chapter 4.

Clarity for the compiler is aided by simplicity and the use of language-defined structured constructs (e.g., rather than **go to** statements) to achieve program flow. Excessive branching, especially inside **do** loops, can often thwart optimization.

Avoid "cute tricks." They are often found in code that may conform to the standard, but take advantage of things like internal data representations, which are not standardized. These tricks have two problems: They obscure what you are trying to compute, from both the compiler and you, and they are very likely not portable, even among different compilers on the same hardware. Many uses of the intrinsic function **transfer** and bit manipulation intrinsic functions fall into this category.

A simple test for whether a program unit is clearly expressed is the Telephone Test (see Reference [45]). If the program can be read over the telephone, and completely understood by the listener, it is likely clear.

2. *Write programs that can be efficiently tested.*

A program must produce correct results when provided valid input. Key to this is to emphasize error detection and correction as early as possible in the development and testing process. The earlier a problem is detected, the less it costs to fix it.

Several techniques can be used to help produce quality code with reduced debugging times. First, when writing code, take advantage of modern features that allow the compiler to detect errors at compile time. Two key items for Fortran programmers are the use of **implicit none**, for avoiding typographical mistakes, and the use of modules for packaging and, doing so, ensuring interface checking. The use of these two features is highly recommended for all code.

Second, it is desirable to modularize and code individual algorithms into procedures in a way that they can be independently tested and verified. Testing procedures independent of the entire application is called "unit testing," and the individual tests are called "unit tests." Unit tests are a fundamental tool for validating a procedure (see Reference [47]).

To be easily unit tested, a procedure should use a minimal number of variables outside its local scope. A test driver can then be written to present the target procedure with different combinations of arguments, and compare the actual returned results with known good results.

Each test driver should indicate in some manner, for example in a log file, each of the tests it has run, and a PASS or FAIL flag. Simple scripts can then be written to run each of the unit test drivers, and to summarize the results.

Regressions, code that worked previously but, after some changes have been made, no longer does, can be quickly spotted and repaired.

A third aspect of reliability is the rejection of inputs that are invalid. For example, it is often possible to include non-time-consuming tests of the input arguments for validity, such as ensuring that arrays have compatible sizes. The routine can then return an error code back to the caller instead of producing incorrect results. This is discussed in more detail in Section 6.4. By returning an error code, instead of aborting, unit tests may be written to test for bad inputs, as well as good inputs.

Finally, once individual components of an application have been tested, tests on complete problems can be made to verify the application as a whole. Inputs representing typical end-user problems can be provided that produce known good results. Tests should encompass the full range of allowable inputs. Tests of numerical algorithms should include very large and small values; decision algorithms should be tested with as many combinations, such as true or false conditions, as practical. For numerical algorithms that will break down with very large arguments, such as computing $\cos(10^{10})$, the documentation should specify to what degree it has been tested and the results of the tests. As an application is developed and maintained, the test base provides a valuable feedback mechanism to look for regressions.

3. *Write programs that will scale to different problem sizes.*

Scalability is the property of a program to accommodate a wide range of problem sizes. In other words, a program should be able to handle small test cases using minimal computer resources, and, ideally, it should also be able to handle the largest problems that a given machine is capable of processing without changing any of the source code. Arrays and other data structures should be able to adjust themselves to any reasonable problem size. This can also result in greater efficiency through better use of cache memory.

Since Fortran 90, Fortran has supported various techniques – pointers, and allocatable variables, assumed shape and automatic arrays – for dynamically allocating memory based on problem size. These should be used instead of fixed dimensions wherever an array size may vary (instead of the earlier practice of hard-coding maximum sizes).

Scalability is also often used to describe how well a program takes advantage of multiple processors and the multiple cores of modern processors. Many schemes for executing portions of a code in parallel have been implemented by the Fortran community, including OpenMP and MPI. Section 12.2.2 covers OpenMP in more detail; Section 12.2.3 does the same for MPI. Fortran 2008 introduces the **do concurrent** variant of the **do** construct for shared memory parallelism (that is, all the processors share a common memory address space). It also introduces the coarray, which allows multiple copies of a program to run in both shared and distributed memory environments. These are covered in more detail in Section 12.3.

4. *Write code that can be reused.*

Human time is expensive. Computer hardware and software is cheap in comparison. It is therefore advantageous to write code in such a way that it can be reused in new applications and in new environments with minimal change.

Some well-known techniques that aid reuse include:

- Following the current Fortran standard. The standard is the contract between the compiler writer and the application developer. When nonstandard code is used, there are no guarantees that the code will run with future hardware or software.
- Maximizing the use of local variables. Generally, low-level procedures should both accept their inputs and return their results through the dummy argument list of subroutines and function return values. Use of variables outside the procedure's local scope often creates application-specific dependencies, which can limit reuse.
- Using derived types, and their type-bound procedures and procedure components. These allow code to be reused and even extended, using object-oriented techniques. Components within objects can be added, changed, or removed while limiting the scope of changes in existing code to places that actually use the changed components.

5. *Document all code changes, keeping a history of all code revisions.*

Auditability refers mostly to the commentary within the code and to its revision history. It is quite useful to understand how and why a particular area changed and to verify that the correct version of a routine is in use. In some environments, such as in organizations that need to conform to Sarbanes-Oxley standards (see Reference [68]), it is critical to maintain a revision history. It is also useful for a program to be able to indicate its own version to a user upon demand.

Source code control systems are very useful for inserting version numbers into source code on a per file basis. For example, in one such system, CVS (see Reference [16]), one can embed the string $Id: $ into a comment line in the source:

```
! File version:  $Id: $
```

The sentinel "Id" is a keyword. When CVS encounters it surrounded by dollar signs, it expands the line by adding a header when extracting the source file. The previous line would expand to something like:

```
! File version:  $Id: version_mod.f90,v 1.4 2009/02/02
! 02:55:10 wws Exp $
```

In addition, each change to the file via the source code control system allows the insertion of commentary describing the change. The text is maintained for future review.

A version numbering scheme should also be maintained for the program or library as a whole. Typically these version numbers will use digits separated by periods indicating major, minor, and bug-fix levels. A major release is one where the new features are of such significance that a shift in how a user uses the code may occur. A minor release may signify that features with little impact to existing use have been added and that a large number of bugs have been fixed. Sometimes developers release a very small number of changes purely to fix specific bugs that have been discovered since the previous major or minor releases.

A common convention is to allow a user to specify an option on the command line, such as -V or --version, that causes the program to print out its version. Programs might also print their version on one of the output files or on the screen. Note that programs can read arguments from the command line with the **get_command_argument** intrinsic procedure.

```
$ prog1—version
prog1 (Elements utilities) 3.1.4 $
```

Additionally, especially in the case of libraries that are used by a number of applications, it is useful to maintain a module variable within the library containing the version string. A module procedure can be written to return the string so that a caller can determine which version of the library is in use. Likewise, the CVS Id can be placed into a character string that can be extracted with tools such as the Unix strings command. By doing this you can ensure that the source file and the object file match.

```
! wws Exp $

module Version_mod
  implicit none
  private
  public :: Check_version_option, Get_version

  ! Because of space requirements, literal constant
  ! CVS_ID is shown on 2 lines. CVS will write it on
  ! one line.

  character(*), parameter :: CVS_ID = &
    '$Id: ProgForAuditability.tex,v 1.16 2010-12-18 &
    &23:26:02 clerman Exp $'
  character(*), parameter :: VERSION_STRING = '3.1.4'

contains
```

```fortran
function Get_version () result (return_value)
  character(len (VERSION_STRING)) :: return_value

  return_value = VERSION_STRING
end function Get_version

subroutine Check_version_option ()
  character(128) :: arg_string
  integer :: i

  do, i=1, command_argument_count ()
    call get_command_argument (number=i, &
      value=arg_string)
    if (arg_string == '--version') then
      print *, 'Version: ', Get_version ()
      exit
    end if
  end do
end subroutine Check_version_option
end module Version_mod
```

3.

Formatting Conventions

3.1 Source Form

6. *Always use free source form.*

Fortran 90 introduced free source form. We recommend that it always be used in new code. Free source form offers a number of advantages over the older fixed source form code:

- Free source form is more compatible with modern interactive input devices than fixed form. The maximum line length is 132 characters, compared to the older limit of 72 characters. This reduces the possibility of text exceeding the limit, which could lead the compiler to misinterpret names.

- Line continuations in free form are performed by using a trailing ampersand character, &, rather than entering a character in column 6 of the following line. As an additional visual reminder and safeguard, a leading ampersand, placed in any column, is also allowed to precede the remaining source code.

- In fixed source form, the first six columns are reserved for statement labels, with column 1 also used to indicate comment lines. In modern code, using structured control statements, statement labels are rare. The first five columns are therefore wasted because they are rarely used. These last two features, combined with the next, provide much greater flexibility laying out the code.

- In free source form, any statement can begin in column 1. Free source form always uses the "in-line" comment style, indicated by using an exclamation mark. In-line comments can begin in any column. Here is the same code in fixed format and in free format:

```
C FIXED SOURCE FORM COMMENT
      DO 10, I = 1, SIZE (DTARR)
      . . .
   10 CONTINUE
```

```
   ! Free format comment
do, i=1, size (dtarr) ! comments begin in any column
   . . .
end do
```

- With free source form, the concept of "significant blanks" was introduced. In fixed form source, blanks were insignificant in most contexts. This could lead to code that was very difficult to read. For example, statement

9

or variable names might be split across line continuations. By requiring blanks to be significant in free form code, code becomes more uniform and readable, leading to better clarity and reliability. Here is a sample of a fixed form statement showing what are now considered significant blanks followed by an equivalent statement without the blanks:

```
DO ITER = 1, MAX ITER S
. . .
DO ITER = 1, MAXITERS
```

3.2 Case

7. *Adopt and use a consistent set of rules for case.*

It is essential when discussing case in Fortran to emphasize that it is a case-insensitive language. The following variations all represent the same variable: VORTICITY, vorticity , Vorticity , VortiCity. Compilers that, as an optional feature, permit distinguishing entities based solely on case are not standard; you should not use this option.

Strictly speaking, prior to Fortran 90, standard-conforming code had to be written in uppercase letters. The Fortran character set described in the older standards specified only the 26 uppercase letters.

Beginning with Fortran 90, lowercase letters have been formally permitted, and all known compiler vendors supported them. However, because so much old code is still in use, it is still common to encounter code that conforms to the original restriction. Here is a snippet of code from the *LINPACK Users' Guide* (see Reference [20]):

```
 20 M = MOD (N, 4)
    IF (M .EQ. 0) GO TO 40
    DO 30 I = 1, M
       DY(I) = DY(I) + DA * DX(I)
 30 CONTINUE
    IF (N .LT. 4) RETURN
 40 MP1 = M + 1
```

Nowadays, programmers can use lowercase letters, and the underscore is part of the character set. The maximum number of characters that can be used to form a name has grown from the original number of 6, to 31 in Fortran 90/95, to 63 in Fortran 2003. It is now common to see a variable such as molecular_weight.

Even though the language is case-insensitive, you will often see that programs, especially large ones, are written with specific case conventions. Using different combinations of case, such as using all one case for certain types of program entities and the opposite case for others, capitalizing certain types of entities, or using a consistent set of combinations of uppercase letters and underscores, helps differentiate between the different types of entities. On the other hand, modern text editors have greatly obviated this; they automatically recognize different types of entities, and the programmer can configure the editor to highlight them by using different fonts and colors, both foreground and background, and by using underlining. Furthermore, the careful naming of all entities, as described in Chapter 4, decreases the need to use different case rules for different program entities.

A wide range of opinion exists on this subject. A survey of professional literature reveals the use of many different conventions. Rather than strictly prescribing a particular set of case rules, we suggest here, in several subrules, some alternatives. They are only a few of the many possibilities. The important point is that whatever rule you choose, you should use it consistently.

7.1   *Use lowercase throughout.*

As implied earlier, writing all entities using solely lowercase characters is being widely adopted. Words spelled with all lowercase letters tend to be more legible than those spelled using only uppercase ones. Furthermore, there is little chance of confusing the letter "i" with the numeral "1," the letter "B" with the numeral "8," etc., which can be a problem with some fonts.

Because case is not used to distinguish between types of program entities, the importance of using a clear naming scheme, as described in Chapter 4, grows. It also encourages the use of underscores in names, which some programmers prefer not to use. If underscores are used, the editor should not be configured to underline entities that contain them; the underscore would then be difficult to see. Most, but not all, of the entities in this book are written using lowercase letters.

7.2   *Capitalize the names of all user-written procedures.*

Capitalizing the first character of the names of all subroutines and functions makes them stand out in the code. For the most part, this isn't a problem with subroutines because they are normally preceded by the keyword **call**. Their names can, however, be passed as arguments to procedures. With functions, capitalizing the names is more useful; it helps distinguish them from array references in expressions. So, in the following two lines of code, the first is a reference to a function, the second to an element of an array:

```
a_name = Employee_name (i)

items = item_list(i, j)
```

You may prefer to not use underscores. If this is the case, consider writing the function name using what is commonly called UpperCamelCase, where each word has the first letter capitalized, like this:

```
a_name = EmployeeName (i)
```

Capitalizing procedure names has the additional advantage of helping to distinguish between derived-type components that are data objects and those that are functions referenced using the notation new to Fortran 2003.

Here are two snippets of code: in the first, the assignment statement is to an element of component protein_codes of derived type cell_t, identifiable by the lowercase component name protein_codes; the second is a function reference, identifiable by the capitalized function name, to the type-bound function Next whose first argument is a data object of type cell_t (see Section 11.3):

```fortran
type cell_t
   integer, allocatable :: protein_codes(:)
   type (cell_t), pointer :: neighbor => null ()
contains
   procedure :: Next => Next_neighbor
end type cell_t

type (cell_t) :: this, next_cell
integer :: protein

   ! component reference
protein = this%neighbor%protein_codes(i_p)
...
   ! function reference
next_cell = this%neighbor%Next ()
```

You can use two other schemes to emphasize that a name is a function: one is to name the function using a verb. So, a better name for the function Employee_name would be Get_employee_name. The second, as in the example, is to separate the name of the function from the opening parentheses by a space and to not do so when referencing an array. In this book, we capitalize all procedure names. We also separate the name of the procedure from the opening parentheses with at least one space. (See also Rules 26 and 16.)

7.3   *Write all named constants using uppercase letters.*

Named constants (entities declared using **parameter**) stand out in your code if you write them using all uppercase characters. The use of all uppercase differentiates them from, say, variables read in from a file. All uppercase characters are used in the code in this book when writing named constants:

```fortran
integer, parameter :: MAX_ELEMENTS = 200
...
read (unit=10, fmt=*) max_elements
```

7.4   *Begin the name of all data entities using a lowercase letter.*

To set off data entities from the other entities discussed so far, begin them with a lowercase letter. If you are using underscores, the entire name can be lowercase like this: loop_voltage, or, if underscores are not used, write the name using lowerCamelCase like this: loopVoltage. In this book, we employ all lowercase characters when writing data entities, separating words using underscores.

3.3 Indentation

8. *Use a consistent number of spaces when indenting code.*

The next few rules discuss the indentation of code: the use of two or three spaces is recommended. Be consistent. A single space is not large enough for clarity. More than three may result in code being pushed to the right when various code constructs are nested, for example, an **if**−**else**−**end if** construct nested inside a **do**−**end do** construct, nested inside a **case** statement in an internal subprogram of a module procedure. If you use a four-space indentation in such an instance and follow the guidelines in this chapter, the most-nested statements would begin in column 20.

9. *Increase the indentation of the source code every time the data scope changes.*

A typical example of such indentation would be to indent module procedures in modules and internal subprograms from their host, like this:

```
module Element_mod

   ! indent all entities whose scope is module.
   type element_t
      real :: drag_vector(3)
      ...more components
   end type element_t

   integer, parameter :: MAX_ELEMENTS = 10000
contains

   ! indent module procedures after the contains
   ! statement.
   pure subroutine Compute_drag_vector (this, error_flag)

      ! indent code within procedures.
      type (element_t), intent (in out) :: this
      integer,          intent (out)    :: error_flag
      real :: vorticity
      error_flag = NO_ERROR
      vorticity  = Compute_vorticity (this)
   contains

      ! indent internal subprograms that follow the
      ! contains statement.
```

```
    pure function Compute_vorticity (this) &
        result (ret_val)
      type (element_t), intent (in) :: this
      real (WORKING_PREC) :: ret_val
        ...
    end function Compute_vorticity
  end subroutine Compute_drag_vector
end module Element_mod
```

10. *Indent the block of code statements within all control constructs.*

Structured control constructs comprise an initial and a terminal statement between which is a block of executable statements. Some may also include intermediate statements with statements following them. They include the **do**, **if**, **select case**, **select type**, **associate**, **where**, and **forall** constructs. In Fortran 2008, the interior of the **block** construct may also be indented. Align the statements that define the bounds of the block and indent the interior statements:

```
i_code = bisect_first_entry
try_bisect: do i = 1, MAX_ITERS
  call Bisect (z, zst, zf, i_code)
  x = z
  if (i_code == BISECT_EVAL_REQD) then
    if (func1 (x) > 0.0) then
      i_code = BISECT_POS_EVAL
    else
      i_code = BISECT_NEG_EVAL
    end if
  else
    exit try_bisect
  end if
end do try_bisect

type (element_t) :: elems(:, :)
  ...
hilite : where (Get_temp (elems) >= melt_pt)
  call Highlight (elems, RED)
else where (Get_temp (elems) >= plastic_pt) hilite
  call Highlight (elems, MAGENTA)
else where hilite
  call Highlight (elems, GREEN)
end where hilite

choose_shape : select case (shape)
case (SHP_CIRCLE) choose_shape
  x_dist = 2.0 * dimensions(1)
```

```
  y_dist = x_dist
case (SHP_RECTANGLE, SHP_SQUARE) choose_shape
  x_dist = dimensions(1)
  y_dist = dimensions(2)
case default choose_shape
  x_dist = 0.0
  y_dist = 0.0
end select choose_shape
```

11. *Indent all the code after a named construct so the name stands out.*

For short names, maintain the initial construct statement on the same line as the name and align all other block construct statements with the first letter of the initial statement:

```
each_pt: do i = 1, max_points
     . . .
     if (x <= 0.0) cycle each_pt
     . . .
     if (x > x_max) exit each_pt
end do each_pt
```

In order that the indentation not be excessive when using longer names, consider the block label to be part of the construct:

```
until_converged: do i = 1, max_points
  . . .
  if (x <= 0.0) cycle until_converged
  . . .
  if (x > x_max) exit until_converged
  . . .
end do until_converged
```

12. *Consider using one indentation for block constructs and a different one for statement continuation.*

You may wish to differentiate between the code contained in block constructs and continuation lines by using a different number of spaces for each. One simple rule is that continuation lines are doubly indented, that is, their indentation is four or six spaces if, respectively, two or three spaces is the regular indentation. In the following code, two spaces are used for an **if** −**else**−**end if** block construct and four for a single-line **if** statement:

```
if (present (arg_1) ) then
  arg_1_local = arg_1
else
  arg_1_local = DEFAULT_ARG_1
end if
. . .
```

```
if (present (return_stat) ) &
    return_stat = return_stat_local
```

13. *Left-justify major documentation blocks; indent short comments the same as the code it describes or one additional indentation level.*

You may choose to use the following guidelines to indent comments:

Reference [53] strongly recommends indenting comments at the same level as the code it describes and not left-justifying it. In general, indenting to the level of the code is clearer. For major documentation blocks, however, such as the one Rule 43 prescribes for every file unit and procedure, left-justifying the block may make more sense. It clearly segregates the documentation from the code, and you can extract the block as a whole to be included in a program user's guide. Here is the beginning of the example from that rule:

```
subroutine Bisect (x, xP, xN, mode, max_attempts, &
    zero_crit )
    real (WORKING_PREC), &
        intent (in out) :: x, xP, xN
    integer, intent (in out) :: mode
    integer, intent (in), optional :: max_attempts
    real (WORKING_PREC), &
        intent (in), optional :: zero_crit

!_____

! Purpose: determine the next point at which a function
!          should be evaluated by bisecting xN and xP.

! Author: N. S. Clerman, Dec. 1983
```

Three forms for indenting short comments are shown in the following code: (1) Indentation to the level of the code. (2) Indentation to one extra level. (3) Indentation to one extra level without a following blank line. This last compresses all the code vertically and may make the code logic easier to follow:

```
! indentation form 1: at the code level.

! start timing

call cpu_time (t1)

    ! indentation form 2: one additional level.

    ! start timing

call cpu_time (t1)
```

Table 3.1. Using optional separating blanks

Use	Instead of	Use	Instead of
block data	blockdata	double precision	doubleprecision
else if	elseif	else where	elsewhere
end associate	endassociate	end block data	endblockdata
end do	enddo	end enum	endenum
end file	endfile	end forall	endforall
end function	endfunction	end if	endif
end interface	endinterface	end module	endmodule
end procedure	endprocedure	end program	endprogram
end select	endselect	end subroutine	endsubroutine
end type	endtype	end where	endwhere
go to	goto	in out	inout
select case	selectcase	select type	selecttype

```
! indentation form 3: one additional level
! without blank line.

! start timing
call cpu_time (t1)
```

3.4 White Space

14. *Use all optional white space in keywords*.

The Fortran standard allows optional blanks between some keywords; you should take advantage of this to improve readability. For example, the **endif** and the **elseif** statements may have a blank before the **if**:

```
if (flag == ITERATE) then
  do, i = 1, MAX_COUNT
    . . .
  end do
else if (flag == COMPUTE) then
  . . .
else
  . . .
end if
```

Table 3.1 shows statements and keywords that may have separating blanks for better readability.

15. *Align similar code*.

You can make your program easier to read by paying attention to the alignment of the code. To assist in doing this, when declaring the dummy arguments of procedures, always specify their attributes in the following order so they can be aligned. First, specify the type, either intrinsic or derived, and kind of the argument. Second, indicate the argument's intent. A dummy argument's intent is not required in its declaration. Its default value if you do not specify it is **intent** (**in out**) as long as the actual argument is definable (see Rule 50). But you should always include it so that the compiler can check for the proper usage and to provide additional documentation. Follow this with the arguments that are required only as needed. These are the **dimension** attribute for arrays, and the **target**, **pointer**, **allocatable**, and **optional** attributes. Always place these in a consistent order so they may be aligned as shown here:

```
subroutine Sub_a (arg_1, arg_2, arg_3, error_flag)
   real,     intent (in),      pointer        :: arg_1
   integer, intent (in out), dimension(:)  :: arg_2
   real,     intent (out)                     :: arg_3
   logical, intent (out),     optional       :: error_flag
   . . .
end subroutine Sub_a
```

In some situations, the type specification of the arguments may be of greatly different lengths, and strict adherence to this rule may push the code far to the right and cause long blank spaces. This is the case for argument arg_3. You may prefer this format:

```
   integer, intent (in out) :: arg_2 (:)
   real,     intent (out)    :: arg_3
   logical, intent (out), optional :: error_flag
```

In the same manner, align the beginning and ending keywords of all constructs, program units, and other code elements that have beginning and ending keywords. Here is an example:

```
type, public :: node_t
   type (node_t), pointer :: pt_next => null ()
   . . .
end type note_t
```

In the next example, the symbols => used in an **associate** construct are aligned, as are the equal signs in the assignment statements:

```
associate (cv => this%elements (elem_num)%curv,      &
            cc => this%elements (elem_num)%con_con,  &
            ht => ray (ray_number)%y_height)
   y2  = ht * ht
   ecc = 1.0 + cc
   cv2 = cv * cv
   . . .
end associate
```

The following example shows the alignment of relational and logical operators. Notice here that the keyword **then** of the **if** statement is put on a separate line so the end of this particularly long statement is clearly indicated:

```
if (       Get_velocity (element) > velocity_limit    &
   .or.   Comp_turbul (element)  > upper_turb_limit &
   .and. (       Graph_is_active (graph_id)          &
           .and. Highlighting_is_on () ) )           &
then
   call Graph_element (element, graph_id)
   ...
end if
```

Rule 21 advises against placing comments at the end of lines except under a limited number of conditions. Here are three lines of code from that rule. In such multiline instances, the code and comments will be clearer if you align the comments as shown:

```
read   (rep_unit, *, iostat=io_error)    ! skip title
read   (rep_unit, *, iostat=io_error_1)  ! skip col. title
read   (rep_unit, *, iostat=io_error_2)  ! skip hyphens
```

16. *Consider using white space to differentiate between the use of parentheses to enclose the argument list in calls to subprograms and their use to enclose the index list of arrays.*

To make your code clearer, you or your program team may wish to adopt one form of using parentheses with arrays and a different one with subprogram calls. In this example, a space is placed between the end of the procedure name and the opening parenthesis, and no space is placed after an array name:

```
call Calc_luminosity (trace_result, viewport, &
     error_flag)

x(i, j, k) = coefs(i, j, k) * Calc_density (elems, &
     i, j, k)
```

An alternative way to distinguish the procedure call is to place the space between the opening parenthesis and the first argument and to leave a space between the end of the last argument and the closing parenthesis:

```
call Calc_luminosity( trace_result, viewport, &
     error_flag )
```

17. *Place a space after all commas.*

There are many places in Fortran where lists of entities are separated by commas. Placing a space after each comma makes the lists easier to read:

```
use element_m, only : add_elem, create_elem, real_var_1

subroutine Bisect (x, xp, xn, mode, max_tries, &
     zero_crit)
```

18. *Do not use "hard" tabs.*

Tabulation characters, "tabs," can be a convenient way to insert multiple columns of white space into source code with a single keystroke. However, the use of tabs is not specified by the Fortran standard. Different environments and editors display and compile tab characters in different manners. Code that appears well laid out in one editor may appear skewed in a second. Some compilers may treat a tab as a single character, while others might treat it as representing multiple blank characters. This is a problem when calculating line length limits and when tabs appear in character literals. Use spaces instead of tabs or set the editor to replace tabs with an equivalent number of spaces when the tab key is pressed.

3.5 Statements and Expressions

19. *Consider using leading ampersands (&) to mark continuation lines.*

Some programmers may prefer to place the optional leading ampersand on continuation lines; doing so highlights them when reading down the left margin. At least one text editor known to the authors automatically places leading ampersands when wrapping code lines:

```
character(len=20), parameter :: line_strings(3) = &
  & [ "first line of text  ", &
  &   "second line of text ", &
  &   "third line of text  " ]
```

One use for leading ampersands occurs when you must include the same text in old fixed format code as well as more modern free format code. Then, the leading ampersand allows you to embed new code in old fixed format code, either directly or by using the **include** statement. Place the leading ampersand in column 6 and the trailing ampersand after column 72 like this:

```
      character(len=20), parameter :: LINE_STRS(3) = ...&
  & [ "first line of text  ",              ...&
  &   "second line of text ",              ...&
  &   "third line of text  " ]
```

The points of ellipsis (...) indicate blank spaces to column 72. This code will compile both as fixed source form and as free source form code.

You should also be aware that leading ampersands are required when breaking a long character literal constant into several lines:

```
error_message = "The velocity exceeds the turbulence&
                & limit on the following blade sections:"
```

Neither the blanks that follow the trailing ampersand nor the blanks that precede the leading ampersand are part of the character literal. In both examples there is only one blank between the word "turbulence" and the word "limit."

As an alternative you can use a concatenation operator (//):

```
error_message = "The velocity exceeds the turbulence" &
            // " limit on the following blade sections:"
```

20. *Place each program statement on its own line.*

You can now place more than a single line of code on a line by separating them by semicolons. In general, this is not recommended. Placing each coding statement, especially an executable statement, on a separate line aids you in seeing the code logic. Placing more than one on a line makes modifying the code more difficult. You might make an exception to this in the case of a data structure, such as a matrix, where placing several lines of code on one line, separated by semicolons, actually promotes clarity, as in the following rotation matrix:

```
real, dimension(2, 2) :: a, an
! ...
a(1, 1) = cos (an); a(1, 2) = -sin (an)
a(2, 1) = sin (an); a(2, 2) =  cos (an)
```

21. *In general, avoid putting comments at the end of lines containing source code.*

In general, the best location for comments is immediately before the code being described. Comments at the end of lines may not be visible in the editor or they may cause line-wrapping when the code is printed, thereby ruining the code's logical typographical layout. Comments placed at the end of the line, even though annotating only one line, sometimes form part of a group of similarly commented lines, like this:

```
real (kind=double), intent (in) :: real1  ! input args
character (len=*), intent (in) :: char1   ! will not be
integer, intent (in), optional :: int1    ! modified.
integer, intent (in out) :: int2          ! input arg
                                          ! will be
                                          ! modified.
```

If the intents of either argument int1 or int2 are changed, the comments at the end of line need to be moved.

However, for very short lines of code that require a brief comment, placing the comment at the end of the line may be appropriate. For example, in Rule 109, the code includes the following three lines. Even if these three lines need to be moved as a block, the three end-of-line comments logically move with them:

```
read (rep_unit, *, iostat=io_error)   ! skip title
read (rep_unit, *, iostat=io_error_1) ! skip col. title
read (rep_unit, *, iostat=io_error_2) ! skip hyphens
```

3.6 Symbols and Numbers

22. *Use the symbolic relational operators,* <, <=, /=, ==, >=, >.

It is fitting in the computer language of math and science to use symbols expressing the relationship between numbers in place of the older letter abbreviations delineated by periods. The code then more closely resembles the mathematics. Use the first set of three lines of code here instead of the second set of three:

```
if (a <= b) ...
first_quad = x > 0.0 .and. y > 0.0
near_axis  = abs (z) <= EPSILON
...
if (a .le. b) ...
first_quad = x .gt. 0.0 .and. y .gt. 0.0
near_axis  = abs (z) .le. EPSILON
```

Be aware, however, that the proper relational operators for the **logical** data type are .eqv. and .neqv. These operators did not exist prior to FORTRAN 77. So it is not unusual to find compilers that have extended the use of .eq. and .ne. for logical data, often by treating the logicals as integers. The result is a program that inadvertently uses the wrong operator. This can cause portability problems because different compilers use different internal representations of values for .**true**. and . **false** .:

```
logical :: a, b, c
...
c = a .eqv. b
if (a .neqv. c) ...
```

23. *Use the square bracket notation,* [ ], *introduced in Fortran 2003, for array constructors.*

Parentheses are used for many purposes in Fortran. For example, they enclose the argument list of procedures; they enclose format specifications; and they are used in the declarations of arrays, characters, and types. They are also used as part of the notation for array constructors.

In Fortran 2003, square brackets can be used to specify array constructors. Use the first two assignment statements instead of the last two:

```
integer, parameter :: NO_OF_ELEMS = 3
integer, dimension(NO_OF_ELEMS) :: array_a, array_b
integer :: i
    ! use these two assignments instead of the last two
array_a = [0, 1, 5]
array_b = [ (i, i=1, size (array_b)) ]
...
array_a = (/ 0, 1, 5 /)
array_b = (/ (i, i=1, size (array_b)) /)
```

Use of square bracket array constructors adds clarity to the code by reducing the appearance of multiple uses of parentheses. Visually, this makes the code easier to read. Note, though, that the coarray data entities in Fortran 2008 also use square brackets as part of their notation (see Rule 169).

24. *Write at least one digit on each side of the decimal point of floating-point literal constants*.

```
real , save  ::  a = 0.0
```

The advantage is that the dot will be seen and cannot be confused with any other token, for example, with an operator.

4.

Naming Conventions

4.1 Modules, Procedures, and Types

25. *Use detailed names for data objects whose scope is global, less detailed names for those whose scope is a module, and simple but clear names for those whose scope is a single procedure.*

Symbolic names are used in many places. At the outermost level are the names of modules, the main program, and external procedure program units. Within the confines of a program unit are derived-type definitions, named constants, and variables. In addition, there are also internal procedures and interface blocks.

Within individual procedures, there are statement labels for control flow and I/O purposes.

Generally, the more global the name, the longer and more descriptive it should be. And, likewise, the more limited the scope of a name is, the shorter it should be. For example, a module name should indicate the use of the definitions and related procedures it contains, for example: Triangular_solver_mod , whereas a simple loop index variable may be called i or j.

26. *Name user-written procedures using verbs.*

Almost all procedures perform some task. Name them using one or more verbs that succinctly describe the operation carried out. If appropriate, follow each verb with a specific noun that describes the object being used. This method is especially useful when you name functions; it aids in distinguishing them from arrays. (See also Rules 7.2 and 16.)

subroutine Perform_alpha_sort (list)

function Calc_dir_cosines (ray) **result** (dir_cosines)

Be as specific as possible without making the function name overly long. And be mindful that a procedure specific to a certain data type has a specific name. Write:

subroutine Read_temperature_data (input_port)

And, likewise, for a generic procedure or for a type-bound procedure that might be used in an extended type, a more generic name should be used (see Rule 149):

subroutine Read_data (input_port)

27. *Use a consistent set of verbs throughout to name common procedures.*

Many categories of subprograms are used throughout programs. The following subrules suggest naming guidelines for some of them.

27.1 *Name accessor procedures using either the verb "Set" or "Put" and the verb "Get" followed by the component name.*

In the following example, a parameterized derived type is defined; the two accessor procedures are type-bound.

```
module Polynomial_mod
  use Kinds_mod , only : WORK_PREC
  implicit none
  private

  type , public :: poly_t (degree)
    integer , len :: degree = 2
    real (WORK_PREC) :: coefs(degree) = 0.0_WORK_PREC
  contains
    procedure :: Get_coef
    procedure :: Set_coef
  end type poly_t

contains
  elemental function Get_coef (this , power) &
      result (return_value)
    class (poly_t), intent (in) :: this
    integer (kind (this%degree)), &
        intent (in) :: power
    real (kind (this%coefs)) :: return_value

    return_value = 0.0
    if (0 < power .and. power <= this%degree) &
        return_value = this%coefs(power)
  end function Get_coef

  subroutine Set_coef (this , power, coef)
    class (poly_t), intent (in out) :: this
    integer (kind (this%degree)), &
        intent (in) :: power
    real (kind (this%coefs)), intent (in) :: coef

    if (0 < power .and. power <= this%degree) &
        this%coefs(power) = coef
  end subroutine Set_coef
end module Polynomial_mod
```

27.2   *Name procedures that traverse data structures using the verbs that are commonly used – "Next, Previous, Pop, Push," and so on.*

Your code will be clearer to anyone reading it if you name the procedures operating on data structures using names such as these:

```
function Next_element (this) result (return_value)
function Previous_element (this) result (return_value)
function Pop_node (this) result (return_value)
```

27.3   *Use the same verb for all final procedures followed by the name of the derived type.*

For clarity, use verbs like "Finalize," "Destroy," "Remove," or "Clean" for all final routines (see Rule 147). Whichever the word chosen, use it solely throughout the program so as not to cause confusion.

```
module Node_mod
  implicit none
  private

  type, public :: node_t
    integer :: id
    type (node_t), pointer :: next_node => null ()
  contains
    final :: Clean => Clean_node
  end type node_t

contains
  subroutine Clean_node (this)
    type (node_t), intent (in out) :: this
    integer :: alloc_stat

    if (associated (this%next_node) ) &
        deallocate (this%next_node, stat=alloc_stat)
  end subroutine Clean_node
end module Node_mod
```

27.4   *Name functions that return a logical result using verbs such as "Is," or "Has."*

```
module Data_packet_mod
  implicit none
  private

  type, public :: data_packet_t
    private
    logical :: init = .false.
    ... more components
```

```
contains
   procedure :: Is_initialized
end type data_packet_t

contains
   function Is_initialized (this) result (ret_val)
      class (data_packet_t), intent (in) :: this
      logical :: ret_val

      ret_val = this%init == .true.
   end function Is_initialized
   ...
end module Data_packet_mod
```

4.2 Supplemental Notation

In this section we set forth guidelines for adding prefixes and suffixes to data object names to assist the person reading the code in identifying the type of an object and its function. The motivation is that at one glance the reader can do this; he or she does not have to refer to the data declarations at the beginning of a module or procedure or to search through other program units to determine its characteristics.

28. *Add an identifying tag to all module names.*

The names of modules are used in only a few contexts. One is the **module** and bracketing **end module** statements; another is in **use** statements. They should rarely be a point of confusion. On the other hand, if you follow this rule as well as the next one of adding a tag to the names of derived types, one possible system of naming is to append _mod as a suffix to the module name, _t as the type name, and then to name objects of the derived type using the base name. In the following code outline, the local variable element in subroutine Calculate_evaporation is such an object.

```
module Element_mod
   implicit none
   private

   type, public :: element_t
   ... components
   contains
      procedure :: Calculate_evaporation
      ... other type-bound procedures
   end type element_t

contains
   subroutine Calculate_evaporation (this, temperature)
```

```
      class (element_t), intent (in out) :: this
      real , intent (in) :: temperature
      type (element_t) :: element

        ! copy to temp. variable in the event of an
        ! exception.
      element = this
      ...code calculating the evaporation for element.
    end subroutine Calculate_evaporation
end module Element_mod
```

29. *Add an identifying tag to all derived type names.*

Type names can appear in several different contexts in a program. In some, the fact that they are derived types is obvious because the keyword **type** appears in the statement. One example is the definition of the type; a second is the declaration of a dummy argument that is a derived type. Here, there is no question that particle is the name of a derived type.

```
type particle
   real (WORKING_PREC) :: weight , momentum
end type particle

elemental function Calc_force (this)
   result (return_value)
   type (particle), intent (in) :: this
   real (WORKING_PREC) :: return_value
end function Calc_force
```

In other situations, however, this may not be clear. For example, structure constructors have the same appearance as functions. Here is an assignment:

```
new_command = command (init=.false., no_of_pars=0)
```

There is no way to know just by reading this line if it is a normal function call or an initialization of a variable of derived type command with a structure constructor. Adding a suffix to form the name makes this clear.

```
new_command = command_t (init=.false., no_of_pars=0)
```

An additional situation where the use of a type name is not obvious and adding a suffix assists in identification is their inclusion in a list of objects following the **only** option in **use** statements.

```
use element_mod , only : Add, element_t , Print
```

Extended derived data types present another instance where adding a suffix clarifies code. Here are two derived types:

```
type , public :: plane_point_t
   real (WORKING_PREC) :: x, y
end type plane_point_t
```

```
type,  public,  extends  (plane_point_t)  ::  space_point_t
   real  (WORKING_PREC)  ::  z
end type  space_point_t
```

You can refer to the inherited x component of an object of derived type space_point_t in this manner:

```
type  (space_point_t)  ::  rotation_pt
...
rotation_pt%x  =  3.2_WORKING_PREC
```

It can also be referred to in this manner:

```
rotation_pt%plane_point_t%x  =  3.2_WORKING_PREC
```

Even though the latter is longer, you may prefer to use this nomenclature. The presence of the intermediate component plane_point_t, identifiable as a type by its _t suffix, draws your attention to the fact that the variable rotation_pt is of a derived type extended from type plane_point_t, and that the component x is inherited from it (Rule 149).

30. *Consider adding an identifying tag to all pointers.*

When a data object that is a pointer appears in a pointer assignment, there is no confusion.

```
real,  target   ::  matrix(:,:)
real,  pointer  ::  row(:)
...
row  =>  matrix(i,  :)
```

However, this is also a valid assignment:

```
real,  pointer  ::  row(:)
...
row  =  matrix(i,  :)
```

In the first case, the pointer row is pointing to a row of matrix, serving as an alias to it; it need not have been previously allocated. The opposite is true in the second case – where the data is copied. To immediately identify the context, and to emphasize that the variable row is a pointer and not an array, it helps to name the pointer using a suffix.

```
real,  pointer  ::  row_p(:)
...
row_p  =  matrix(i,  :)
```

This supplemental notation also can be helpful in indicating if a pointer or an allocatable object is being allocated in an **allocate** statement.

```
type (element_t), pointer :: elements_p(:)
integer :: alloc_stat, no_of_elements
...
allocate (element_t :: elements_p(no_of_elements), &
          stat=alloc_stat)
```

4.3 Data Objects

31. *Use plural nouns to differentiate arrays from scalars.*

Name individual objects using a singular noun

```
type (atom_t) :: carbon
```

and name arrays using a plural noun

```
type (atom_t) :: carbons(4)
```

An exception to this rule would be the naming of arrays using terms commonly associated with aggregates, such as "vector" and "matrix."

```
real (WORKING_PREC) :: velocity_vector(3)
```

This manner of naming objects is especially useful whenever you refer to an entire array by its name only. Here is a call to a routine where a single oxygen atom and arrays of both carbon and hydrogen atoms are passed as arguments:

```
call Combine_atoms (oxygen, carbons, hydrogens, &
     return_val)
```

32. *In modules in which a derived type is defined, use either the name "this" or the name "self" for the* **pass** *argument in all type-bound procedures and procedure pointer components and for the dummy argument of the type in all module procedures.*

In many object-oriented programming languages, names such as "this" and "self" are used within a procedure to refer to the object by which the procedure was invoked. These names may even be reserved for the purpose.

In Fortran, the object passed to a type-bound procedure is the argument that has the **pass** attribute. By default, this is the first argument. (See Rule 142.) There is no default naming requirement. However, if you use either "this" or "self," your code will be clearer to someone who is not familiar with Fortran but is knowledgeable in other languages. Here is an accessor subroutine that sets the component of a type:

```
module Node_mod
  use Numerical_kinds_mod, only: WORKING_PREC
  implicit none
```

```
  private

  type, public :: node_t
    real (WORKING_PREC) :: temperature
  contains
    procedure :: Set_temp => Set_temp_node
  end type node_t

contains
  subroutine Set_temp_node (this, temperature)
    class (node_t), intent (in out) :: this
    real (kind (this%temperature)), &
        intent (in) :: temp

    this%temperature = temperature
  end subroutine Set_temp_node
end module Node_mod
```

33. *Establish pairs of logical named constants to replace the values of* .true. *and* .false. *in cases where this will clarify the code.*

There are situations where using the logical values .**true**. and .**false**. in your code can lead to ambiguity. For example, in the following code, the Fortran floating-point exception handling halting mode is turned off, a division is performed, after which, the Fortran underflow flag is tested. If an underflow has occurred, the result is set to 0.0. Finally, the flag is reset:

```
use, intrinsic :: IEEE_Exceptions
use, intrinsic :: IEEE_Features, only : &
    IEEE_invalid_flag, IEEE_underflow_flag

logical :: flag
real    :: x, a, b

call IEEE_Set_halting_mode (IEEE_UNDERFLOW, &
    halting = .false.)
x = a / b
call IEEE_Get_flag (IEEE_UNDERFLOW, flag)
if (flag) x = 0.0
call IEEE_Set_flag (IEEE_UNDERFLOW, &
    flag_value = .false.)
```

One may question if the final line is setting the flag to be signaling or quiet, its two possible values. Here, four logical named constants are defined and used:

```
use, intrinsic :: IEEE_Exceptions
use, intrinsic :: IEEE_Features, only : &
    IEEE_invalid_flag, IEEE_underflow_flag
```

```
logical  ::  flag
real     ::  x, a, b

logical , parameter  ::  SIGNALING = .true., &
    QUIET = .false.
logical , parameter  ::  ON = .true., OFF = .false.

call  IEEE_Set_halting_mode  (IEEE_UNDERFLOW, &
    halting = OFF)
x = a / b
call  IEEE_Get_flag  (IEEE_UNDERFLOW, flag )
if ( flag == SIGNALING) x = 0.0
call  IEEE_Set_flag  (IEEE_UNDERFLOW, flag_value = QUIET)
```

34. *Consider using a unique name or a limited number of names throughout a program as the names of the value returned by a function.*

In a large program, containing hundreds or even thousands of functions, you
or your programming team may find it useful to always use a single name
or one of just a few names for the result variable in the **result** clause. This
can assist, especially in long procedures, in immediately identifying the object
returned when reviewing your own code or the code of a fellow programmer.
Use the term regardless of the type, be it intrinsic or derived, or the kind of
value returned. (An obvious disadvantage of doing this is that the name is less
descriptive than may be desirable [see Rule 129].)

```
function  Calc_vorticity ( this , method_flag) &
      result ( return_value )

    type (element_t), intent (in) ::  this
    integer,         intent (in), optional :: method_flag
    real (WORKING_PREC) ::  return_value
    . . .
end function  Calc_vorticity

function  State_is_active ()  result ( return_value )

    logical  ::  return_value

end function  State_is_active

function  Get_employee (employee_name) &
      result ( return_value )
    character (*), intent (in) ::  employee_name
    type (employee_t) ::  return_value
    . . .
end function  Get_employee
```

When returning an array, consider using a plural name like return_values .

```
function Get_salaried_employees (this) &
    result (return_values)
  type (employee_t), intent(in) :: this (:)
  type (employee_t), allocatable :: return_values (:)
  . . .
end function Get_salaried_employees
```

A third suggestion is to remove the verb from the function name, salaried_employees or vorticity , for example.

35. *Use common names for variables that represent accepted mathematic, scientific, and engineering terms. Spell out the names of quantities whose symbol is not part of the Fortran character set.*

Programmers with the appropriate expertise will more easily be able to read your code if you adhere to this rule. Those who are less familiar with the subject will more easily be able to follow the code while referring to reference material.

For example, in structural engineering the stress σ at a point along a loaded beam is

$$\sigma = \frac{M\,z}{I} \tag{4.1}$$

where M is the bending moment, z is the distance from the neutral axis, and I is the moment of inertia with respect to this axis (see Reference [65]). In Fortran write this as

```
sigma = M * z / I
```

Recall that you don't want to try to distinguish names by case. Here the symbol for the bending moment, M, is capitalized because that is the standard notation used in structural engineering.

36. *Consider beginning the names of all do, index, and subscript variables using the letters "i" through "n."*

It is often the practice for Fortran programmers to begin the names of do variables with the letters "i" through "n." This is logical for a language used for writing scientific and engineering software. The subscripts used in mathematics for many operations such as summations are written using these letters, and these subscripts become the do variable in loops.

As a legacy of premodern Fortran, if the **implicit none** statement is not present in a program unit, the typing of entities is determined by what is called "implicit typing." In this method, all entities that begin with the letters "i" through "n" are of type default integer; all others are of type default real.

As Rule 72 states, every program unit you write should contain an **implicit none** statement. In modules, a single **implicit none** suffices at the beginning of the module for the procedures contained within it.

Beginning with Fortran 2003, as Rule 194 explains, do loop variables may not be of type **real** or **double precision**. If you configure your compiler to conform to the standard, it should detect any instances of nonconformance. If not so configured, the compiler may not report this. In any case, if you begin all do variables with the letters "i" through "n," your program will always be correct even if you ignore our **implicit none** recommendation. So, instead of writing:

```
do col = 1, ubound (element_grid , dim=2)
  do row = 1, ubound (element_grid , dim=1)
    call Calc_average_temp (element_grid(row, col) )
  end do
end do
```

write:

```
do j_col = 1, ubound (element_grid , dim=2)
  do i_row = 1, ubound (element_grid , dim=1)
    call Calc_average_temp (element_grid(i_row , j_col) )
  end do
end do
```

4.4 Construct Blocks

37. *Name all executable construct blocks with a name describing the purpose of the construct.*

To all block constructs that are more than a few lines long, names should be added to all that allow them. These constructs are **associate**, **select case**, **do**, **if**, **select type**, **forall**, and **where**. This is especially true of nested **do** constructs. They are required if you wish to use either the **exit** *do-construct-name* statement to exit from a specific **do** construct or the **cycle** *do-construct-name* statement to loop to its beginning. Furthermore, Fortran 2008 allows exit from block constructs other than **do** constructs. As with any name you provide, use the name to convey some information about the program to the reader. Choose a name that describes the purpose of the construct in the same manner that you choose a procedure name to describe the purpose of a procedure (see Rule 11).

```
each_column: do k_column = 1, column_limit
  each_row: do i_row = 1, row_limit
    call Proc1 (i_row , kerr)

    if (kerr < 0) then
      exit each_column
    else if (kerr > 0) then
```

```
      cycle each_column
    else
       ...
    end if
  end do each_row
end do each_column
```

Also, where constructs may be nested, a compiler can give better diagnostics if construct names appear at the end of the construct.

38. *Always use optional names on end statements.*

Several Fortran syntax forms in addition to constructs allow names on the final statement as an option. For example, you can write the type name at the end of an **end type** statement, and when there are many components, doing so better delineates them.

```
type, extends (genus_t), public :: specie_t
! ... components
end type specie_t
```

39. *Make liberal use of the* associate *construct.*

In sections of code that include extensive use of both data and procedure components, you can clarify your code to a great extent by using the **associate** construct to assign them one-word names. For example, if you had this type definition

```
type, public :: pt2d_t
  real :: x, y
contains
  procedure :: Get => Get_x_coordinate
end type pt2d_t
```

and you had a long section of code in a subroutine with the following interface

```
subroutine Calculate_val (this)
  type (pt2d_t), intent (in) :: this
end subroutine Calculate_val
```

the code will read much better if it is enclosed in an **associate** construct block if there's a long section of code in which there are numerous reference to the x and y components of argument this, that is,

```
a = this%x + b
e = this%y + d
... many more references
```

```
comp_assign: associate (x=>this%x, y=>this%y)
  a = x + b
  e = y + d
  ... many more references
end associate comp_assign
```

In object-oriented code (see Chapter 11) this rule is even more applicable. Here a new type pt3d_t extends type pt2d_t

```
type, public, extends(pt2d_t) :: pt3d_t
  real :: z
end type pt3d_t
```

In code where the variable this is one of type pt3d_t, you can easily have code that is calling the type-bound binding Get of type pt2d_t that looks like this:

```
coords = this%pt2d_t%Get ()
```

This is especially confusing. The entity this is a variable of type pt3d_t; because type pt3d_t is extended from type pt2d_t, the entity pt2d_t is a component of this; and Get is a type-bound procedure. Even if this is used only once, the following nomenclature makes the code clearer:

```
associate (comp_2d => this%pt2d_t)
  coords = comp_2d%Get ()
end associate
```

The following code snippet, taken from a program manipulating pieces on a chess board, uses the **associate** construct advantageously:

```
comp_assoc: associate (row => this%row, &
    column => this%column)
  if (row == test_row) then
    return_value = .true.
  else

      ! test diagonals.
      column_difference = test_column - column
      if (     (row + column_difference == test_row) &
          .or. (row - column_difference == test_row) ) &
              return_value = .true.
  end if

      ! this queen cannot attack a queen at test_row /
      ! test_column; investigate if its neighbor can.
  if (.not. return_value) then
    neighbor_pointer => this%neighbor
    if ( associated (neighbor_pointer) ) &
        return_value = neighbor_pointer% &
        Can_attack (test_row, test_column)
  end if
end associate comp_assoc
```

In the standard, the specification for the aliasing is

associate-name=>selector

Be especially aware that, even though the => operator is used in both the **associate** statement and in pointer assignments, the name assigned is *not* a pointer; rather, it is an alias.

The selector can be a variable or an expression, such as a function. It can be an array. It cannot be the name of a subroutine. Furthermore, the selector can be allocatable, but, in this case, the associate name is not allocatable. The same applies if the selector is a pointer; the associate-name does not acquire the pointer attribute. This means that if you have the following derived type:

```
type, public :: element_t
  real, allocatable :: real_array(:)
end type element_t
```

you can use the following associate construct:

```
type (element_t) :: object
...
associate (real_item => object%real_array(i))
  ... code using real_item
end associate
```

But the following code is not valid because real_item is not allocatable:

```
type (element_t) :: object
...
associate (real_item => object%real_array(i))
  if (allocated (real_item) ) then
    ... code using real_item
  end if
end associate
```

5.

Documentation Conventions

40. *Write self-documenting code.*

Well-written code, that which is written following the rules in Chapter 4, documents itself. A person reading it can understand the operations the code performs with little or no supplemental code documentation. It also passes the "telephone test." (See Rule 1.)

Here is an instructive example, one that uses an old graphics standard, the Graphical Kernal System (GKS) from the 1980s that was used for creating two-dimensional graphics (see Reference [34]). It demonstrates how the appropriate naming of data entities and procedures produces code that documents itself. The original language binding for GKS was FORTRAN 77. The members of the standards committee that created it, constrained by the limitations of the FORTRAN standard, were forced to develop a set of procedure names of six characters or fewer in length. A further constraint was that the first letter of all procedures be the letter "G" and that the second letter represented a particular action. The letter "S," for example, was used for procedures that set the value of an entity.

Here is a short section of code.

```
CALL  GSWN  (TRNNUM,XMINW,YPOSW+8.0,XMIN_WINDOW,
+   YPOSW+8.0)
CALL  GSVP  (TRNNUM,XMINVP,XMAXVP,YMINVP,YMAXVP)
CALL  GSELNT  (TRNNUM)
CALL  GSTXI  (TXTIDX)
CALL  GSCHH  (0.8*CHH)
CALL  GSTXP  (RGTXP)
CALL  GSCHUP  (CHUX,CHUY)
CALL  GSPLI  (LINIDX)
```

Only a person familiar with GKS or one who refers frequently to a GKS manual would be able to understand this without supplemental documentation in the form of comments.

Had modern Fortran been available when the standard was written, the code might have looked like this:

```
call  GKS_Set_window (transform_num , window_limit_data)
```

```
call  GKS_Set_viewport  (transform_num,  vwport_limit_data)
call  GKS_Set_element_trans_matrix  (transform_num)
call  GKS_Set_text_index  (text_index)
call  GKS_Set_char_height  (0.8*char_height)
call  GKS_Set_text_path  (TEXT_PATH_RIGHT)
call  GKS_Set_char_up_vector  (char_up_vector)
call  GKS_Set_polyline_index  (line_index)
```

where window_limit_data and vwport_limit_data are data objects of the following type:

```
type  GKS_limit
   real  ::  x_min,  x_max,  y_min,  y_max
end  type  GKS_limit
```

and char_up_vector is one of this following type:

```
type  GKS_vector
   real  ::  delta_x,  delta_y
end  type  GKS_vector
```

The longer names clarify the purpose of the code. Additionally, the GKS prefixes make it clear that the derived types and calls are intended for the GKS library.

41. *Add comments to your code to allow other programmers to understand its purpose. It is especially important to explain what cannot be read from the source text itself.*

Writing code in adherence with the precepts of the previous rule makes its operation clear. However, it does not necessarily explain the purpose of the code; for this, you need to add supplementary documentation. Here is a code example:

```
y_sqrd    = y_ht ** 2
eccen     = 1.0 + this%con_const
curv_sqrd = (this%curv) ** 2
dis = 1.0 - eccen * y_sqrd * curv_sqrd
if (dis < 0.0) then
  max_radius = sqrt (1.0 / (eccen * curv_sqrd) )
  sag_data   = sag_values_t (y_ht, max_radius, 0.0, &
       0.0, 0.0, SAG_YgtR)
else
  denom  = 1.0_DOUB_PREC + sqrt (dis)
  sag    = this%curv * y_sqrd / denom
  denom  = 1.0_DOUB_PREC - this%curv * eccen * sag
  sag1By = Divide (this%curv, denom)
  sag_prime      = sag1by * y_ht
  sag_doub_prime = sag1by * &
       (1.0_DOUB_PREC + sagP**2 * eccen)
```

```
      max_radius = HUGE_DP
      sag_data   = sag_values_t (y_ht, max_radius, sag, &
           sag_prime, sag_doub_prime, SAG_SUCCESS)
end if
```

This code may or may not be clear to someone reading it – it would depend on
his or her familiarity with the program. Here is the same code with explanatory
comments added.

```
      ! determine the perpendicular distance from the
      ! tangent plane to the conic surface at y_ht from the
      ! tangent point. (this%con_const = 0 for sphere)
y_sqrd     = y_ht * y_ht
eccen      = 1.0 + this%con_const
curv_sqrd  = (this%curv) ** 2
dis        = 1.0 - eccen * y_sqrd * curv_sqrd

      ! two possibilities:
      ! SAG_YgtR: y_ht > maximum height at which there is an
      !           intersection - set the sag and the first
      !           and second derivatives to 0.0
      ! SAG_SUCCESS: otherwise.
if (dis < 0.0) then
   max_radius = sqrt (1.0 / (eccen * curv_sqrd) )
   sag_data   = sag_values_t (y_ht, max_radius, 0.0, &
        0.0, 0.0, SAG_YgtR)

else

      ! compute distance (sag) and 1st & 2nd derivatives
      ! (sag_prime, sag_doub_prime)

      ! (use lib. function Divide to trap floating-point
      !  problems.)
   denom   = 1.0 + sqrt (dis)
   sag     = this%curv * y_sqrd / denom
   denom   = 1.0 - this%curv * eccen * sag
   sag1By  = Divide (this%curv, denom)
   sag_prime      = sag1by * y_ht
   sag_doub_prime = sag1by * (1.0 + sagP**2 * eccen)
   max_radius     = HUGE_DP
   sag_data = sag_values_t (y_ht, HUGE_DP, sag, &
        sag_prime, sag_doub_prime, SAG_SUCCESS)
end if
```

42. *Always synchronize the documentation with the code.*

As you make changes to your code, an important, even crucial task is to update any explanatory comments that describe it. Comments that do not agree with the code, or even worse, contradict it, are extremely confusing.

43. *Write a documentation block for every program unit.*

You should include a general documentation section with every program, module, submodule, and subprogram. It should comprise at least the following items:

- A brief description of the function of the unit. This should be a few sentences, at most, describing the purpose of the unit.
- The author.
- The date.
- A dated list of brief explanations of code revisions and their authors.
  This explanation should be a general one. More specific descriptions, if necessary, are better embedded in the code.

You also may want to include the following items:

- A description of the interface to the subprogram.
  If you have chosen good names for the arguments, you need not list them; they are self-documenting. Because the type and kind of arguments may change, as may other attributes assigned to them, such as **intent**, **optional**, or **pointer**, you need not document these here. Let their declarations, carefully laid out, be the documentation.
- A version number.
  This number would be a version number you or your project team have adopted.
- A number used by the version control system used to maintain file updates.
  This number would be the version number assigned by whatever program you are using (such as CVS), if any, to synchronize and manage changes to your code. You may want to include this as part of the revision list (see Rule 5).
- The names of any references.
  Mention here any texts, papers, or articles you are using as a basis for your code. These might be the source of the algorithm, engineering or scientific calculations, or a data structure you are using. List the chapters or sections here, if applicable, but embed references to specific equations or calculations in the code.

Here is an example:

```
subroutine Bisect (x, xP, xN, mode, max_tries, &
    zero_crit)
  real (WORK_PREC), intent (in out) :: x, xP, xN
  integer, intent (in out) :: mode
  integer, intent (in), optional :: max_tries
  real (WORK_PREC), intent (in), optional :: zero_crit
```

```
!──────────────────────────────────────────
! Purpose: determine the next point at which a function
!          should be evaluated by bisecting xN and xP.

! Author: N. S. Clerman, Dec. 1983

! Revisions:

    ! 1) N. S. Clerman, Nov. 1984: error logging added
    ! 2) C. R. Crawford, June 1987: add arguments
    ! max_tries and zeroCrit. save i. Add the necessary
    !    code.

! Release: 52.4.3int

! Line wrapped because of space limitations. CVS will
! write it on one line.

! File Version: $Id: Bisect.f90,v 1.26 2008/12/22
! 03:01:42
!                    clerman Exp $

! Args:

! x — on input: the current point at which the function
                ! was evaluated.
!       on output: the next point at which the function
                ! should be evaluated.
! xP,xN — x−values where the function is positive and
            ! negative, respectively. set to x on entry
            ! based on the value of mode.
! mode — control value
!           on input:
!               mode = BISECT_FIRST_ENTRY
!               mode = BISECT_NEG_EVAL
!               − the function at x was negative.
!               mode = BISECT_POS_EVAL
!               − the function at x was positive.

!           on output:
!               mode = BISECT_FAILS
!               − max. number of iterations exceeded.

!               mode = BISECT_EVAL_REQD
!               − evaluate function at x.
```

```
!            mode = BISECT_FINISHED
!              - convergence
!_____
!   ... type declaration and specification statements
!   ... excutable statements
end subroutine Bisect
```

6.

Programming Principles

6.1 Standards Conformance

44. *Always write standard-conforming code.*

Adherence to no other guideline in this book will make your code more portable than adhering to this one. Over the years, compiler vendors and others have added numerous nonstandard extensions to the language. There is no guarantee that every compiler will support them or that any given compiler will continue to do so in the future.

When you write code that conforms to the standard, you can expect and demand that a "standard-conforming" compiler will successfully compile it. If it cannot, you have a good indication that either your code is in error, that it does not conform to the standard, or that there is a problem with the compiler itself. Most compilers can provide warning messages when encountering nonstandard code. If possible, do not depend on a single compiler as a reference. Compiling code through several different vendors' compilers can often expose additional errors. (See also Rule 4 and Section 15.3.)

45. *Do not rely on compiler switches that change code semantics.*

Many compiler vendors have added switches to their compiler directives that provide a capability that the programmer must otherwise provide by writing code. Some compilers, for example, have a switch that will automatically initialize all variables or change the default kinds of variables. Others have switches that remove the necessity for explicitly including the **implicit none** statement in every program unit. You should not use these; they make your code nonportable.

6.2 Module Design

46. *Order the statements in modules in a fixed and consistent manner.*

The standard dictates a specific ordering of statements in all program units. (See Reference [39].) For consistency, it is best to further arrange the order of the various elements. A general scheme is:

module *module-name*

alphabetical sequence of **use** *statements of the following form:*

use *module-name*, **only** : *only-list*

implicit none

44

private

protected :: *access-id-list*

public :: *access-id-list*

declaration of named constants

derived type definitions

interfaces

variables whose scope is the entire module

contains

alphabetical ordering of all module procedures, both public and private.

end module *module-name*

Here is an example:

```
module  Rect_mod
    use  Object_mod ,  only  :  object_t
    use  Point_mod ,  only  :  point_t
    use  Sys_kinds_mod

    implicit  none
    private
    public      ::  Comp_area ,  Init_calls

    type ,  extends ( object_t ),  public  ::  rect_t
        private
        real  (WORKING_PREC)  ::  dimensions (2)
        type ( point_t )          ::  center
    contains
        procedure  ::  Comp_area  =>  Comp_area_rect
    end type  rect_t

    interface  Init_Calls
        module  procedure  Init_calls_rect
    end  interface

        ! monitor the number of calls.
    integer ,  protected  ::  number_of_area_calls = 0

contains
    elemental  function  Comp_area_rect ( this ) &
            result ( return_value )
        class ( rect_t ),  intent ( in )  ::  this
        real  (WORKING_PREC)  ::  return_value
        return_value  =  this%dimensions (1)  *  &
            this%dimensions (2)
        number_of_area_calls  =  number_of_area_calls + 1
    end  function  Comp_area_rect
```

```
  subroutine Init_calls_rect ()

    number_of_area_calls = 0
  end subroutine Init_calls_rect
end module Rect_mod
```

47. *Place data objects that require global accessibility in modules.*

Module-scope variables have the **public** attribute by default. They can be both read and updated by any user of the module. While convenient, numerous problems can result: The variables are visible outside the module, thus violating the concept of "information hiding." The names may conflict with those from other modules. And finally, an errant user of a module variable may update it in unexpected manner, potentially causing unexpected program behavior. Alternatively, variables may be given the **private** attribute, and public accessor procedures may be written, similar to those that allow access to the private components of public derived types (see Rule 135).

Using the **protected** attribute, you can give public "read only" access to a module variable, allowing only procedures within the module to actually update the variable. A public accessor procedure can be written to provide unified services such as assigning values, verifying data correctness, and logging updates for debugging purposes. Here is a module that sets state variables for program debugging:

```
module Debug_state_mod
  use state_mod, only : FAILURE, FATAL, INFO, &
      NO_LEVEL, OFF, ON, SUCCESS, WARN
  implicit none
  private
  public :: Set_debug_state

  integer, protected :: debug_state = OFF, &
      debug_level = NO_LEVEL

contains
  subroutine Set_debug_state (new_state, return_stat)
    integer, intent (in) :: new_state
    integer, intent (out) :: return_stat

    if (new_state == ON .or. new_state == OFF) then
      debug_state = new_state
      return_stat = SUCCESS
    else
      return_stat = FAILURE
    end if
  end subroutine Set_debug_state
    ...
end module Debug_state_mod
```

Note that the **save** attribute was not explicitly specified; the variables debug_state and debug_level both possess this attribute by virtue of their being initialized in their declarations.

A stipulation in the standard pertaining to modules is that the module-scope variables within them are allowed to become undefined when no module or procedure using their containing module (for example, via a **use** statement) is active. To ensure that the contents of such a module does not inadvertently go out of scope, the module should either be used in the main program, or the **save** attribute should be specified for the entire module, accomplished using a simple **save** statement. The Fortran 2008 standard specifies that module-scope variables possess the **save** attribute by default (see Rule 75).

48. *Include a default* private *statement in the specification section of all modules. Provide either public or read-only access to module entities on an as-needed basis.*

The default access for entities in modules is public. It is preferable to limit access to only those items that other program units need via use association. This is done by either listing them in **public** or **protected** statements or by specifying one of these two attributes in definitions such as derived-type definitions. Provide this access solely to those entities that are defined in the module. This reduces the possibilities of naming conflicts with items in other modules. Use this rule and the rule for using the **only** option to maintain strict control over access to all module entities (see Rules 49 and 135).

Here are skeleton outlines of three modules:

```
module A_mod
  implicit none
  private
  public :: Proc_a1
contains
  subroutine Proc_a1 (arg_a1)
    real, intent (in out) :: arg_a1
    ...
  end subroutine Proc_a1
end module A_mod

module B_mod
  use A_mod, only : Proc_a1
  implicit none
  private
  public :: Proc_b1
contains
  subroutine Proc_b1 (arg_b1)
    real, intent (in out) :: arg_b1
    ...
    call Proc_a1 (arg_b1)
```

```
      . . .
      end subroutine Proc_b1
end module B_mod

module C_mod
   use B_mod, only : Proc_b1
   implicit none
   private
   public :: Proc_c1
contains
   subroutine Proc_c1 (arg_c1, arg_c2)
      integer, intent (in out) :: arg_c1
      real,    intent (out)    :: arg_c2
      . . .
      call Proc_b1 (arg_c2)
      . . .
   end subroutine Proc_c1
end module C_mod
```

Note that the subroutine Proc_a1 is not made public in module B_mod. If in module C_mod it was necessary to call it from subroutine Proc_c1, C_mod should explicitly use it as shown here:

```
module C_mod
   use A_mod, only : Proc_a1
   use B_mod, only : Proc_b1
   implicit none
   private
   public :: Proc_c1
contains
   subroutine Proc_c1 (arg_c1, arg_c2)
      integer, intent (in out) :: arg_c1
      real,    intent (out)    :: arg_c2
      . . .
      call Proc_b1 (arg_c2)
      . . .
      call Proc_a1 (arg_c2)
      . . .
   end subroutine Proc_c1
end module C_mod
```

The contents of some categories of modules make the inclusion of the **private** statement optional. One example is a module that contains only named constants. The program cannot modify the values of named constants, so it is logical to allow all items in a module such as this to have the default public attribute.

```
module Global_par_mod
   implicit none
```

```
  integer ,  parameter  ::  MAX_EMPLOYEES  =  20000
  real ,     parameter  ::  MAX_PAY_RATE   =  75.00
end module  Global_par_mod
```

A second category is a module whose sole purpose is to provide the interface to procedures, such as this example (see Rule 122):

```
module  Interface_mod
  implicit none
  interface
    subroutine  Sub_a  ( arg_a1 ,  arg_a2 ,  arg_a3 )
      real ,      intent ( in )       ::  arg_a1
      real ,      intent ( in out )  ::  arg_a2
      logical ,  intent ( in ) ,  optional  ::  arg_a3
    end subroutine  Sub_a

    function  Func_b  ( arg_b1 )  result  ( return_value )
      integer ,  intent ( in )  ::  arg_b1
      integer  ::  return_value
    end function  Func_b
  end interface
end module  Interface_mod
```

In this case, the module's purpose is to provide the interface information to those program units that need it, and there is no reason to make any of this information private. Bear in mind, however, that there could be a naming conflict in program units where modules such as these are used. In that case, if the accessibility of all entities in the module is **public**, the **only** option may be needed, or the public entity may have to be renamed.

```
use  interface_mod ,  Comp_Func_b  => Func_b
```

49. *Use the* **only** *option in* **use** *statements.*

Application of this guideline in conjunction with the use of the **private** attribute, as explained in Rule 48, provides complete control over the access to module entities. Each module then has a directory of the references made to entities in other modules along with their location. Except for possible naming conflicts, there is no reason to use the **only** option with modules whose default access is **public**. As explained in the Rule 48, these would be modules that contain only named constants or interfaces.

One drawback of applying this rule is that its use could possibly increase the work involved in maintaining a program. Here is a **use** statement that provides access in B_mod to entity var_a in module A_mod. If, for some reason, you have to move variable var_a from module A_mod to another module, every **use** statement like this in the program needs to be changed:

```
module B_mod
   . . .
   use A_mod, only : var_a
   . . .
end module B_mod
```

6.3 Procedure Arguments

50. *Indicate the intent of all dummy arguments.*

Indicating the intent of all the dummy arguments of a procedure aids the compiler in discovering errors in your program. The compiler can verify that values are not assigned to arguments that have the **intent** (**in**) attribute. Furthermore, if a dummy argument with **intent** (**in**) is used as an actual argument to another subprogram, and if the code provides access to that subprogram's interface, the compiler can issue an error message if the corresponding dummy argument in the called procedure is not also **intent** (**in**). Similarly, the compiler can warn if no value is assigned to a dummy argument of **intent** (**out**), or if the calling procedure passed a constant value, an expression result, or a procedure reference as the actual argument.

When the dummy argument has attribute **intent** (**out**) and it is a derived type, the program will initialize all components as specified in the type definition. Note that when the procedure is called, the actual argument will be finalized before the call if it is a derived type for which a **final** procedure exists. In a like manner, if the actual argument is an allocatable variable or a derived type containing allocatable components, the allocatable entities will be deallocated before the procedure is called (see Rules 53, 136, and 147 and Section 7.2.1).

When the **intent** attribute of a dummy argument is not specified, the implied intent is similar to **intent** (**in out**) with an important difference: When **intent** (**in out**) is specified, the actual argument must be "definable," meaning it could appear on the left side of an assignment statement. The program that follows demonstrates this. In module Mod_a_mod, at location *Cmnt-1 in subroutine Set_all_good_calls, there are alternative declarations of the argument calls, one with an **intent** (**in out**) and one without, which also bestows the attribute **intent** (**in out**). There is a call to this subroutine in the main program Intent_exp_imp at the location marked *Cmnt-2. The actual argument is a reference to function Get_good_calls; it is not definable.

Listing 6.1: Program Intent_exp_imp

```
module Mod_a_mod
   implicit none
   private
   public :: Set_all_good_calls
   integer :: all_good_calls = 0
```

```
contains
  subroutine Set_all_good_calls (calls)
      ! *Cmnt-1
      ! with intent: the actual argument must be
      ! definable.
!     integer, intent (in out) :: calls
      ! without intent: the actual argument need not be
      ! definable.
    integer :: calls

    all_good_calls = all_good_calls + calls
    calls = 0
  end subroutine Set_all_good_calls
end module Mod_a_mod

module Mod_b_mod
  implicit none
  private
  public :: Get_probe_reading , Get_good_calls

  enum, bind(C)
    enumerator :: GOOD_PROBE=0, BAD_PROBE
  end enum
  integer, save :: series_good_calls
contains
  subroutine Get_probe_reading (probe_reading , &
      new_series)
    real , intent (out) :: probe_reading
    logical , intent (in) :: new_series

    integer :: i_stat = GOOD_PROBE

      ! for demonstration, return a fixed number.
    if (new_series) &
        series_good_calls = 0
    probe_reading = 6.5
    if (i_stat == GOOD_PROBE) &
        series_good_calls = series_good_calls + 1
  end subroutine Get_probe_reading

  function Get_good_calls () result (ret_val)
    integer :: ret_val
    ret_val = series_good_calls
  end function Get_good_calls
end module Mod_b_mod
```

```
program Intent_exp_imp
  use Mod_a_mod, only: Set_all_good_calls
  use Mod_b_mod, only: Get_probe_reading, Get_good_calls
  implicit none

    ! for demonstration, set a fixed number of calls
  integer, parameter :: NUMBER_OF_CALLS = 5
  integer :: i_tot_cnt
  real    :: probe_reading

  call Get_probe_reading (probe_reading, .true.)
  do i_tot_cnt = 2, NUMBER_OF_CALLS
    call Get_probe_reading (probe_reading, .false.)
  end do
    ! *Cmnt-2
    ! actual argument is undefinable
  call Set_all_good_calls (Get_good_calls () )
  write (*, "(2(A, I0))") "Good calls: ", &
      Get_good_calls (), " total calls: ", i_tot_cnt - 1
end program Intent_exp_imp
```

A good compiler will spot these differences. As an example, version 5.3 of the Numerical Algorithm Group's (NAG) compiler generates the following error message when the intent is explicitly specified:

```
Error: intent_exp_impP.f90, line 68: Argument CALLS (no. 1)
of SET_ALL_GOOD_CALLS is INTENT(OUT) or INTENT(INOUT) but
is not a variable
```

When the intent is *not* explicitly specified, the compiler builds the program, not issuing any error messages, but it generates the following runtime error message when executed:

```
Runtime Error: intent_exp_impP.f90, line 18: Dummy argument
CALLS is associated with an expression - cannot assign Program
terminated by fatal error
```

Another point arises in the following instance, one connected to definable objects: When you enclose parentheses around a simple variable, constant value, or named constant, you are creating an expression; as such, it's not definable. In its simplest form, you can place just a single variable inside parentheses. Here are two calls to a subroutine. In the first, the argument is a variable called int_arg ; in the second, the argument is an expression.

```
call Sub_c (int_arg)
...
call Sub_c ( (int_arg) )
```

The first call to Sub_c is correct. If the interface to procedure Sub_c is available, and the intent assigned to the dummy argument is **intent (in out)**, a good compiler will flag the second call as an error, which it is according to the standard. If the interface does not specify an intent, the standard states the call to Sub_c is correct. However, if the procedure attempts to redefine the argument, an error at runtime is likely to occur.

Be aware that Fortran 2003, unlike Fortran 90 and Fortran 95, allows the **intent** attribute to be specified for dummy arguments that are pointers (see Rule 55). The **intent** refers to the association status of the pointer, not to its target. A final point on intent is that if the argument is a derived type with pointer components, the intent applies to the type object itself, not the targets of the pointers. That is, if, for example, **intent** (**in**) is used, the data area that the pointer is targeted at can be modified:

```
module Mytype_mod
  implicit none

  type mytype_t
    integer, pointer :: int_p (:)
  contains
    procedure :: Sub => Mytype_sub
  end type mytype_t
contains
  subroutine Mytype_sub (this)
    class (mytype_t), intent(in) :: this
      ! Legal assignment to pointer target, even though
      ! intent(in) was specified.
    this%int_p = 42
  end subroutine Mytype_sub
end module Mytype_mod

program Mytype
  use Mytype_mod
  implicit none

  type(mytype_t) :: my_mytype
  integer :: al_stat

  allocate (integer :: my_mytype%int_p(100), &
    stat=al_stat)
  call my_mytype%Sub ()
end program Mytype
```

Even though not required, in a case such as the previous example, it is better to state **intent** (**in out**) to indicate to the reader that modification of data is taking place.

51. *In functions, specify the intent of all dummy arguments as* **intent** (**in**).

The purpose of Fortran functions is to return a value based on the value of its arguments (if there are any). The function should not cause side effects by altering their value. You can ensure this will not occur by declaring all dummy arguments **intent** (**in**). Use a subroutine instead of a function if an argument needs to be modified. The standard mandates that you declare all dummy arguments of a **pure** function to be **intent** (**in**). Otherwise, a standard-conforming compiler will not compile it (see Section 6.6 and Rule 52). Here is an example of a routine written counter to this rule. It calls a function that returns a value in one of its arguments. Following it is code that calls the function:

```fortran
module Calc_mod
  implicit none
  private
  public :: Calc_result , CALL_FOO_1 , CALL_FOO_2 , &
      CALL_FUNC_1 , CALL_FUNC_2 , TERMINATE

  integer , parameter :: CALL_FOO_1 = 1, &
      CALL_FOO_2 = -1, CALL_FUNC_1 = 1, &
      CALL_FUNC_2 = -1, TERMINATE = 0
contains
  function Calc_result (i_state , a) &
      result (return_value)
    integer , intent (in out) :: i_state
    real ,    intent (in)     :: a
    real :: return_value
    real :: old_a
    real , parameter :: EPS = 5.0 * tiny (1.0)

    old_a = a
    if (i_state == CALL_FOO_1) then
      return_value = Foo_1 (a)
    else if (i_state == CALL_FOO_2) then
      return_value = Foo_2 (a)
    end if

    if (abs (old_a - return_value) < eps) then
      i_ret = TERMINATE
    else if (    (return_value > 0.0 .and. old_a > 0.0) &
            .or. (return_value < 0.0 .and. old_a < 0.0))
    then
      i_state = CALL_FUNC_2
    else
      i_state = CALL_FUNC_1
    end if
  end function Calc_result
end module Calc_mod
  . . .
```

```fortran
use Calc_mod, only : Calc_result, CALL_FOO_1, &
    CALL_FOO_2, CALL_FUNC_1, CALL_FUNC_2

integer, parameter :: NO_OF_VALS = 10
real       :: new_val, x(NO_OF_VALS)
integer :: i_flag, j_iter

x = 0.0
each_val: do j_iter = 1, NO_OF_VALS
  new_val = 0.0
  i_flag  = CALL_FOO_1

  make_val: do
    new_val = Calc_result (x(j_iter), i_flag)
    select case (i_flag)
    case (CALL_FUNC_1)
      x(j_iter) = Func_1 (new_val)
      i_flag    = CALL_FOO_1
    case (CALL_FUNC_2)
      x(j_iter) = Func_2 (new_val)
      i_flag    = CALL_FOO_2
    case default
      exit each_val
    end select
  end do make_val
end do each_val
```

This should not be done. Two possible methods can be used to change this: The first is to change the function Calc_result to a subroutine. Its interface and a call would then be:

```fortran
subroutine Calc_result (i_state, a, new_a)
  integer, intent (in out) :: i_state
  real,    intent (in)     :: a
  real,    intent (out)    :: new_a
end subroutine Calc_result
...
call Calc_result (i_state, x(j_iter), new_val)
```

If you wish to retain the use of a function call, which is very suited to use of **forall** and **where** statements and constructs, you can define a derived data type that contains both the returned value and the flag (see Rule 59):

```fortran
type result_t
  real    :: new_a
  integer :: i_state
end type result_t
```

The interface to the procedure Calc_result and the code in the calling procedure would be:

```
function Calc_result (a) result (return_value)
  real, intent (in) :: a
  type (result_t)   :: return_value
end function Calc_result

...

type (result_t) :: new_res
new_res = Calc_result (x(j_iter))
  ! branch based on the value returned in
  ! new_res%i_state
```

52. *Whenever possible, write procedures such that they can be prefixed by the* pure *prefix.*

The Fortran 95 standard introduced the **pure** prefix that can be attached to subprograms (see Reference [42]). The constraints attached to a pure subprogram ensure that the subprogram will not have side effects. They do this by requiring the intent of all function dummy arguments to be **intent** (**in**) (see Rule 51); by stipulating that a pure subprogram not make any assignments to any entities whose scope is not the subprogram itself (but could be accessed by it via host or use association, either directly or via arguments that are pointers or have pointer components); and by dictating that the subprogram not perform any external input/output operations or the **stop** operation. Furthermore, the standard also states that local variables shall not have the **save** attribute (see Rule 128). (Elemental procedures are a special case of pure procedures [see Rule 128].) Here is a pure function that calculates the distance between two points:

```
type point_t
  real :: x, y
end type point_t

pure function Calc_dist (pt_1, pt_2) &
    result (return_value)
  type (point_t), intent (in) :: pt_1, pt_2
  real (kind (pt_1%x)) :: return_value

  return_value = sqrt ( (pt_2%y - pt_1%y) ** 2 + &
                        (pt_2%x - pt_1%x) ** 2)
end function Calc_dist
```

Many compilers provide optimization switches that will optimize your code or permit it to run in parallel on multiple processors and processors that have multiple processing cores. The **pure** attribute assists the compiler in doing this. This is especially so in **forall** statements and constructs. In the following code snippet, knowledge that the function Calc_dist is pure will allow the compiler to distribute the assignments to multiple processors or processor cores.

```
integer, parameter :: NO_OF_POINTS = 20
type (point_t)     :: pt_array (NO_OF_POINTS), base_point
real     :: dists (NO_OF_POINTS)
```

```
integer :: i

forall (i = 1: ubound (pt_array , dim=1)) &
     dists(i) = Calc_dist (base_point , pt_array(i))
```

In Fortran 2008, pure subprograms become especially useful in the **do concurrent** construct. Designed for parallel processing, this construct is similar to **forall** : It specifically permits the program to execute a loop in any order, but adds the restriction, among others, that all procedure references within the construct be to pure procedures (see Reference [43] and Rule 168).

The Fortran 2008 standard introduces impure subprograms, relaxing the restriction that they be pure. In subprograms so defined, input and output is permitted. You use the keyword **impure** in the subprogram specification.

53. *Use caution when specifying derived-type dummy arguments with the* intent (out) *attribute*.

If derived-type components are initialized in the type definition, and a dummy argument of that type is specified to have the **intent** (**out**) attribute, the non-pointer components of the derived type are initialized upon entry to the procedure. Conversely, the components of dummy arguments with the **intent** (**out**) attribute are not initialized if no such initialization is specified in the component definition; they become undefined on entry to the procedure. If care is not taken, both of these situations can cause problems.

Here, in very abbreviated form, are two modules and a main program that make up part of an investment portfolio program:

Listing 6.2: Program Intent_out_test

```
module Equity_mod
  implicit none
  private
  public :: Calculate , Get_active , Get_quote , Print

  type, public :: equity_t
     ! active: indicate if stock is volatile .
    logical :: active = .false.
    real     :: current_price = 1.0
    integer :: no_of_shares  = 0
  end type equity_t

  interface Calculate
    module procedure Calc_equity
  end interface Calculate
```

```fortran
      interface Print
        module procedure Print_equity
      end interface Print
contains

      elemental function Calc_equity (this) &
          result (return_val)
        type (equity_t), intent (in) :: this
        real :: return_val

        return_val = this%current_price * this%no_of_shares
      end function Calc_equity

      elemental function Get_active (this) &
          result (return_val)
        type (equity_t), intent (in) :: this
        logical :: return_val

        return_val = this%active
      end function Get_active

      subroutine Get_quote (this)
        ! call code to obtain online quotation.
        ! set active true if no. of shares traded exceeds a
        ! threshold.

        type (equity_t), intent (out) :: this

          ! simplified code to show intent (out) problem
        this%active = .true.
        this%current_price = 10.0
      end subroutine Get_quote

      subroutine Print_equity (this)
        type (equity_t), intent (in) :: this

        write (*, "(A, L1)") "Active is ", this%active
      end subroutine Print_equity
end module Equity_mod

module Account_mod
   use equity_mod, only : Calculate, equity_t, Get_quote
   implicit none
   private
   public :: Calc_account, Get_quotes

   integer, parameter :: MAX_EQUITIES = 3
```

```fortran
   type, public :: account_t
     type (equity_t) :: equities (MAX_EQUITIES)
     !...components with other account information
   end type account_t
contains

   subroutine Calc_account (this)
     ! intent (out) causes problems.
     type (account_t), intent (out) :: this
     real    :: temp_value
     integer :: i_equity

     do i_equity = 1, size (this%equities)
       temp_value = Calculate (this%equities(i_equity) )
     end do
   end subroutine Calc_account

   subroutine Get_quotes (this)
     type (account_t), intent (in out) :: this
     integer :: i_equity

     do i_equity = 1, size (this%equities)
       call Get_quote (this%equities(i_equity) )
     end do
   end subroutine Get_quotes
end module Account_mod

program Intent_out_test
   use account_mod, only : account_t, Calc_account, &
       Get_quotes
   use Equity_mod, only : Get_active, Print
   implicit none

   type (account_t) :: account
   integer :: i_equity

   call Get_quotes (account)
   do i_equity = 1, size (account%equities)

     if (Get_active (account%equities(i_equity) ) ) &
         call Print (account%equities(i_equity) )
   end do

     ! does not work.
   call Calc_account (account)
   do i_equity = 1, size (account%equities)
     if (Get_active (account%equities(i_equity) ) ) &
```

```
        call Print (account%equities(i_equity))
    end do
end program Intent_out_test
```

In the main program, the loop following the reference to function Calculate will not work correctly. Here is the output of the program:

```
Active is T
Active is T
Active is T
```

Only the values of the first loop, not the second, appear. The culprit is the **intent** (**out**) of subprogram Calc_account in Account_mod. This attribute forces component active of all the elements of component array account%equities to acquire their initialization value of . **false** ..

A programmer most likely would find this error easily because the program simply would not operate as required. A more insidious error could occur if component active were not initialized in the type declaration of derived type equity_t . In this case, according to the standard, the component active would become undefined when Calculate was called, and you could not rely on its maintaining the correct value in the second set of loops. However, it would be likely that it would retain the value set in Get_quotes; the compiler would not generate code that would change it, and, therefore, subroutine **Print** would be called as expected. But this may not be the case for all compilers or, for a particular compiler, the behavior may vary according to the compiler options set. The easiest way to avoid such problems is to assign the **intent** (**in out**) attribute to the dummy argument in place of **intent** (**out**) (see Reference [17] and Rule 86).

54. *When appropriate, assign the* value *attribute to dummy arguments to allow their values to change without affecting the value of the actual argument.*

The **value** attribute forces the compiler to pass an actual argument "by value" and not, as is usually done in Fortran, "as if by reference." The primary motivation for the addition of this feature is for interoperability with C (see Chapter 14). This capability, however, can be effectively used for other purposes. The following code is a simple example. It is the skeleton of a subroutine that moves a cutting tool to a part. The increment by which the tool is moved is dummy argument inc, and the value of the actual argument should not change. This is achieved using the **value** attribute.

```
module Tool_mod
    use Error_codes_mod , only : SUCCESS, FAIL
    use Part_mod , only : part_t

    implicit none
    private
```

```
  type , public :: tool_t
    real      :: location (3) = 0.0
    integer :: move_status = FAIL
  contains
    procedure :: Move_tool_to_part
    procedure :: Move_tool
  end type tool_t
contains

  subroutine Move_tool_to_part (this , part , inc , tol , &
      max_iters )
    class (tool_t ), intent (in out) :: this
    type (part_t ), intent (in)       :: part
    real ,      intent (in ), value    :: inc (3)
    real ,      intent (in ) :: tol
    integer , intent (in ) :: max_iters

      ! iter — iteration counter
      ! distance — current distance of tool from the
      ! part tool — working copy of this
    integer :: iter
    real      :: distance (3)
    real      :: hypot_sqrd , total_dist
    type (tool_t ) :: tool

    interface
      subroutine Change_inc (inc , distance )
        real , intent (in out), value :: inc (3)
        real , intent (in ), :: distance (3)
      end subroutine Change_inc
    end interface

    tool%location = this%location
    loop_to_solution : do iter = 1, max_iters
      call Move_tool (this , inc )

      distance  = Calc_tool_part_distance (tool , part )
      hypot_sqrd = dot_product (distance , distance )
      total_dist = sqrt (hypot_sqrd )
      if (abs (total_dist) <= tol ) then
        tool%move_status = SUCCESS
        this%location    = tool%location
        exit loop_to_solution
      else if (iter >= max_iters ) then
        this%move_status = FAIL
        exit loop_to_solution
      end if
```

```
      call Change_inc (inc, distance)
   end do loop_to_solution
end subroutine Move_tool_to_part

subroutine Move_tool (this, inc)
   class (tool_t), intent (in out) :: this
   real, intent (in) :: inc(3)

   this%location = this%location + inc
end subroutine Move_tool
end module Tool_mod
```

55. *Be attentive to the particular standard specifications regarding arguments possessing either the* pointer *or the* target *attribute.*

Using dummy and actual arguments that possess either the **pointer** or **target** attribute can be confusing. To clarify their use, this rule explains the program behavior when a dummy argument possesses the **pointer** attribute, and Rule 56 details the behavior when it possesses the **target** attribute.

The explanation is first divided into two major sections: the first when the dummy argument has the **pointer** attribute, the second when it is assigned solely to the actual argument. In several instances, the behavior the standard prescribes for arguments that are pointers apply to those that are allocatable too. This is pointed out in the text. Short code sections provide examples.

Dummy Pointer Argument   An explicit interface to a subprogram must be provided if one or more of its arguments is either a pointer or has the **allocatable** attribute assigned to it. The actual argument must also be a pointer and all its non-deferred type parameters and ranks shall agree with those of the dummy argument.

In the following code, a parameterized derived type is defined (see Rule 125); two pointers of this type are declared; and the interfaces of two subroutines, each having two dummy pointer arguments of this type, are given. The explicit interfaces are specified using interface blocks. However, it is normally preferable to have the explicit interface specifications come directly from the procedures themselves – either by residing in the same module as the caller, or from "use association" from another module. Three calls to these routines are shown, and comments within the code explain which are legal calls and which are not.

```
integer, parameter :: MAX_LEN = 100
type, public :: my_typ_t (arr_len)
   integer, len :: arr_len = MAX_LEN
   integer :: int_array(arr_len)
end type my_typ_t

   ! define three variables of type my_typ_t. one with a
   ! deferred type parameter and two without.
   type (my_typ_t, arr_len =:), pointer :: def_var
```

```
type (my_typ_t , arr_len =50), pointer :: non_def_var_50
type (my_typ_t , arr_len =20), pointer :: non_def_var_20

interface
  subroutine Sub_a (arg_a1 , arg_a2)
    import :: my_typ_t
    type (my_typ_t , arr_len =50), intent (in out), &
        pointer :: arg_a1
    type (my_typ_t , arr_len =:), intent (in out), &
        pointer :: arg_a2
  end subroutine Sub_a
end interface

  ! this call is legal:
  ! the type parameter of the first actual argument
  ! is not deferred and it agrees with that of the dummy
  ! argument. the second actual argument has a deferred
  ! type parameter, as does the dummy argument.
call Sub_a (non_def_var_50 , def_var)

  ! this call is illegal:
  ! the first actual argument has a deferred type
  ! parameter but the first dummy argument does not,
  ! and the second actual argument does not have a
  ! deferred type parameter but the second dummy
  ! argument does.
call Sub_a (def_var , non_def_var_50)

  ! this call is illegal:
  ! the non—deferred type parameter of the first
  ! actual argument does not agree with the type
  ! parameter of the first dummy argument.
call Sub_a (non_def_var_20 , def_var)
```

Attention must be paid to the intent of the dummy argument when it is a pointer; the intent affects the behavior as explained in the next three sections covering **intent (out)**, **intent (in)**, and **intent (in out)**.

■ **intent (out)**

If the dummy argument has this attribute, the pointer association of the actual argument becomes undefined when the procedure is invoked. After the procedure has completed, the association status of the actual argument acquires that given the dummy argument during execution of the procedure (see Rule 53). The behavior on invocation is a potential source of memory leaks, a situation where the program loses access to memory without deallocating it, so you must be cautious in this case. Here is the interface of a subroutine with such a dummy argument:

```
! on invocation of this procedure, the actual
! argument associated with dummy argument
! int_arg1 acquires a status of undefined. To use
! it, the procedure first needs to allocate it
! (or it may be nullified).

interface
   subroutine Sub_a (int_arg1)
      integer, intent (out), pointer :: int_arg1 (:)
   end subroutine Sub_a
end interface
```

Here is a code that includes a call to the procedure. It will cause a memory leak.

```
integer, pointer :: int_ptr (:)
integer :: alloc_stat, num_elems

   !allocate memory for the integer pointer
allocate (integer :: int_ptr(num_elems), &
   stat = alloc_stat)

   ! If the allocation is successful, call Sub_a.
   ! access to the memory just allocated is lost.
if (alloc_stat == 0) call Sub_a (int_ptr)
```

Assigning a pointer dummy argument could be an alternative to returning a pointer as a function result. For example, you may have a linked list of a derived type, and you wish to create a new node in the list (the definition of type my_type_t is not shown).

```
type node_t
   type (my_type_t) :: my_type_value
   type (node_t), pointer :: next_node_ptr
end type node_t

subroutine Create_node (this, my_type_object)
   type (node_t),    intent (out), pointer :: this
   type (my_type_t), intent (in) :: my_type_object

   integer :: alloc_stat

   ! the nullified status of this on return
   ! indicates an error.
   nullify (this)

   ! check values of the components of this;
   ! proceed if correct.
   if (Check_components (my_type_object) == 0) then
```

```
    allocate (node_t :: this, stat=alloc_stat)
    if (alloc_stat == 0) then
      this%my_type_value = my_type_object
    else
      !... handle error condition
    end if
  end if
end subroutine Create_node
```

A "dangling" pointer is the result of deallocating the target of a pointer without directly using the pointer itself. To prevent a dangling pointer in the previous calling procedure, you would want to make sure the actual argument that corresponds with argument this is not already associated with a target. (It is too late to do so in Create_node because the actual argument has acquired a status of undefined on entry.) In the sample code here, this is accomplished by a call to a procedure named Destroy (not shown).

```
type (my_type_t) :: my_type_object
type (node_t), pointer :: new_node

nullify (new_node)

  ! code to set components of my_type_object.

  ! code that possibly could allocate, assign,
  ! and use new_node.

if (associated (new_node) ) call Destroy (new_node)
call Create_node (new_node, my_type_object)
```

■ **intent (in)**
The procedure cannot change the association of the pointer to its target during execution. It can, however, change the value of the pointer's target. Here is an example:

```
subroutine Calc_temp (this, temp_pointer)
  type (temp_t), intent (in out)      :: this
  real,          intent (in), pointer :: temp_pointer
  real, target :: local_target

    ! The following code is legal:
  temp_pointer = 5.2

    ! but the following two lines of code are not:
  nullify (temp_pointer)
  temp_pointer => local_target
end subroutine Calc_temp
```

This applies not only to dummy arguments that are pointers, but also to dummy arguments of derived type that are not pointers but have pointer components.

```fortran
type, public :: element_t
  real, pointer :: intensity
end type element_t

subroutine Process_element (this)
  type (element_t), intent(in) :: this

    ! The following code is correct:
  if (associated (this%intensity) ) &
    this%intensity = 0.0

    ! but this is not:
  if (associated (this%intensity) ) &
    nullify (this%intensity)
end subroutine Process_element
```

A further restriction is that the actual argument in a call to a procedure where the corresponding dummy argument is a pointer with **intent (in)** (or **intent (in out)**) must be a pointer and not the result of a call to a function that returns a pointer. The following code snippet shows the interface of two calls followed by an *illegal* reference to the second:

```fortran
interface
  function Clone_element (this) result (return_value)
    type (element_t), intent (in) :: this
    type (element_t), pointer     :: return_value
  end function Clone_element
end interface

. . .

interface
  subroutine Assemble_element (this)
    type (element_t), pointer, intent (in out) :: this
  end subroutine Assemble_element
end interface

. . .

type (element_t) :: element_1

    ! illegal call!
call Assemble_element (Clone_element (element_1))
```

■ **intent (in out)**
When the pointer dummy argument has the intent of **intent (in out)**, both the value and the association of the dummy argument can be changed. On entry to the called subprogram, the dummy pointer argument becomes

associated with the target of the actual pointer argument if it has one. If the dummy pointer becomes associated with a different target during execution, the actual target will be associated with it when control is returned to the invoking routine. Care must be taken, however, if the dummy argument is associated with a local target that ceases to exist on exit. In that case, the actual argument is undefined when execution returns to the calling routine.

The following program demonstrates how this works. It contains a module with a subroutine that has two pointer arguments with **intent** (**in out**). In it, one of the arguments, i_arg_a , is associated with a module variable that has the **save** attribute. Argument int_arg_b , the second dummy argument, is associated with a variable local to the subroutine that does not have this attribute. The code in the main program that follows shows a call to subroutine Point_arg . Comments embedded in the code point out the program behavior.

Listing 6.3:   Program Point_intent_in_out

```
module Proc_mod
   implicit none
   private
   public :: Point_arg

   integer, target, save :: module_saved_int
contains
   subroutine Point_arg (i_arg_a , int_arg_b)
      integer, intent (in out), pointer :: i_arg_a
      integer, intent (in out), pointer :: i_arg_b

      integer, target :: local_non_saved_int

      module_saved_int    = 50
      local_non_saved_int = 60
      i_arg_a    => module_saved_int
      int_arg_b  => local_non_saved_int
   end subroutine Point_arg
end module Proc_mod

program Point_intent_in_out
   use Proc_mod, only : Point_arg
   implicit none

   integer, target  :: int_a , int_b
   integer, pointer :: int_point_a , int_point_b

   int_a = 5
   int_b = 8
```

```
      int_point_a  => int_a
      int_point_b  => int_b
      call Point_arg (int_point_a , int_point_b)
        ! int_point_a is now associated with saved module
        ! variable module_saved_int in module proc_mod.
        ! Its value is 50 (the value of int_a remains 5).
      if (associated (int_point_a) ) print *, &
          "int_point_a: ", int_point_a

        ! Even though int_point_b appears associated,
        ! its target is undefined; any reference to it is
        ! illegal.
      if (associated (int_point_b) ) print *, &
          "int_point_b: ", int_point_b
   end program Point_intent_in_out
```

When this program was built using version 5.3 of the Numerical Algorithm Group compiler, the results of executing the program are:

```
   int_point_a:  50
   Runtime Error: point-intent-in-outP.f90, line 42: Dangling
   pointer INT_POINT_B used as argument to intrinsic function
   ASSOCIATED Target was RETURNed from procedure
   PROC_MOD:POINT_ARG
   Program terminated by fatal error
```

Actual Pointer Argument An actual argument may be a pointer even if the dummy argument is not. In this case, the actual argument must be allocated prior to the procedure reference; you can regard this as if the associated target were the actual argument and not the pointer. (An actual argument that has the **allocatable** attribute must also be allocated if the dummy argument is not also allocatable.) In the following code, the two calls to Sub_a have the same effect on the values of both int_ptr and int_targ ; either could be used.

```
integer , pointer :: int_ptr
integer , target  :: int_targ

interface Sub_a (int_arg)
   integer , intent (in out) :: int_arg
end interface Sub_a

int_targ = 5.2
int_ptr  => int_targ

   ! either of the following two calls could be made.
call Sub_a (int_ptr)
call Sub_a (int_targ)
```

56. *Be attentive to the particular standard specifications regarding arguments possessing the* **target** *attribute; do not rely on pointers that become associated with dummy arguments possessing this attribute to retain their value or their association status.*

This rule explains the behavior of programs where either a dummy or an actual argument, or both, have the **target** attribute (see Rule 55).

An explicit interface to a subprogram must be provided if one or more of its dummy arguments is a target. As opposed to dummy pointer arguments, the actual argument corresponding to a dummy target argument may or may not be a pointer or a target. Furthermore, an actual argument may be a target even though its corresponding dummy argument is not one.

With target actual and dummy arguments, it is important to understand the behavior of pointers that are pointer associated with them. The following sections explain this. In each, the assumption is that the dummy argument has the **target** attribute; each section discusses the behavior based on the characteristics of either the actual or the dummy argument. One behavior common to all occurs when the dummy argument possesses the **value** attribute as well as the **target** one. In this case, any pointers that become assigned to the dummy argument become undefined when program execution exits the invoked procedure. In the following routine, the pointer int_point_a becomes undefined on procedure exit (see Rule 54).

```
subroutine Targ_a (int_targ)
  integer, intent (in out), target, value :: int_targ
  integer, pointer :: int_point

  int_point_a => int_targ
  ...
end subroutine Targ_a
```

actual argument: neither pointer nor target If an entity is neither a target nor a pointer, no pointer can be associated with it. The standard explicitly states that if any pointers become associated with the dummy target argument in the referenced subprogram, they become undefined on return to the calling routine; they cannot become associated with the actual argument (see Reference [39]). This is true regardless of the intent of the dummy argument and the possession of the **save** attribute of any pointers that become associated with the target argument. This behavior is identical to that described above when the dummy argument has the **value** attribute assigned to it.

The following skeleton code shows a module with a subroutine, Sub_a, that has a target integer argument. When invoked, it associates a pointer whose scope is the entire module with it. This pointer is referenced by two other subroutines in the module. When the program exits Sub_a, the pointer data_ptr in module

Sample_mod becomes undefined because the variable int_1, the actual dummy argument, is not a target.

```fortran
Sample_mod
   implicit none
   private
   public :: Sub_a

   integer, pointer, save :: data_ptr:
contains

   subroutine Sub_a (i_targ)
      integer, intent (in out), target :: i_targ:
      ...
      data_ptr => i_targ
      ...
      call Sub_b ()
      call Sub_c ()
   end subroutine Sub_a

   subroutine Sub_b ()
      ! code that accesses data_ptr
   end subroutine Sub_b

   subroutine Sub_c ()
      ! code that accesses data_ptr
   end subroutine Sub_c
end module Sample_mod
```

Here is code showing a call to Sub_a:

```fortran
...
use Sample_mod
implicit none
integer :: i
integer, parameter :: ARR_SIZE = 1000
...
integer :: int_1 (ARR_SIZE)
int_1 = [(i, i=1, size(int_1))]
call Sub_a (int_1)
```

actual argument: target With respect to pointers associated with the actual argument and those associated with the dummy argument, the situation where both arguments possess the target attribute present the programmer with the most difficulties. Here are the possibilities:

- **dummy argument is a scalar or assumed-shape array**
  When a procedure is invoked, pointers associated with the target actual argument become associated with the target dummy argument. When control returns to the calling procedure, any pointers that become associated

with the target dummy argument become associated with the actual target argument, but only if these pointers do not become undefined on completion of the subprogram called (as would be the case, for instance, of a pointer that is local to the subprogram and that does not have the **save** attribute).

Here is the interface to a subroutine with both a scalar and an assumed-shape target dummy argument. Any pointers in it that become associated with the dummy arguments and that do not become undefined will become associated with the actual target argument.

```
interface
   subroutine Targ_b (scalar_targ , assum_shape_targ)
      integer , intent (in out), target :: scalar_targ
      integer , intent (in out), target :: &
         assum_shape_targ (:,:)
   end subroutine Targ_b
end interface
```

None of this applies if the actual argument is an array section with a vector subscript. If this is the case, the standard specifies that any pointers that become associated with a target dummy argument become undefined on subprogram exit. The following code shows an example:

```
integer :: vect_sub(3)
integer :: array_1(100, 100)

interface
   subroutine Sub_a (int_targ)
      integer , intent (in), target :: int_targ(:, :)
   end subroutine Sub_a
end interface

vect_sub = [10, 20, 30]

   ! if any pointers are associated with dummy argument
   ! int_targ in subroutine Sub_a, they will become
   ! undefined after the following call exits.
call Sub_a (array_1(:, vect_sub) )
```

■ **dummy argument is an explicit-shape array or an assumed-size array**

The standard dictates that in this situation it is processor-dependent whether pointers associated with the actual argument become associated with the target dummy argument, and that, on return from the subprogram, the association status of any pointers that become associated with the target dummy argument is also processor-dependent. That would be the case with both of the arguments in the subprogram interface shown here.

```
interface
   subroutine Target_a (exp_targ , assum_size_targ , &
      targ_a_size )
```

```
      integer , intent ( in out ) , target :: &
        exp_targ (20 , 40)
      integer , intent ( in out ) , target :: &
        assum_size_targ ( targ_a_size , *)
      integer , intent ( in ) :: targ_a_size
   end subroutine Target_a
end interface
```

The same qualification pertaining to actual arguments that are array sections with a vector subscript that was noted previously for target dummy arguments that are either scalars or assumed-shape arrays applies here as well: Any pointers that become pointer associated with them become undefined on exit.

A further complication exists when there is a dummy argument that is not a target and it is associated with an actual argument that is a target, and that dummy argument, in turn, becomes the actual argument to a call to a routine where the dummy argument does possess the **target** attribute. That would be the situation shown here:

```
subroutine Targ_a
   integer , target :: targ
   . . .
   call Sub_b ( targ )
end subroutine Targ_a

subroutine Sub_b ( int_arg_b )
   integer , intent ( in out ) :: int_arg_b
   . . .
   call Targ_c ( int_arg_b )
end subroutine Sub_b

subroutine Targ_c ( targ_arg_c )
   integer , intent ( in out ) , target :: targ_arg_c
   integer , pointer :: int_point_c
   . . .
   int_point_c => targ_arc_c
end subroutine Targ_c
```

The standard states that the association of int_point_c in subroutine Targ_c with variable targ_a in subroutine Targ_a is processor-dependent.

This multitude of possibilities make the use of pointers associated with dummy arguments having the **target** attribute problematical. The code that follows demonstrate one of the potential difficulties. This one is especially egregious because the behavior of one call in some cases depends on the argument characteristics of the previous one.

```
module Proc_mod
   implicit none
```

```fortran
   private

   public :: Target_arg

      ! saved_int_ptr has the save attribute because
      ! it is initialized in its declaration;
      ! non_saved_int_ptr does not.
      ! Fortran 2008 stipulates that module variables
      ! have the save attribute.
   integer, pointer :: saved_int_ptr => null ()
   integer, pointer :: non_saved_int_ptr
contains

   subroutine Target_arg (i_targ)
      integer, intent (in out), target :: i_targ

         ! loc_saved_ptr has the save attribute because
         ! it is initialized in its declaration;
         ! loc_non_saved_ptr does not.
      integer, pointer :: loc_saved_ptr => null ()
      integer, pointer :: loc_non_saved_ptr

         ! In the first call to Target_arg, these
         ! references to the intrinsic function
         ! associated will work because both
         ! loc_saved_ptr and saved_int_ptr are
         ! initialized in the declarations as nullified.

         ! On subsequent calls, the references will not
         ! work if the actual argument of the most recent
         ! call did not have the target attribute.
      if (associated (loc_saved_ptr) ) then
         print *, "loc_saved_ptr is ", loc_saved_ptr
      else
         print *, "loc_saved_ptr is not associated"
      end if

      if (associated (saved_int_ptr) ) then
         print *, "saved_int_ptr is ", loc_saved_ptr
      else
         print *, "saved_int_ptr is not associated"
      end if

         ! this call to intrinsic function associated
         ! will always cause a problem. The variable
         ! loc_non_saved_ptr has a processor-dependent
         ! state on entry and, therefore, its use is
         ! unreliable.
```

```
   if (associated (loc_non_saved_ptr) ) then
     print *, "loc_non_saved_ptr is ", &
       loc_non_saved_ptr
   else
     print *, "loc_non_saved_ptr is not associated"
   end if

     ! this reference to associated will cause a
     ! problem in the first call to Target_arg
     ! because it is not initialized in its
     ! declaration.

     ! variable non_saved_int_ptr does not possess
     ! the save attribute, but it is a module
     ! variable.
     ! Subsequent calls to associated will cause
     ! a problem if it becomes undefined, by,
     ! for example, going out of scope, or if
     ! the actual argument in the most recent
     ! call did not possess the target
     ! attribute.

   if (associated (non_saved_int_ptr) ) then
     print *, "non_saved_int_ptr is ", loc_saved_ptr
   else
     print *, "non_saved_int_ptr is not associated"
   end if

   saved_int_ptr      => i_targ
   non_saved_int_ptr  => i_targ

   i_targ = 98

   loc_saved_ptr      => i_targ
   loc_non_saved_ptr  => i_targ
 end subroutine Target_arg
end module Proc_mod
```

57. *Consistently place subprogram arguments in the following order:* the pass *argument,* intent (in out) *arguments,* intent (in) *arguments,* intent (out) *arguments,* optional *arguments.*

By default, the first argument of both procedure pointer components and type-bound procedures is an object of a class. The actual argument passed must be one of the types of the class, either the base type or one extended from it (see Rule 149). It makes sense, therefore, that such an argument be made the first one whenever possible (see Rule 152). Here is part of a module for a structural beam:

```
module Beam_mod
  type beam_t
  ... components describing geometry, structural
  ... properties, material, etc.
  contains
    procedure :: Compute_deflection
  end type beam_t

  subroutine Compute_deflection (this, load, deflection)
    class (beam_t),intent (in) :: this
    type (load_t), intent (in) :: load
    type (deflection_t), intent (out) :: deflection
    !... code to compute beam deflection.
  end subroutine Compute_deflection
end module Beam_mod
```

The first argument, this, possesses the **pass** attribute by default. The type-bound procedure Compute_deflection would be called as shown in this code:

```
type (beam_t) :: a_beam
type (load_t) :: load_1
type (deflection_t) :: deflection_1
call a_beam%Compute_deflection (load_1, deflection_1)
```

Regarding the placing of optional arguments at the end, here's the interface of a subroutine with one optional argument:

```
subroutine Put_a (r_arg, i_arg1, i_arg_op)
  real,     intent (in out) :: r_arg
  integer, intent (in)      :: i_arg1
  integer, intent (in), optional :: i_arg_op
end subroutine Put_a
```

Calls to this subroutine, both with and without the optional argument, would appear as follows:

```
integer :: int1, int2
real    :: real1
call Put_a (real1, int1)
...
call Put_a (r_arg=real1, i_arg1=int1, i_arg_op=int2)
```

If during program development you need to add an optional argument to the argument list, you should add one to the end. Then only the calls that need to pass the new argument need be modified.

```
subroutine Put_a (r_arg, i_arg1, i_arg_op, k_arg_op)
  real,     intent (in out) :: r_arg
  integer, intent (in)      :: i_arg1
  integer, intent (in), optional :: i_arg_op, k_arg_op
end subroutine Put_a
```

```
! a new call to Put_a
call Put_a (r_arg=real1, i_arg1=int1, k_arg_op=int3)

! an old call to Put_a, which still works
call Put_a (real1, int1)
```

Note that if keywords are always used for all optional arguments in all procedure calls, new optional arguments can be placed in any position after the non-optional arguments. But if there are cases where keywords are not used, it would be possible for an actual argument to be passed to an unintended dummy argument. If the previous new call was written without keywords, the argument int3 would mistakenly be passed to dummy argument i_arg_op :

```
call Put_a (real1, int1, int3)
```

One technique that can assist in avoiding this problem is shown in the following code segments taken from the Earth System Modeling Framework (ESMF) (see Reference [23]). The first segment of code shows the definition in a utility module of a derived type having public access:

```
module ESMF_UtilMod
   . . .
   ! define a derived type of public access
   type ESMF_KeywordEnforcer
     private
     integer :: quiet
   end type ESMF_KeywordEnforcer
   . . .
end module ESMF_UtilMod
```

In all subprograms containing optional arguments, a dummy argument of this type separates the required arguments from the optional ones. The next segment presents the interface to such a subprogram:

```
use ESMF_UtilMod
. . .
subroutine ESMF_FieldRedistStore (srcField, dstField, &
    routehandle, factor, keywordEnforcer, &
    srcToDstTransposeMap, rc)

    ! input arguments
    type (ESMF_Field),        intent (in)      :: srcField
    type (ESMF_Field),        intent (inout)   :: dstField
    type (ESMF_RouteHandle),  intent (inout)   :: &
        routehandle
    integer (ESMF_KIND_I4),   intent (in)      :: factor
```

```
        ! must use keywords below
   type (ESMF_KeywordEnforcer), optional :: &
        keywordEnforcer
   integer, intent (in), optional :: &
        srcToDstTransposeMap (:)
   integer, intent (out), optional :: rc
end subroutine ESMF_FieldRedistStore
```

Even though it is possible to declare and pass a variable of type ESMF_KeywordEnforcer to this routine (because the type possesses the **public** attribute), as policy, this is never done, and, therefore, keywords must be used for all the arguments that follow the argument keywordEnforcer in the interface. Here is one such call:

```
call ESMF_FieldRedistStore14 (src_field, dst_field, &
     route_handle, factor, &
     srcToDstTransposeMap = transpose_map, rc = rc_out)
```

58. *Assign a default value to all dummy arguments possessing the* optional *attribute.*

Rather than using the intrinsic procedure **present** to test throughout a subprogram for the presence of an optional argument with the attribute **intent** (**in**) or **intent** (**in out**), declare a local variable of a type and kind compatible with it. Then, at the beginning of the procedure, assign it the value of the optional argument if it is present, or a default value if it is not, and use it in its place in the remainder of the routine.

```
function Calc_val (this, arg_1, o_flg_1) &
     result (ret_val)
   type (object_t), intent (in) :: this
   real,            intent (in) :: arg_1
   integer,         intent (in), optional :: o_flg_1
   real :: ret_val

   integer (kind (o_flg_1)), parameter :: &
        DEFAULT_FLAG_1 = 0
   integer (kind (o_flg_1)) :: local_flag_1

   if (present (o_flg_1)) then
      local_flag_1 = o_flg_1
   else
      local_flag_1 = DEFAULT_FLAG_1
   end if
   !... code that may use local_flag_1
end function Calc_val
```

Had this been a subroutine instead of a function, and had the argument o_flg_1 been assigned an intent of **in out** instead of **in**, you would also test for its presence at the function exit and set its value to the local variable as explained next for the case of **intent** (**out**).

For **optional, intent** (**out**) dummy arguments, declare a local variable and set it to a default value at the beginning of the subprogram. In the case of a derived-type object, component initializations may be used to perform this automatically. Set the local variable as needed throughout the procedure and then set the optional argument, if present, at program exit (see Rule 127).

```
subroutine Sub_a (this , arg_1 , error_flag)
  type (object_t), intent (in out) :: this
  real ,            intent (in)      :: arg_1
  integer ,         intent (out), optional :: error_flag

  integer , parameter :: DEFAULT_ERROR_FLAG = 0
  integer :: local_error_flag

  local_error_flag = DEFAULT_ERROR_FLAG

  ... code that may set local_error_flag

  if (present (error_flag)) &
     error_flag = local_error_flag
end function Sub_a
```

59. *Reduce long argument lists by placing arguments in derived types.*

Before Fortran 90 introduced derived types, you would often see procedures with long argument lists. This made them difficult to maintain and test. As new pieces of information needed to be maintained, extra arguments would have to be added to every related routine – tedious and error-prone work. Alternatively, **common** blocks might have been used, but this also had negative ramifications with regard to testability and reusability. When derived-type objects are passed between procedures, additional information can be included within the derived-type object and no modifications are needed to procedures that pass the object around.

Here, as a simple example, is the interface to the subroutine GSVP (SET VIEWPORT) in the Graphical Kernel System (GKS). The Fortran language binding was for FORTRAN 77 (see Reference [34]).

```
SUBROUTINE GSVP (TRNUM, X_MIN , X_MAX , Y_MIN , Y_MAX)
  INTEGER TRNUM
  REAL X_MIN , X_MAX , Y_MIN , Y_MAX
END
```

The argument TRNUM is the transformation number, and the arguments XMIN, XMAX, YMIN, and YMAX are the viewport limits in normalized device coordinates. They are all input arguments. In the GKS specification for the C language binding, the prototype for the same function is:

```
void gset_vp (Gint tran_num , const Glimit *vp );
```

where Glimit is defined as follows:

```
typedef struct {
  Gfloat x_min ;
  Gfloat x_max ;
  Gfloat y_min ;
  Gfloat y_max ;
} Glimit ;
```

(See Reference [36].)

If you were writing a Fortran 2003 version of GKS, you would most likely mimic the C struct with a derived type and create a new interface to the routine:

```
type glimit_t
  real :: x_min , x_max , y_min , y_max
end type glimit_t
 . . .
subroutine GKS_svp (trnum , vp )
  integer (kind=g_int ), intent (in ) :: trnum
  type (glimit_t ),       intent (in ) :: vp
end subroutine GKS_svp
```

Where appropriate, organize arguments to all procedures in this manner.

This rule is especially pertinent when the arguments are arrays. For example, had the original interface in FORTRAN 77 been written like this:

```
SUBROUTINE GSVP (TRNUM, XLIM , YLIM )
  INTEGER TRNUM
  REAL XLIM (2) , YLIM (2)
END
```

This subroutine, as written, could not be prefixed by **elemental** (although it could be made **pure**). However, when it is rewritten using argument vp of derived type glimit_t , it can be an elemental routine because all the arguments are scalars (see Rule 128).

60. *In all calls to subprograms, use the form* $dummy-argument-name$ = $actual-argument-name$ *with all optional arguments.*

Using keywords for all optional arguments clearly distinguishes between required arguments and those that are optional. Strictly speaking, however, keywords are required for optional arguments in only two situations: in a procedure reference where you do not place the optional arguments in the order that conforms to the procedure's interface; or where you skip some optional arguments when calling it. In the following example, keywords are required in the first call to subroutine Calc_energy because the optional actual arguments are out of order; in the second call because the first optional dummy argument, o_flg_1, is skipped, that is, there is no corresponding actual argument. The third call does not require keywords; they are included to distinguish between the required arguments and the optional ones (see Rule 57).

```fortran
subroutine Calc_energy (this, arg_1, arg_2, o_flg_1, &
    op_err_2)
  type (object_t), intent (in out) :: this
  real,     intent (in)  :: arg_1
  real,     intent (out) :: arg_2
  integer, intent (in),  optional :: o_flg_1
  integer, intent (out), optional :: op_err_2
end subroutine Calc_energy

call Calc_energy (a_object, in_arg, out_arg, &
    op_err_2=err_ind, o_flg_1=switch)

call Calc_energy (a_object, in_arg, out_arg, &
    op_err_2=err_Ind)

call Calc_energy (a_object, in_arg, out_arg, &
    o_flg_1=switch, op_err_2=err_ind)
```

Using keywords offers some additional benefits: They enhance the clarity of your code; when you choose good names for dummy arguments, a reader can quickly determine the purpose of passing the various variables to the procedure. Using keywords also forces the compiler to look for an explicit interface to the called routine, which the standard requires when there are optional arguments. The availability of the interface can be either via use association of public procedures in other modules, or through an explicit interface block to an external subprogram, or use association with a module whose sole purpose is to provide interface information (see Rule 48).

And, finally, as arguments are added to the procedure over time, keywords prevent you from inadvertently passing an actual argument to an unintended dummy argument. With this in mind, a more stringent rule you may wish to adopt for references to external subprograms, but not necessarily to module procedures, is to always specify keywords to arguments, whether they are optional or not, thereby forcing the compiler to require access to an explicit interface.

61. *Use assumed-shape arrays as dummy array arguments in subprograms.*

The Fortran 90 standard (see Reference [40]) introduced assumed-shape arrays as a new method of passing arrays of different shapes to subprograms, improving on and supplanting both explicit-shape and assumed-size arrays. The preferred method to pass arrays is to use these assumed-shape arrays. An explicit interface must be provided for subprograms that have assumed-shape array dummy arguments. Either they must be module subprograms with the **public** attribute or an interface block must be be provided to the calling routine. These assumed-shape arrays help prevent array violations that result when there is a mismatch between the actual array shape and the dummy argument array boundaries when using the older-style array-passing methods. You should note, however, that assumed-size arrays need to be used when inter-operating with a C array of unspecified size (see Chapter 14). Here is an example of a subprogram with an assumed-shape array dummy argument:

```
subroutine  Process_array  (array_dum)
   real ,  intent  (in  out)  ::  array_dum(:,  :)
   . . .
end  subroutine  Process_array
```

In this case, any rank 2 array of default intrinsic type **real** can be passed to subroutine Process_array, and the shape of the dummy array takes on the shape of the actual array argument. For example:

```
real  ::  array_act_1(15,  22)
. . .
call  Process_array  (array_act_1)
```

Note that if, for some reason, you need to maintain the lower and upper bounds of the actual array argument in the called subprogram, the lower bound can be explicitly specified in the called subprogram or passed to it as an argument. Otherwise it defaults to a value of 1. For example, in this call:

```
real  ::  array_act_2(-15:  15,  22)
. . .
call  Process_array  (array_act_2)
```

the lower and upper bounds of the first dimension of array_dum will be 1 and 31, respectively. If, however, the interface to Process_array and a call to it are modified as shown here, the lower and upper bounds of the first dimension of array_dum will be -15 and 15, respectively (see Rule 84).

```
subroutine  Process_array  (array_dum ,  lower_bound_1)
   real ,  intent  (in  out)  ::  array_dum(lower_bound_1:,  :)
   integer ,  intent  (in)        ::  lower_bound_1
   . . .
end  subroutine  Process_array

. . .
real  ::  arr_act_2(-15:  15,  22)
. . .
call  Process_array  (arr_act_2 ,  lbound  (arr_act_2 ,  &
      dim=1))
```

62. *Use assumed-length or deferred-length allocatable character dummy arguments.*

When passing character arguments, it is far better to use either of two methods that allow strings of varying length instead of declaring a fixed-length value that is "big enough." One method is to declare assumed-length arguments of subprograms that are of intrinsic type character as shown in this example:

```
subroutine Process_array (string)
    character (len=*), intent (in) :: string
```

When you do so, an actual character argument of any length, including length 0, can be passed to the subprogram, and the dummy argument takes on the length of the actual argument. In the subprogram, you can pass the dummy argument to all the intrinsic character functions if necessary. Use the intrinsic function **len** to determine the length of the dummy argument character variable if needed.

Another possibility is assigning the argument the **allocatable** attribute and using a deferred-length parameter specification of **len**=:. In this case, the string length can be changed within the routine either by using the **allocate** statement or by assignment. As with any allocatable argument, the actual argument in the calling procedure must also have the **allocatable** attribute:

```
subroutine Process_array (str)
    character (len=:), intent (in out), allocatable :: str
    . . .
    str = "Fortran"
        ! If not previously allocated with an allocate
        ! statement, str now has a length of 7.
    deallocate (str)
    allocate (character(5) :: str)
        ! str now has a length of 5.
```

6.4 Argument Verification

63. *Provide simple runtime argument checking at the beginning of procedures.*

The use of explicit interfaces provides a great deal of compile time checking to ensure that procedures are called with the correct number and type actual arguments. Yet there are often ways that procedures can still be called incorrectly. These could include, but are not limited to, passing arrays with incompatible sizes, providing bad argument values, specifying incompatible optional arguments, and so on. Simple argument checking, performed on entry to procedures, ensure that the arguments are valid.

In the case of array sizing, most Fortran compilers offer options to check array bounds. This is a very useful option for debugging code, but can significantly slow down production code. A single quick test at the beginning of the procedure will usually suffice and offers the opportunity to provide better problem-specific error messages.

As an example of argument verification, the following code implements a Fast Fourier Transform (FFT) with an optional work array. It checks the direction argument for validity. If the caller provides the work array to avoid the overhead of allocating and deallocating internal work space, it must have a certain minimum size. The code contains a simple check that executes quickly, and will immediately detect problems (*Cmnt-1).

<u>Listing 6.4: Program Arg_par_test</u>

```
module FFT_mod
  implicit none
  private
  public :: FFT_ALLOC_ERR, FFT_BAD_WRKSPACE, &
      FFT_SUCCESS, FFT_UNKNOWN_DIR, FFT_1d

  enum, bind(C)
    enumerator :: FFT_SUCCESS = 0, FFT_UNKNOWN_DIR, &
        FFT_BAD_WRKSPACE, FFT_ALLOC_ERR
  end enum

contains
  subroutine FFT_1d (sig_data, direction, &
      work, ret_stat)
    complex,         intent(in out) :: sig_data(:)
    character(*), intent(in)        :: direction
    real,        intent(in), optional, target :: work(:)
    integer,     intent(out), optional        :: ret_stat

    integer :: alloc_stat, min_size, i_exit, err_flg
    real, allocatable, target :: work_local(:)
    real, pointer :: workp(:)

    integer, parameter :: MAX_FACTORS = 256

    err_flg = FFT_SUCCESS
    ! Single-pass loop provides structured error exit
    ! (Alternative: use F2008 checks: block statement)
    checks: do i_exit = 1, 1

      ! *Cmnt-1: Check arguments for sanity.
```

```fortran
      select case (direction)

      case ('forward', 'FORWARD', 'reverse', 'REVERSE')
      case default
        print *, "invalid direction"
        err_flg = FFT_UNKNOWN_DIR
        exit checks
      end select

      min_size = 2 * size (sig_data) + MAX_FACTORS
      if (present (work)) then
        if (size (work) >= min_size) then
          workp => work
        else
          err_flg = FFT_BAD_WRKSPACE
          print *, "insufficient workspace"
          exit checks
        end if
      else
        allocate (real :: work_local(min_size), &
            stat=alloc_stat)
        if (alloc_stat == 0) then
          workp => work_local
        else
          err_flg = FFT_ALLOC_ERR
          print *, "allocation problem"
          exit checks
        end if
      end if
      ! (Alternative: use F2008 end block checks
      ! statement)
    end do checks

    if (err_flg /= FFT_SUCCESS) then
      if (present (ret_stat)) then
        ret_stat = err_flg
        return
      else
        stop 1
      end if
    end if

      ! compute FFT using workp for scratch space.
      print *, "Computing FFT"
  end subroutine FFT_1d
end module FFT_mod
```

```
program  Arg_par_test
   use FFT_mod, only : FFT_1d
   implicit none

   integer , parameter :: ARR_SIZ = 3, &
       WORKSPACE_SIZE = 300

   complex :: dat_arr(ARR_SIZ)
   real    :: work_space(WORKSPACE_SIZE)
   integer :: call_stat

   dat_arr = [(2.0, 3.0), (3.0, 4.0), (4.0, 5.0)]
   call FFT_1d (dat_arr, "forward", work_space, &
       call_stat)
   call FFT_1d (dat_arr, "backward", work_space, &
       call_stat)
end program Arg_par_test
```

The results from running this program are:

```
Computing FFT
invalid direction
```

64. *Create private "argument parameter" types for better compile-time checking of valid values.*

It is often useful to create private derived types specifically for the purpose of providing better compile-time diagnostics and avoiding the need to write runtime validity checks. An example of this is the case of procedures that have a dummy argument that indicates which of several options need to be performed. We saw an example of this in Rule 63, the FFT example, with the argument direction .

To prevent a caller from entering an incorrect argument value, the derived type itself is made **private**, yet named constants of the type can be **public**. The caller of the routine uses the parameterized values that are legal for the procedure. Because the type itself is private, a caller cannot define new variants of the argument.

Using the program from Rule 63, the first argument check (*Cmnt-1) can be entirely eliminated if the following code is added to module FFT_mod:

```
integer , parameter :: LEN_DIRECTION = 7
type FFT_dir_t
   character(len=LEN_DIRECTION) :: direction
end type FFT_dir_t

type (FFT_dir_t), public , parameter :: &
    DIR_FOR  = FFT_dir_t ("FORWARD"), &
    DIR_REV  = FFT_dir_t ("REVERSE")
```

and the main program Arg_par_test is rewritten:

```
program Arg_par_test
    use FFT_mod, only : DIR_FORWARD, DIR_REVERSE, FFT_1d
    implicit none

    integer, parameter :: ARR_SIZ = 3, &
        WORKSPACE_SIZE = 300

    complex :: dat_arr(ARR_SIZ)
    real    :: work_space(WORKSPACE_SIZE)
    integer :: call_stat

    dat_arr = [(2.0, 3.0), (3.0, 4.0), (4.0, 5.0)]
    call FFT_1d (dat_arr, DIR_FORWARD, work_space, &
        call_stat)
end program Arg_par_test
```

Any call to subroutine FFT_1d whose second actual argument is not one of the named constants made available in the **use** statement will be flagged by the compiler as an error instead of requiring detection at runtime (see also *Cmnt-1 in program Type_bound_demo, Listing A.1).

6.5 Recursive Procedure Design

Recursive procedures (see Reference [66]) are analogous to mathematical induction. In mathematical induction, the result for a simple-to-specify initial case is defined. Then, for a larger problem, a rule is then defined to break the problem into two portions – a simple case, and a smaller remaining problem. The latter rule is repeatedly applied until the end of the problem has been reached.

In a recursive procedure, steps similar to mathematical induction are followed; however, steps also can be applied in reverse. The rule can be repeatedly applied until the simple end case is found, and additional steps can be performed as the procedure unwinds itself.

When using data structures that are more complicated than simple arrays, such as lists and trees, it is common to use recursion to walk through the structure while processing the elements. Clarity can be achieved by abstracting away some of the local data management and focusing on the steps needed to solve the problem (see *Cmnt-1 in Program Unlimited_demo in Listing A.2).

65. *Write recursive procedures so they have a beginning, a middle, and an end.*

The following code illustrates one way to write a simple factorial function. The function Factorial provides the public interface to the caller, and performs sanity checks for bad inputs. It then calls the private function Factorial_worker to apply the rules to solve the problem.

```
module Math_function_mod
  implicit none
  private
  public :: Factorial
contains

  function Factorial (n) result (res)
    integer, intent(in) :: n
    integer :: res

      ! Initial sanity check.
    if (n <= 0) then
      res = 0
      return
    else
      res = Factorial_worker (n)
    end if
  end function Factorial
```

In the worker routine, a test is made to determine whether it is time to terminate the recursion and unwind the instances of it, or to apply the rule and call itself again.

```
  recursive function Factorial_worker (n) result (res)

      ! Worker function implements the recursive
      ! algorithm
    integer, intent(in) :: n
    integer :: res

      ! Define the processing step for this case,
      ! also identify case that ends the recursion.
    if (n == 1) then
      res = 1
    else
      res = n * Factorial_worker (n-1)
    end if
  end function Factorial_worker
end module Math_function_mod
```

66. *Use recursion to simplify locally scoped data.*

Each invocation of a recursive procedure provides a fresh set of automatic data objects. This allows the processing step to be simplified because storage management can be automated to a great degree. Where code might have needed to declare and allocate arrays or perform other data management tasks, with recursion much of this work can be automatically performed as part of the procedure call mechanism.

One example is reading in a file with an unknown amount of data in it. The program described here uses recursion to create a linked list to hold the data.

```fortran
type data_list_t
   character(len=:), allocatable :: data_string
   type (data_list_t), pointer   :: next => null ()
end type data_list_t
...
contains
   subroutine Read_file_list (this, unit_num)
      type(data_list_t), intent(in out) :: this
      integer,           intent(in)      :: unit_num

      logical :: is_opened
      logical :: i_am_last

      inquire (unit_num, opened=is_opened)
      if (.not. is_opened) then
         this%next => null ()
         return
      else
         call Read_worker (this, unit_num, i_am_last)
      end if
   end subroutine Read_file_list

   recursive subroutine Read_worker (this, unit_num, &
         i_am_last)
      type (data_list_t), intent (in out) :: this
      integer,            intent (in)      :: unit_num
      logical,            intent (out)     :: i_am_last

      integer, parameter :: MAX_DATA_LENGTH = 80
      integer :: alloc_stat, ioerr, i_one_pass
      character(MAX_DATA_LENGTH), save :: data_string

      ! (F2008 Alternative: use routine : block statement)
      routine: do i_one_pass = 1, 1
         i_am_last = .false.
         read (unit_num, '(a)', iostat=ioerr) data_string
         if (ioerr /= 0) then
            i_am_last = .true.
            exit routine
         else
            this%data_string = data_string
         end if
```

```
  allocate (data_list_t :: this%next, &
    stat=alloc_stat)
  if (alloc_stat /= 0) then
    i_am_last = .true.
    exit routine
  end if

  call Read_worker (this%next, unit_num, i_am_last)
  if (i_am_last) then
    deallocate (this%next, stat=alloc_stat)
    this%next => null ()
  end if
  ! (F2008 Alternative : end block routine statement)
  end do routine
end subroutine Read_worker
```

You do not need a separate copy for each instance of data_string : Once it is assigned to this%data_string, it is no longer needed. Only the copy current to a particular call in the chain of recursive calls is required, and this is accomplished by giving it the **save** attribute. Also, a flag is passed from the final instance of the procedure to the next previous invocation to allow deallocation of the node with no data attached to it. Note that the **stat**= option is used in all references to the **allocate** and **deallocate** statements. In the first two instances, the program processes an allocation problem as if the **read** statement had returned a nonzero reply in the **iostat** = option, thereby terminating the recursion. In the last case, the recursion has terminated; the **stat**= option is included, but not processed, so the program will not abnormally terminate if there is a problem with deallocation (see Rule 95).

67. *Take advantage of tail recursion when possible.*

As recursion depth increases, the memory used by the active instances can add up to a significant amount. Also, the procedure call mechanism is costlier in time than the branching in a simple **do** loop. Some compilers can recognize an optimization called "tail recursion," which allows the generation of an iterative loop, rather than a recursive one.

A tail recursive procedure is one where the only call to itself is the final statement in the procedure. Since no local storage is being modified after the call, it is safe to compile the code as if it has a simple branch to the top of the routine. Each instance reuses the memory allocated by the very first instance.

Here is a tail recursive version of the factorial function. A second argument, current_product is added to keep track of the accumulated product:

```
recursive function Factorial_worker &
    (n, current_product) result (ret_value)
  integer, intent(in) :: n, current_product
  integer :: ret_value
```

```
if (n == 1) then
   ret_value = 1
   return
end if
res = Factorial_worker (n-1, n*current_product)
end function Factorial_worker
```

6.6 State, Side Effects, and Thread Safety

One of the characteristics of a procedure is whether or not it maintains visible internal "state." Given a set of inputs, does the procedure return the exact same results each time or can the results vary from call to call? A simple example of a stateless procedure is the intrinsic trigonometric function **sin**. It may be invoked many times with many different argument values. Yet the results will always be consistent and identical given identical input values.

A common example of a routine that maintains visible state is a pseudo-random number generator, such as the **random_number** intrinsic subroutine. Every time the routine returns a value, it updates its internal state so that the next call will return a different value.

68. *Write code that avoids side effects.*

Side effects may occur when a procedure modifies global variables, such as those at module scope (or in **common** blocks in older code), when variables have the **save** attribute, and, in the case of functions, when a function modifies its arguments.

Consider the first line of the following code, where multiple function calls and usages of an actual argument exist within a single expression. There are no parenthesis being used to control the order of evaluation, and Fortran does not prescribe strict left to right evaluation of the expression. The order of operations are limited to operator precedence; for example, the multiplications will be performed before the additions. If it is known that the function is visibly stateless (for example, **pure**) and that it has no other side effects, a compiler might optimize this code to either of these two statements that follow it:

```
return_value = My_func (arg) * My_func (arg) + arg + 2

! two possible optimizations:
return_value = (My_func (arg) ** 2) + (arg + 2)

return_value = (arg + 2) + (My_func (arg) ** 2)
```

Semantically, the compiler generates only a single call to the function. And because it knows that arg is not changed by the call, the program can compute arg + 2 before or after the call. Optimizations such as this are often performed as a result of inlining, which eliminates the call altogether, and subsequent common subexpression elimination optimization.

According to the Fortran standard, if an actual argument in a call to a function is modified by the function and it is also used elsewhere within the same expression, the result is undefined. This would be the case if function My_func alters the value of the dummy argument corresponding to the actual argument arg. *Therefore, it is an error to write such code.*

The use of procedures possessing the **pure** attribute is a good way to ensure there will be no side effect. Pure procedures are written with a specific set of restrictions that guarantee this (see Rule 52).

69. *Separate initialization from computation to maintain computational purity.*

Some procedures require initialization and need to keep track of whether they have been initialized or not. For example, the procedure may need to read in some data from a file and populate a lookup table. It only needs to be done once, after which the data is available for the remainder of the run. However, this is enough to render a procedure as not pure. Such is the case in the following code, where the **save** attribute precludes assigning the the function the **pure** attribute.

```
module Trig_function_mod
  implicit none
  private
  public :: Trig_compute
contains
  . . .
  function Trig_compute (arg) result (ret_values)
    real, intent(in) :: arg(:)
    real :: ret_values(size (arg))

    real, allocatable, save :: data_table(:)
    logical :: initialized = .false.

    if (.not. initialized) then
      ! ... Initialize data_table here
      initialized = .true.
    end if
    ! ... Calulate function here
  end function Trig_compute
  . . .
end module Trig_function_mod
```

To avoid this problem, you can either use a separate initialization call, combined with a module-scope state variable; or you can carry the state in a derived-type object.

The first technique, using a separate call for initialization, is made possible by the fact that pure procedures are allowed to access module-scope data; they simply must not modify it. In this example, the state is maintained implicitly within the allocated status of the allocatable array data_table:

```fortran
module Trig_function_mod
  implicit none
  private
  public :: Trig_compute, Trig_function_init

  real, allocatable, save :: data_table(:)
contains
  subroutine Trig_function_init (data_file)
    character(*), intent(in) :: data_file

    integer :: data_unit, table_size, alloc_stat

    if (allocated (data_table)) &
        deallocate (data_table, stat=alloc_stat)

    ! Use F2008 newunit to assign temporary
    ! unit number
    open (newunit=data_unit, file=data_file, &
        status='old', access='read', form='unformatted')
    read (data_unit) table_size
    allocate (real :: data_table(table_size), &
        stat=alloc_stat)
    read (data_unit) data_table
    close (data_unit)
  end subroutine Trig_function_init

  pure function Trig_compute (arg) &
      result (ret_values)
    real, intent(in) :: arg(:)
    real :: ret_values(size (arg))
    ...
  end function Trig_compute

end module Trig_function_mod
```

You need to first call Trig_function_init. Then Trig_compute can be called.

```fortran
call Trig_function_init (file='data1.dat')
...
r = Trig_compute (a)
```

The second technique involves using derived-type objects to maintain their own state data. Consider the case where multiple calls to Trig_compute need to be made, yet each may need to have a different set of initializations.

```
module Trig_function_mod
  implicit none
  private

  type, public :: trig_state_t
    real, allocatable :: data_table(:)
  contains
    procedure :: Init    => Trig_function_init
    procedure :: Compute => Trig_compute
  end type trig_state_t
contains

  subroutine Trig_function_init (this, data_file)
    class(trig_state_t), intent(in out) :: this
    character(*),        intent(in)     :: data_file

    integer :: alloc_stat

    if (allocated (this%data_table)) &
        deallocate (this%data_table, stat=alloc_stat)
    ... ! Initialize data_table from the file
  end subroutine Trig_function_init

  pure function Trig_compute (this, arg) &
      result (ret_values)
    class(trig_state_t), intent(in) :: this
    real,                intent(in) :: arg(:)
    real :: ret_values(size (arg))
    ...
  end function Trig_compute

end module trig_function_mod
```

The caller of this code would need a trig_state_t object for each case that it needs to keep track of. Each object may be initialized with its own state as needed. Type-bound procedure names are used to simplify the calls (see Section 11.3).

```
type (trig_state_t) :: trig_1, trig_2
real, dimension(:) :: a, b, r, s

call trig_1%Init (data_file='data1.dat')
call trig_2%Init (data_file='data2.dat')

r = trig_1%Compute (a)
s = trig_2%Compute (b)
```

70. *Use subroutines instead of functions when returning results through the argument list.*

When a function is written in such a way that it must return values through its argument list, it is almost always better to use a subroutine instead. This avoids ambiguous cases where multiple calls and usages of the output variables are used within a single expression. Consider the following example, keeping in mind that addition is associative, and that Fortran does not mandate left-to-right processing of expressions:

```
return_value = Trig_compute (x) + x + Trig_compute (x)
```

If the actual argument x is modified in the Trig_compute routine, the result of the above statement is undefined. If the function were recoded as a subroutine, the problem could not exist in the first place. The revised interface and calling code are shown next. If a function really does need to return multiple values, consider coding it to return a derived type containing all the data items that need to be returned as described in Rule 59.

```
subroutine Trig_compute (arg, ret_val)
   real, intent (in out) :: arg (:)
   real, intent (out)     :: ret_val
end subroutine Trig_compute

call Trig_compute (x, ret_val=temp)
return_value = x + temp
call Trig_compute (x, ret_val=temp)
return_value = return_value + temp
```

71. *Avoid unintentional aliasing.*

Aliasing refers to the case where a single data item is known under multiple symbolic names, called aliases. Fortran only allows aliasing when the programmer specifically states that it is possible, such as when using pointers to objects, the **target** attribute, the **associate** construct, and, in older programs, the **equivalence** statement. Otherwise, the compiler is allowed to assume that there is no aliasing. While this may sound obvious, it is one of the key assumptions that allow Fortran compilers to optimize code that executes faster than code written in most other computer languages. Consider the following simple procedure. Note that the programmer did not specify **intent** attributes for the dummy arguments:

```
subroutine Compute_42 (a, b, d)
   real :: a (:)
   real :: b (:)
   real :: d (:)

   integer :: i
```

```
  do, i=1, size (a)
    b(i) = a(i) + 42.0
    d(i) = a(i) - 42.0
  end do
end subroutine Compute_42
```

A compiler with limited optimization capabilities, or perhaps a more advanced one with its optimization capabilities disabled, may compile the loop as written, that is, the variable a(i) is loaded from memory twice per loop iteration. However, in most computers, references to memory can be costly compared to arithmetic operations. By taking advantage of Fortran's aliasing rules, a good compiler might perform an optimization, called common sub-expression elimination, and compile the above loop to use a high-speed processor register to avoid loading a(i) from memory a second time:

```
  do, i=1, size (a)
    register_temp = a(i)
    b(i) = register_temp + 42.0
    d(i) = register_temp - 42.0
  end do
```

If the caller of the above routine happened to use the same array for both input and output arguments, thereby creating an illegal, but perhaps undiagnosed, aliasing situation, you would likely get different results depending on the particular compiler in use, and even on the optimization level.

Many other languages require the compiler to assume that aliasing is always possible unless told otherwise. The compiler would be required to reload a(i) from memory, and the code would not run as fast as a program written in Fortran.

Many cases of illegal aliasing can be devised that are unintended and undiagnosed by compilers. As just a single example, here is one where the procedure reads a variable via the argument list, yet through **use** association, the same variable is also modified under the name used at module scope.

```
module Compute_mod
  implicit none
  private
  public :: Compute_42, d

  real, allocatable :: d(:)
contains

  subroutine Compute_42 (a, b)
    real, intent(in)  :: a(:)
    real, intent(out) :: b(:)
```

```
      integer :: i

      do, i=1, size (a)
         b(i) = a(i) + 42.0
         d(i) = a(i) - 42.0    ! updates module scope data
      end do
   end subroutine Compute_42
end module Compute_mod

program Main
   use Compute_mod, only: d, Compute_42
   implicit none

   real, allocatable :: b(:)
   . . .
      ! ILLEGAL
   call Compute_42 (a=d, b=b)
   . . .
end program Main
```

If you require that the integrity of particular variables be rigorously preserved
during program execution, the **volatile** attribute may be used. The standard
states that an object possessing this attribute may be referenced, defined, or
become undefined, by means not specified by the program. When confronted
with an object having this attribute, the compiler should generate code that
guarantees its value and state. Such a requirement could possibly arise, for
example, in the situation in which a shared-memory parallel processing construct depends on the memory references to take place in a coherent fashion
between threads.

```
   subroutine Spin_wait (shared_lock)
      integer, volatile :: shared_lock

         ! Loop until some other process changes the lock
         ! value.
      do
         if (shared_lock) exit
      end do
   end subroutine Spin_wait
```

In this example, if **volatile** were not used, there are several optimizations a
compiler might perform that would render the code problematic.

The **volatile** attribute is often stronger than needed because it accommodates
situations not defined by the Fortran standard. Most likely its use will decrease
the speed of the program. The **target** and **asynchronous** attributes cover cases
that are defined within the standard. Because they cover defined cases, they

can be implemented in a weaker fashion than **volatile** , potentially leading to better performance. Their use also documents the intended use of the variable. The **target** attribute is required for variables that are to be associated with one or more pointers. And the **asynchronous** attribute is required for buffers that are used as part of asynchronous I/O (see Rule 111).

7.

Programming Conventions

7.1 Declaration and Initialization of Data Objects

This section contains guidelines that pertain to all types of data objects, both of intrinsic type and derived type. Section 11.2 is reserved for the same topic as it applies to objects of derived type.

72. *Declare all variables. To enforce this rule, always include the statement* implicit none *in all program units.*

The original FORTRAN implicit data typing scheme, where names beginning with the letters I through N were considered integers, and all others were considered reals, has proven to be a major source of errors (see Rule 36). All variables should be explicitly declared.

When an **implicit none** statement is present in a program unit, the compiler will require an explicit declaration of the type and kind of every data entity. In modules, it is most convenient to place the **implicit none** statement once, at module scope.

Note that procedure specifications defined within interface blocks require their own **implicit none** statements. By default, they do not import anything from the surrounding module or procedure. When access to an entity in the surrounding scope is required, the **import** statement may be used.

```
module My_mod
    ! use statements precede implicit none
    use Kinds_mod , only : WORK_PREC
    implicit none

    interface
      subroutine Sub_1 (a)
        import :: WORK_PREC
        implicit none
        real(WORK_PREC), intent (in out) :: a
      end subroutine Sub_1
    end interface
contains
    . . .
end module My_mod
```

98

73. *Assign data objects attributes on the same statement as their declaration.*

Most attributes that can be assigned to a variable or to a constant can be made in its declaration or definition. Here are several examples:

```
integer , private , save          :: int_1
real ,        public ,  allocatable  :: real_1 ( : )
integer , public ,  parameter    :: IPAR_1 = 5
complex , private , pointer    :: pt_1 ( : ) => null ( )
integer , public ,  target      :: int_2 ( IPAR_1 )
character (64) , dimension (100) :: input_buffer , &
   output_buffer

type , public :: a_type_t
   ! ... components
end type a_type_t
```

As an alternative, and for compatibility with old codes, Fortran allows separate statements for assigning attributes to data objects. However, for clarity and simplicity, always use the previous form to keep all the information about an object in one place.

In the case of the **dimension** attribute, we generally use the traditional notation of placing the array specification as a suffix on the variable name. However, in some places, using an explicit **dimension** attribute can make the code clearer when several variables of identical shape are declared in the same statement.

74. *Initialize all pointers to have an initial association status of disassociated using the intrinsic function* null.

Unless pointers are initialized in their declaration, their initial association status is undefined. In this undefined state, their status cannot be reliably queried using the instrinsic function **associated**. Likewise, pointers cannot be reliably referenced until they are nullified or associated with a target by using either the **allocate** statement or pointer assignment =>. Here are examples of a pointer to an array being initialized using **null** () and pointer components of a derived data type being similarly initialized in the type definition (see Rules 136 and 144):

```
real , pointer :: array_ptr ( : ) => null ( )

type node_type_t
   type ( node_type ) , pointer :: next_ptr => null ( )
end type node_type_t
```

Note that the first example causes the program to assign the **save** attribute to the variable array_ptr . It is the association status, not the value, of the pointer that is saved. This can have serious ramifications: The user cannot rely on the value of the target to which the pointer is pointer assigned to be retained. Much worse, the target can be deallocated and the pointer become dangling.

The standard does not permit this type of initialization for dummy arguments that are pointers or for functions that return pointers. There are other situations, a local pointer in a recursive procedure, for example, where this **save** attribute may not be desired. In all these cases, the pointer should be nullified in the initial stages of the routine in the following manner:

```
integer ,  pointer  ::  array_ptr (:)
 . . .
nullify ( array_ptr )
! Alternative
array_ptr => null ()
```

75. *Do not initialize variables in their declaration unless necessary.*

Variables that are initialized in their declarations acquire the **save** attribute. If you initialize r_array as shown in the first line of the following code, it acquires the **save** attribute; and the program must retain its value, or in the case of a pointer, its association status, during the entire execution of the program. With local variables, this is wasteful of memory and can cause inefficiencies, so it should be avoided. (In Fortran 2008, all variables whose scope is the module acquire the **save** attribute by default.) However, an example of a situation where variable initialization could be useful is a counter in a procedure (see Rule 74 and Section 6.6).

```
real  ::  r_array (MAX_ELEMENTS) = 0.0


subroutine  Calc_x (x, y)
   real ,  intent (in out)  ::  x
   real ,  intent (in)        ::  y

   integer  ::  i_counter = 0

   i_counter = i_counter + 1
   ! ... code to calculate x
end subroutine  Calc_x
```

A second example could be a state variable declared in a module as shown in this code:

```
module System_state_mod
   implicit none
   private
   public  ::  Is_system_Inited ,  Init_system

   logical  ::  system_inited  = .false .
contains

   subroutine Init_system  ()
      system_inited  = .true .
      ! ...  other initialization operations
   end subroutine Init_system
end module System_state_mod
```

76. *Use assumed-length character notation when declaring named constants of intrinsic type* character.

To avoid having to count characters, use a declaration such as the following one to declare scalar named constants of instrinsic type **character**. In the following statement, the compiler will assign a length to named constant STR according to the length of the literal constant to which it is assigned:

```
character (len=*), parameter :: STR = "string1"
```

You can use assumed-length character notation when declaring named constants that are arrays. The array constructor requires that a specific string length be specified if the elements are of different lengths. The length must be equal to or greater than the length of the longest element.

```
integer, parameter :: NO_OF_CMNDS = 3
character(len=*), parameter :: CMND_NAMES(NO_OF_CMNDS) = &
    [character(len=8) :: "REPLACE", "CONTINUE", "QUIT"]
```

**77. *Use named constants instead of "magic numbers" and frequently used character strings.*

Good programming practice encourages that named constants be used for fixed values and character strings. These may be scientific constants, array bounds, character string lengths, and so forth. For example, the energy per unit area radiated from a body is expressed by the Stefan-Boltzmann equation,

$$\frac{P}{A} = e\sigma T^4 \tag{7.1}$$

where e is the emissivity of the object, σ is the Stefan constant and is 5.6703×10^{-8} when expressed in units of $\frac{watts}{m^2 K^4}$, and T is the absolute temperature. In your program, specify the constant as a parameter (see Rule 35):

```
real, parameter :: STEFAN_CONST = 5.6703E-8

P = e * STEFAN_CONST * A * T**4
```

Whenever possible, use named constants that you have already defined to define new ones. This applies to integer constants, where there is no possibility of losing precision (see Rule 78). For example:

```
integer, parameter :: MAX_HORIZ_PIXELS = 1600, &
    MAX_VERT_PIXELS = 900, &
    MAX_TOTAL_PIXELS = MAX_HORIZ_PIXELS * MAX_VERT_PIXELS
```

Here's an example of a named constant used for an upper bound of an array (see Rule 92):

```
integer, parameter :: MAX_SAMPLING_UNITS = 5000
real :: pop_densities(MAX_SAMPLING_UNITS)
```

Named constants of intrinsic type character can also be used for format specifications. For example, if your program often prints a character string followed by an integer, create a well-named named constant for the format specification and use it throughout.

```
character (len=*), parameter :: FRMT_STR_INT = "(a, i0)"
integer, allocatable :: atoms(:)
write (*, FRMT_STR_INT) "Atoms: ", size (atoms, dim=1)
```

Note that using named constants is more flexible than using **format** statements. A named constant may be placed at module scope, so it can be shared by many customers.

78. Set mathematical constants using known precise values.

Obtain the value of mathematical constants from trusted sources, rather than an intrinsic function result.

For example, find π in the *CRC Handbook* (Reference [78]), rather than using an expression such as $4.0 * tan^{-1}(1)$. By using two digits more than the precision of your variables in the literal, you can guarantee a "last bit" fit, modulo the compiler's rounding mode.

```
real (DBL_K), parameter :: PI = 3.14159265358979324_DBL_K
```

7.2 Allocatable and Pointer Attributes

Allocatable arrays were introduced in Fortran 90. The need for enhancing their capabilities was the impetus for *Technical Report TR 15581* (Reference [31]). This report added the capability of assigning the **allocatable** attribute to components of derived type, to function results, and to dummy arguments. Fortran 2003 incorporates these capabilities and adds some additional ones.

This section comprises two subsections: The first contains a list and accompanying explanation of the characteristics of allocatable arrays and scalars that in most cases makes them superior to pointers in both their behavior and memory management capabilities. There are some situations where either pointers must be used or they are useful; they are listed in the second subsection along with some rules pertaining to cautions about using pointers.

7.2.1 Allocatable Data Objects

Allocatable variables have a single owner of an allocation – the procedure or module in which the variable is declared. When the owner of the allocated space goes out of scope, the allocation is automatically deallocated. Association with a pointer does not change ownership. In fact, it is illegal to attempt to deallocate an allocatable variable through a pointer to it. Ownership of the allocated space can change by using the **move_alloc** intrinsic subroutine. In this case, only the new owner may explicitly deallocate the space.

79. *Wherever possible, use allocatable variables rather than data pointers.*

Automatic Deallocation of Local Allocatable Variables An allocatable variable local to a subprogram is automatically deallocated when the program exits the subprogram unless the variable possesses the **save** attribute. This prevents "memory leakage." Here is a type definition whose components represent the initial conditions of a particle:

```
type , public :: start_conds_t
  real , dimension(3) :: coords , dir_cosines
end type start_conds_t
```

In the following code, the program allocates an allocatable array of type start_conds_t as well as an allocatable array of real variables, random_nums. The program populates the latter with random numbers, and then calls a function called Init_particles (not shown) to initialize the components of the array of particles. When the program exits the function, it will automatically deallocate both allocatable variables.

```
function Comp_disp ( no_of_particles ) &
    result ( return_value )
  integer , intent ( in ) :: no_of_particles
  real :: return_value

  type ( start_conds_t ), allocatable :: particles (:)
  real , allocatable :: random_nums (: ,:)
  integer :: alloc_stat
  integer , parameter :: RAND_NUMS_PER_TYPE = 6

  allocate ( start_conds_t :: &
      particles ( no_of_particles ), stat=alloc_stat )
  alloc1: if ( alloc_stat == 0 ) then
    allocate ( real :: random_nums(RAND_NUMS_PER_TYPE, &
        no_of_particles ), stat=alloc_stat )
    alloc_check: if ( alloc_stat == 0 ) then
      call random_seed ()
      call random_number ( random_nums )
      particles = Init_particles ( random_nums )
    else alloc_check
    ! ...code to handle allocation error
    end if alloc_check
  else alloc1
  ! ...code to handle allocation error
  end if alloc1
  ! ...code to compute return_value
```

```
      ! arrays , particles , and random_nums automatically
      ! deallocate on procedure exit .
   end function Comp_disp
```

Allocatable variables whose scope is an entire module, that is, their declarations precede the **contains** statement separating the specification part from the module procedures, are *not* necessarily deallocated in this manner when the module goes out of scope. The standard stipulates that this behavior is dependent on the processor (see Reference [39]). The burden is upon the programmer to ensure this array is deallocated when it goes out of scope if that is the behavior desired. An example might be an allocatable module variable that is used by several of the module's subprograms. In Fortran 2008, all such variables acquire the **save** attribute by default.

In the next example, a module has an allocatable array of a derived type that contains information about employees. It might be populated by one of the module's subprograms, sorted by a second, and statistical information calculated from it by a third. The pertinent parts of the module may look like this:

```
module Employee_mod
   implicit none
   private
   public :: ! ... list of public entities

   integer , parameter :: MAX_NAME_LEN = 100

   type , public :: employee_t
      character (MAX_NAME_LEN) :: full_name
      integer :: id_numb
      real    :: salary
   end type employee_t

   type (employee_t) , save , allocatable :: work_data ( : )
contains
   ... subprograms that reference work_data
end module Employee_mod
```

Automatic Deallocation of Allocatable Derived-Type Components In Fortran 90 and Fortran 95, the only method for dynamically sizing components of derived types was to use pointers. With the development of *TR 15581* (see Reference [31]) and its inclusion into Fortran 2003, derived-type components may alternatively be declared as **allocatable**.

Allocatable components enjoy the usual advantages of allocatable variables. That is, when you deallocate an allocatable variable of derived type, and that type contains allocatable components at any level, all such components will be automatically deallocated. So, if you have an allocatable array of type screen_t

that is currently allocated, the following program will also deallocate the pixels
component when the array is deallocated.

```
type, public :: pixel_t
  private
  integer :: rgb(3) = 0.0
  ! ... other components
contains
  ! ... type-bound procedures
end type pixel_t

type, public :: screen_t
  type (pixel_t), allocatable :: pixels(:,:)
  integer :: resolutions(2) = [1024, 768]
  real    :: dimensions(2)  = [0.1, 0.1]
contains
  ! ... type-bound procedures
end type screen_t

type (screen_t), allocatable :: screens(:)
integer :: alloc_stat, num_scrns

allocate (screen_t :: screens(num_srcns), &
    stat=alloc_stat)
if (alloc_stat == 0) &
  allocate (pixel_t :: &
      screens%pixels(vert_resol, horiz_resol), &
      stat=alloc_stat)
  ! ... Code operating on variable screens and
  ! ... its components
  ! ... Then deallocate screens, which also deallocates
  ! ... screens%pixels.
deallocate (screens, stat=alloc_stat)
```

Allocatable Scalars and Character String Lengths Scalar variables may be
declared allocatable. Allocatable scalars are useful for scalar derived-type variables, which might be used only part of the time, yet take up a significant
amount of memory.

```
type (huge_type_t), allocatable :: scalar_huge_obj
```

Character string lengths may also be allocatable (see Rule 80). In the employee_t
derived type used in the previous example, the following declaration could be
used for the full_name component to remove the fixed-length restrictions:

```
type, public :: employee_t
  character(len=:), allocatable :: full_name
  ...
end type employee_t
```

Allocatable Function Results Fortran 2003 permits function results to be declared allocatable. Any allocation that occurs is automatically deallocated after the execution of an expression in which the function reference occurs. For example, in the following code, the program retrieves the number of temperature samples from an instrumentation port.

```fortran
type, public :: port_t
   integer :: port_number
   real    :: avg_temp
   real    :: locations(3)
   ... other components
contains
   procedure Get_port_temps
end type port_t
contains

   pure function Get_port_temps (this) result (ret_vals)
      class (port_t), intent (in) :: this
      real, allocatable :: ret_vals(:)
      integer :: num_samps, alloc_stat

      associate (port_no => this%port_number)
         num_samps = Get_no_of_samples (port_no)
         allocate (real :: ret_vals(num_samps), &
            stat=alloc_stat)
         if (alloc_stat == 0) then
            ret_vals = Get_temp_samples (port_no)
         else
            ... code handling the allocation error
         end if
      end associate
   end function Get_port_temps
```

The next example shows code that calls a pure function, Calc_avg_temp (code not shown) that computes the average temperature at a port. The allocatable array created by a call to function Get_port_temps is the second actual argument in the call. First, there is the interface to the function Calc_avg_temp, followed by the code that calls both it and the function Get_port_temps. When this code executes, there will be no_of_ports calls to the function Get_port_temps and, as a result, no_of_ports allocations. After completion of the **forall** statement, all of these allocations will have been automatically deallocated.

```fortran
interface
   pure function Calc_avg_temp (this, temps) &
      result (ret_val)
      implicit none
      import :: port_t
      type (port_t), intent (in) :: this
```

```
      real , intent ( in )    :: temps ( : )
      real ( kind ( temps ) ) :: ret_val
   end function Calc_avg_temp
end interface

type ( port_t )  :: ports ( no_of_ports )
real      ::  temps ( no_of_ports )
integer  :: i_port

forall ( i_port = 1: no_of_ports )     &
   temps ( i_port ) = Calc_avg_temp ( ports ( i_port ), &
        ports ( i_port )% Get_port_temps ( )  )
```

Automatic Deallocation of Temporary Expressions Allocations of allocatable variables that are done during the calculations of intermediate temporary expressions are automatically deallocated.

In the following example the functions Get_probe_temps and Calc_wts are both functions that return a rank 2 allocatable array of default type **real**.

```
real , allocatable  :: crnt_tmps ( : , : )
real      ::  amb_temp
integer  :: grid_bnds ( 2 ) , plate_no

   grid_bnds = Get_bnds ( plate_no )
   crnt_tmps = amb_temp + Calc_wts ( plate_no , grid_bnds ) &
      * Get_probe_temps ( plate_no , grid_bnds )
```

The program will form a temporary variable to hold the result of the multiplication and will automatically deallocate it after it computes the array crnt_tmps.

Contiguous Storage of Allocatable Arrays Storage of allocatable arrays is contiguous in memory, whereas pointer targets may or may not be contiguous.

When a pointer is used in an operation, the compiler cannot assume that the data is stored in contiguous memory when it generates the executable code. Here a pointer points to every second element in row i of a rank-2 array.

```
real , pointer  :: ptr_row ( : )
ptr_row => real_array ( i , 1: n_cols: 2 )
```

If an allocatable array is used instead, the program will store it in a contiguous manner, resulting in more efficient code in most cases (see Rule 97).

Automatic Adjustment of the Size of Allocatable Arrays in Assignments Allocatable variables automatically adjust size in assignments when the entire array is referenced on the left hand side. This includes both allocatable variables as well as those of derived types containing allocatable components. Here is a derived type containing an allocatable component followed by two variables of type screen_t, with one assigned to the other:

```
type, public :: screen_t
   type (pixel_t), allocatable :: pixels(:, :)
   integer :: resolutions(2) = [1024, 768]
   real    :: dimensions(2)  = [0.1, 0.1]
end type screen_t
...
type (screen_t) :: screen_a, screen_b
...
   ! reallocation of pixels component may occur
screen_a = screen_b
   ! no reallocation of pixels
screen_a%pixels(:) = screen_b%pixels(:)
```

When the program executes the assignment, the allocatable component pixels of variable screen_a will be deallocated if it is allocated. Then, if the pixels component of screen_b is allocated, the pixels component of screen_a will be allocated to the same shape as the pixels of screen_b and the copy will take place. If, on the other hand, the pixels component of screen_b is not currently allocated, the same component of screen_a will acquire the status of being not currently allocated.

Fortran 2003 uses this procedure for all levels of nesting of derived types, and it uses the same mechanism when assigning allocatable variables, not just variables of derived type containing allocatable components.

Here we have mentioned just the shape of the expression. However, not only is the shape of the variable set to that of the expression when it is allocated, or reallocated; the lower bounds of the variable are set equal to those of the expression, and, moreover, deferred type parameters also are set to conform to the values of the expression. The type parameters must be deferred. The following allocatable intrinsic variable can appear on the left side of an assignment statement (see Rule 125):

```
character(len =:), allocatable :: temp_var(:)
```

The length type parameters of parameterized derived-type variables can also be deferred. Here is a derived type with length type parameters:

```
type temp_grid_t (rows, cols)
   integer, len :: rows, cols
   real :: nodes(rows, cols)
   ...
end type temp_grid_t
```

and here's a declaration of an allocatable variable of type temp_grid_t where the length type parameters rows and cols are deferred, as indicated by the colons:

```
type (temp_grid_t(rows =:, cols =:)), allocatable :: plate
```

The variable plate can appear on the left side of an intrinsic assignment statement. In the assignment, the program will deallocate plate if it is allocated. The variable will be allocated, and the value of the type parameters rows and cols will be set to those of the expression. In the following assignment, the values of rows and cols in plate will both be set to 20.

```
type (temp_grid_t , rows=20, cols=20) :: template_plate
plate = template_plate
```

Automatic Deallocation of Allocatable Actual Arguments That Correspond to intent (out) Dummy Arguments When calling procedures, allocatable variables and the allocatable components of variables of derived types will automatically be deallocated when the variables are the actual arguments of dummy arguments having the **intent** (**out**) attribute. The called procedure must reallocate the allocatable dummy arguments to the desired size.

In the following code, variables hd_screen and crt_screen are of the derived type screen_t defined in the previous point. Before the call to procedure Clone, whose interface is shown, the the program will deallocate component pixels of variable crt_screen if it is allocated (see Rule 53).

```
subroutine Clone (screen_in , screen_out )
  type (screen_t), intent (in) :: screen_in
  type (screen_t), intent (out), allocatable :: &
      screen_out
end subroutine Clone

type (screen_t), allocatable :: hd_screen , crt_screen
...
call Clone (hd_screen , crt_screen )
```

Reallocation Using the move_alloc Intrinsic Subroutine The intrinsic subroutine **move_alloc** provides a simple capability for reallocation and memory management using allocatable arrays. Fortran 2003 introduces this subroutine as a simple method to transfer ownership of an allocation from one allocatable variable to another. Its general form is:

```
subroutine move_alloc (from , to )
```

where the argument **from** is allocatable, is of any type, and has an intent of **in out**, and the argument **to** is the same type and rank as argument **from**, is also allocatable, and has an intent of **out**. After execution, the program deallocates the actual argument corresponding to the dummy argument **from**.

This subroutine will be most useful in changing the size of an allocation, as the following example demonstrates. The allocation of the variable node_id is changed to n_rows by n_cols . After execution of **move_alloc**, the size of

variable node_id will be n_rows by n_cols, and the allocatable array hold_id will
be automatically deallocated.

```fortran
integer , allocatable :: node_id (: , :) , hold_id (: , :)
integer :: n_rows , n_cols , num_move_rows , &
    num_move_cols
integer :: alloc_stat

! ... code in which node_id is allocated and its elements
! ... are assigned values.

! ... code to assign values to both n_Rows and n_Cols

num_move_rows = min ( n_rows , ubound ( node_id , dim=1))
num_move_cols = min ( n_cols , ubound ( node_id , dim=2))

allocate ( integer :: hold_id (n_rows , n_cols ) , &
    stat=alloc_stat )
if ( alloc_stat == 0) then
  hold_id (1: num_move_rows , 1: num_move_cols) = node_id
  call move_alloc (from=hold_id , to=node_id )
else
  ! ... code to handle the allocation error
end if
```

Sourced Allocation of Variables For variables, sourced allocation provides
a simple method of copying the values of one object to an allocatable one
during the allocation process. The allocatable object may be either allocatable
variables or pointers. When a program executes a sourced allocation, it makes
all necessary allocations and copies data from the source variable to the allocated
variable. The form of the statement can be seen in the following code. (Here,
both the allocatable object and the source object are polymorphic variables;
this is not a requirement of sourced allocation):

```fortran
subroutine Compute_density ( crnt_elems , ... )
  class ( elem_t ) , intent ( in ) :: crnt_elems (:)

  class ( elem_t ) , allocatable :: tmp_elems (:)
  integer :: alloc_stat

  ! allocate the temporary array for the computation.
  allocate ( tmp_elems , source=crnt_elems , &
    stat=alloc_stat )
  ! ... code to process alloc_stat
end subroutine Compute_density
```

Fortran 2008 adds some additional features to sourced allocation: First, the bounds of the allocate object are set to the bounds of the source expression. You have to set this explicitly in Fortran 2003. Second, if you wish to allocate without performing the copy, you can use the keyword **mold** in lieu of **source** (see Rule 153):

```
allocate (tmp_elems, mold=crnt_elems, stat=alloc_stat)
```

80. *Use allocatable deferred-length character strings wherever possible.*

Fortran 2003 allows the length specification of allocatable character strings to be deferred until their assignment. This makes them in essence variable-length strings. To specify this, use a length parameter specification of **len=:** and give the string the **allocatable** attribute. In the following example, after the first assignment, the variable error_message will have a length of 18, and after the second, one of 43. An **allocate** statement was not necessary. Moreover, on exit, the program will automatically deallocate error_message if it is a local variable in a subprogram and also if it does not possess the **save** attribute. These allocatable characters can also be used as derived-type components (see Rule 62).

```
character(len=:), allocatable :: error_message
error_message = "allocation failure"
...
error_message = "file unit number is already allocated."
```

Functions can return variable length strings using the same mechanism. Here is a short program that demonstrates this:

Listing 7.1: Program Return_string

```
module String_utils_mod
  implicit none
  private
  public :: ASCII_BLANK, Extract_printables

  integer, parameter :: ASCII_BLANK  = iachar (" "), &
                        ASCII_LOWERZ = iachar ("z")
contains
  function Extract_printables (string) &
      result (new_string)
    character(*), intent(in) :: string
    character(:), allocatable :: new_string

    character :: c
    character (len (string)) :: string_temp
    integer :: i, new_len
```

```
      new_len = 0
      do, i=1, len_trim (string)
        c = string(i:i)
        if (         ASCII_BLANK <= iachar (c) &
            .and. iachar (c)  <= ASCII_LOWERZ) then
          new_len = new_len+1
          string_temp (new_len: new_len) = c
        end if
      end do
      new_string = string_temp (: new_len)
    end function Extract_printables
end module String_utils_mod

program Return_string
  use String_utils_mod , only : ASCII_BLANK , &
      Extract_printables
  implicit none

  character(len=:), allocatable :: test_str , &
    print_string

  test_str = char (ASCII_BLANK - 1) // "12_bB45)"
  print *, "test_str length: ", len (test_str)
  print_string = Extract_printables (test_str)
  print *, "new string: " // print_string // &
      " , length: ", len (print_string)
end program Return_string
```

The program output is:

```
test_str length:  9
new string: 12_bB45), length:  8
```

Assignment to a character variable as an entity can cause the length to change; however, assignment to a substring of the variable will not. Neither would assignment to an individual element of a character array. In the following code, the character variable text is allocated to a length of 6 by virtue of an intrinsic assignment. The next two lines will replace, respectively, the second through fourth characters and the first through fourth characters in the variable, but neither will reallocate the length, which will remain 6.

```
character (:) , allocatable :: text
text      = "123456"   ! length becomes 6.
text (2:4) = "pqr"      ! length does not change.
text (:)   = "mnop"     ! length does not change.
```

There are situations in which deferred-length character strings do *not* automatically allocate: a **read** statement; the **iomsg** string that Fortran 2003 introduces to many I/O routines such as **open**, **close**, and so on; and an internal **write** statement. The length of the string must be specified in advance, either in the declaration, by having been assigned in advance to a character string, or in an **allocate** statement. Here is an example that uses a fixed-length string set to a length that is "large enough" for use by the **read** statement, then copies just the needed characters into the final resultant string.

```
integer, parameter :: STR_LEN = 64
character(STR_LEN) :: io_string
character(:), allocatable :: final_string
integer :: ioerr
...
read (*, '(a)', iostat=ioerr) io_string
if (ioerr /= 0) then
  ! ... code to handle the I/O error
else
  final_string = trim (io_string)
end if
```

81. *Create simple data structures using derived types with allocatable components.*

Fortran 2008 extends the advantages of allocatable components over pointers by allowing self-referential data structures to be built using derived types that contain allocatable components in lieu of pointers. Doing so provides the advantages of allocatable variables: Arrays are contiguous, there is no danger of aliasing unless the **target** attribute is assigned, and there is no danger of memory leaks.

The following code shows a derived type for a node on a stack of part purchase orders:

```
type order_t
  integer :: purchase_order_number = 0, part_number = 0
end type order_t

type node_t
  type (order_t) :: purchase_order
  type (node_t), allocatable :: next_node
end type node_t
```

A stack, a subroutine to push a node onto it, and a call to do so would be:

```
type (node_t), allocatable :: orders_stack

subroutine Push_node (this, pur_order)
  type (node_t), intent (in out), allocatable :: this
```

```
type (order_t), intent (in) :: pur_order
type (node_t), allocatable :: new_node

new_node = node_t (pur_order, new_node)
call move_alloc (from=this, to=new_node%next_node)
call move_alloc (from=new_node, to=this)
end subroutine Push_node

type (order_t) :: order_obj

call Push (orders_stack, order_obj)
```

A cautionary note is in order here: It would have been possible to write the three executable lines of code in subroutine Push_node in the following manner:

```
this = node_t (pur_order, this)
```

The danger here is that the program may execute what is known as a "deep copy." This means that the assignment will generate the copying of every node on the stack, not just the top one. This could be extremely time-consuming. The code in the procedure uses a single node of type node_t and then, employing two calls to **move_alloc** places it at the top.

For more complex data structures, such as those that require the structure to be traversed, it may be best to use pointers; otherwise, many time-consuming copy operations would have to be performed.

7.2.2 Pointers

Pointers are used for a variety of purposes, some of which are shown in the next few rules. Pointers associate names with "targets," and often multiple pointers can point to a single target. Thus, "ownership" of the target data can move at the programmer's discretion. Pointers may also point to strided data, such as every other element in an array or the diagonal of a matrix. Pointers can also allow a simple name to be used instead of specifying a component of a deeply nested derived type. Finally, pointers are a key requirement when interoperating with code written in C (see Chapter 14).

As pointers are a very general mechanism, they can place a burden on programmers to manage them. In particular, there are the issues of memory "leakage," where ownership of target data is lost and the data is never freed. A second problem is "dangling pointers," where a pointer might point to an area of memory that is in an unknown state. As Fortran has advanced, several of the original uses of pointers have been supplanted with safer language features, such as an increasing number of places where **allocatable** arrays may be used, and with the **associate** construct (see Section 7.2.1).

82. *Use pointers to create dynamic data structures.*

You should use pointers to create standard, possibly self-referential, dynamic data structures such as linked lists, trees, and queues. Here, for example, are two derived types that can be used to create a linked list of integers (see Rule 85):

```fortran
type, private :: int_node_t
  integer :: int_value
  type (int_node_t), pointer :: ptr_next_node => null ()
end type int_node_t

type, public :: int_linked_list_t
  private
  type (int_node_t), pointer :: first_node => null ()
end type int_linked_list_t
```

83. *Use pointers to access array sections and to form arrays of components of nested derived types.*

Numerous numerical methods use sections of arrays to perform algebraic manipulations. You may find it useful to use pointers to point to these sections. Here is part of the code to solve a system of linear equations using Gauss elimination (see Reference [77]). Not all the code is shown here, and neither is the checking that you would want to include.

```fortran
subroutine Gauss_solve (c_mat, rhs, x)
  real, intent (in),  :: c_mat(:,:)
  real, intent (in),  :: rhs (:)
  real, intent (out), :: x(:)
  integer :: n_eqns, i_piv, j_targ
  real :: factor
  real (kind=kind (c_mat)), pointer :: piv_ptr (:), &
      targ_ptr (:)

  n_eqns = ubound (c_mat, dim=1)
    ! loop through the pivot equations
  eqn_loop: do i_piv = 1, n_eqns - 1

      ! for all rows below the pivot equation:
      ! 1) determine the multiplication factor.
      ! 2) point at a section of pivot row
      !    and a section of the target row.
      ! 3) subtract.
    do j_targ = i_piv + 1, n_eqns
      factor   = c_mat(j_targ, i_piv) / c_mat(i_piv, &
          i_piv )
      piv_ptr  => c_mat(i_piv, i_piv + 1: n_eqns)
      targ_ptr => c_mat(j_targ, i_piv + 1: n_eqns)
```

```
        targ_ptr = targ_ptr − factor * piv_ptr
        rhs(j_targ) = rhs(j_targ) − factor * rhs(i_piv)
      end do
    end do eqn_loop
end subroutine Gauss_solve
```

Pointers can also be used to create shortcuts to components of derived types, especially when they are deeply nested. Here is a segment of code where a pointer to an array of integer postal codes is formed:

```
subroutine Sort_mailing (employees)
    type (employee_t), intent (in), target :: employees(:)
    integer, pointer :: codes_ptr(:)

    codes_ptr => employees%address%post_code
    . . .
end subroutine Sort_mailing
```

Note that the **associate** construct could also be used (see Rule 39).

84. *Use pointers to arrays as dummy arguments when it is necessary to maintain the array bounds of the actual argument.*

When you pass arrays as arguments to subprograms, the upper and lower bounds of the actual argument are not maintained in the call unless the lower bound is 1. However, when passing pointers, the lower and upper bounds are maintained. The following code shows the interface to a subroutine and a reference to it; the lower and upper bounds of the dummy argument array_1 in the subroutine will be 1 and 21, respectively.

```
interface
    subroutine Sub_a (this, array_1)
        type (element_t),     intent (in out) :: this
        real, dimension(:), intent (in)      :: array_1
    end subroutine Sub_a
end interface

. . .
type (element_t) :: elem_1
real :: velocities(−10: 10)

call Sub_a (elem_1, velocities)
```

If you change the interface to Sub_a so the second argument is a pointer to an array, the code and reference are as follows:

```
interface
    subroutine Sub_a (this, array_1)
        type (element_t), intent (in out) :: this
        real, pointer,    intent (in)     :: array_1(:)
    end subroutine Sub_a
end interface
    . . .
```

```
type (element_t) :: elem_1
real , target   :: velocities(-10: 10)
real , pointer :: velocities_ptr

velocities_ptr => velocities
call Sub_a (elem_1, velocities_ptr)
```

The dummy argument array_1 will retain the bounds of the actual variable velocities_ptr, that is, the lower bound will be −10 and the upper bound will be 10 (see Rule 61).

85. *When needed, create an array of pointers by defining a supplemental derived type with a single component.*

In some types of data structures, tree structures for example, operations can be more efficiently performed if you use an array of pointers. Fortran does not possess the ability to form such an array; you can only declare a pointer to an array as in the following statement:

```
integer , pointer :: ptr_int (:)
```

To create an array of pointers, define a derived type comprising a single component of the type you wish to point to. Here is a derived type that might be used for a binary tree:

```
type , public :: node_t
  type (node_t), pointer :: left_child   => null ()
  type (node_t), pointer :: right_child  => null ()
  type (node_t), pointer :: parent       => null ()
end type node_t
```

To create an array of pointers of type node_t, first define a new type. Then define an array of pointers of type node_t in this manner:

```
type , public :: p_node
  type (node_t), pointer :: a_node
end type p_node
. . .
type (p_node) :: node_ptr_array (NUM_OF_ARRAYS)
```

86. *Avoid assigning an* intent (out) *attribute to a dummy argument that is a derived type containing pointer components.*

This rule is a more restrictive form of Rule 53. This owes to the fact that assigning **intent** (**out**) to a dummy argument that is a derived type that contains pointer components at any level can easily cause a memory leak if the pointer component is nullified in its component definition.

The following code outlines two derived types, each in its own module. The first defines type photograph_t, whose components are the name of the file containing a photograph and a type-bound procedure for performing a defined assignment of the name. The second is a module describing an animal.

One of its components is a pointer to an object of type photograph_t. It also contains a type-bound procedure for a defined assignment of the file name of the photograph (see Section 11.3).

```
module Photograph_mod
  implicit none
  private

  type, public :: photograph_t
    private
    character(:), allocatable :: file_name
  contains
    procedure :: Photo_assign_name
    generic :: assignment(=) => Photo_assign_name
  end type photograph_t

contains
  subroutine Photo_assign_name (this, file_name)
    class (photograph_t), intent (out) :: this
    character(len=*), intent (in) :: file_name

    this%file_name = file_name
  end subroutine Photo_assign_name
end module Photograph_mod

module Organism_mod
  use Photograph_mod, only : photograph_t
  implicit none
  private

  type, public :: organism_t
    private
    real     :: average_life = 0.0
    real     :: average_mass = 0.0
    logical :: can_move      = .true.
    logical :: is_extinct    = .false.
    character(:), allocatable :: name_organism
    type(photograph_t), pointer :: image => null ()
  contains
    procedure :: Organism_assign_name
    generic :: assignment(=) => Organism_assign_name
  end type organism_t
contains

  subroutine Organism_assign_name (this, file_name)
    class (organism_t), intent(out) :: this
    character(len=*), intent(in) :: file_name
    integer :: alloc_stat
```

```
if (.not. associated (this%image)) then
  allocate (photograph_t this%image, &
      stat=alloc_stat)
  if (alloc_stat == 0) then
    this%image = file_name
  else
    print *, "allocation problem"
  end if
end if
end subroutine Organism_assign_name
end module Organism_mod
```

The following snippet of code will cause Organism_assign_name to be called.

```
type (organism_t) :: aardvark

aardvark = "aardvark.bmp"
```

The problematic code is the **intent** (**out**) attribute assigned to the dummy argument this in subroutine Organism_assign_name. The program will invoke this procedure in assignment statements. If this is not the first such call for variable aardvark, execution of this assignment will cause a memory leak. On entry to subroutine Organism_assign_name, the pointer component image will be nullified as specified in the definition of type organism_t because the intent of argument this is **intent** (**out**). If no other pointer is associated with the photograph_t object to which image was associated at entry, all reference to it will be lost. To avoid this problem, the intent needs to be **intent** (**in out**).

A better technique is to write a **final** procedure that automatically deallocates the pointer components. If a dummy argument possesses the **intent** (**out**) attribute, and the corresponding actual argument of a subprogram is a variable of a derived type that has a final subroutine, the final subroutine will execute prior to the call to the subprogram (see Rule 147).

87. *Do not use defined assignments for pointer assignment.*

It is possible to overload a pointer assignment (=>) using a defined assignment. The following code is a slight modification of the code from the previous rule. Here, we show the differences.

In subroutine Photo_assign_name, the intent of argument file_name is **intent** (**in out**), in accordance with the previous guideline.

```
subroutine Photo_assign_name (this, file_name)
  class (photograph_t), intent (in out) :: this
  character(len=*),      intent (in)     :: file_name

  this%file_name = file_name
end subroutine Photo_assign_name
```

The procedure Organism_assign_name is rewritten as Organism_assign_image. Its second dummy argument is now of type photograph_t.

```
subroutine Organism_assign_image (this , image)
    type (organism_t),    intent(in out)      :: this
    type (photograph_t), intent(in), target  :: image

    this%image => image
end subroutine Organism_assign_image
    . . .
end module Organism_mod
```

In the following code, a photograph_t object, aardvark_photo, is created using a structure constructor. Execution of the second assignment will invoke subroutine Organism_assign_image.

```
type (photograph_t) :: aardvark_photo
type (organism_t)   :: aardvark

aardvark_photo = photograph_t ("aardvark.bmp")
aardvark = aardvark_photo
```

The potential problem here is the use of the assignment operator. The Fortran standard stipulates that the right-hand side of an assignment statement need only exist for the duration of the call (see Reference [39]). So, as written, aardvark%image may point to a transitory object, one that disappears as soon as the program moves to the next executable statement. In this case, its intended association with aardvark_photo is not accomplished. Instead of the assignment, the correct way to do this is to call the subroutine.

```
call Organism_assign_image (aardvark , aardvark%photo)
```

88. *In a hierarchy of derived types containing allocatable components, begin allocation with the component of the parent type and proceed through the hierarchy; deallocate in the reverse order.*

The following code sketches an outline of three modules. The first, Widget_mod, defines a type called widget_t; the second, Widget_list_mod, creates a linked list of widget_t objects by defining derived type widget_node_t; and the final module, assembly_mod, defines type assembly_t, one of whose components is an allocatable array of such linked lists.

```
module Widget_mod
    implicit none
    private

    type, public :: widget_t
        private
        character(len=:), allocatable :: widget_name
```

```fortran
      ... other components
  contains
    ! ... procedure binding statements
  end type widget_t
  ...
contains
  ! module procedures
end module Widget_mod

module Widget_list_mod
  use Widget_mod, only : widget_t
  implicit none
  private

  type, public :: widget_node_t
    private
    type (widget_t) :: widget
    type (widget_node_t), pointer :: &
        next_widget_ptr => null()
    ! ... other components
  contains
    ! ... procedure binding statements
  end type widget_node_t
  ...
contains
  ! module procedures
end module Widget_list_mod

module Assembly_mod
  use Widget_list_mod, only : widget_node_t
  implicit none
  private

  type, public :: assembly_t
    private
    type (widget_node_t), allocatable :: widget_lists (:)
    ! ... other components
  contains
    procedure :: Get_no_of_lists
    ! ... other procedure binding statements
  end type assemble_t
  ...
contains

  elemental function Get_no_of_lists (this) &
      result (ret_val)
    class (assembly_t), intent (in) :: this
```

```
   integer :: ret_val
   ...
end function Get_no_of_lists

! other module procedures
end module Assembly_mod
```

When you wish to populate a linked list of widget_t objects and assign it to an element of the component widget_lists of type assembly_t, you need to allocate the components beginning with the most inclusive component, which in this case is component widget_lists, and proceed to the least inclusive, which here would be the component next_widget_ptr of type widget_node_t. Therefore, the first allocation must be:

```
type (assembly_t) :: wing
   ...
allocate (widget_node_t :: &
    wing%widget_lists(wing%Get_no_of_lists ()), &
    stat=alloc_stat)
```

Now, in the following code, the the first element of the widget_lists array that was allocated is populated with a list of two widgets, aileron and flap. Here you can see the second, inner, allocation, which is the pointer to the next node in the widget list.

```
type (widget_t) :: aileron , flap
associate (crnt_list => wing%widget_lists(1))
  crnt_list%widget = aileron
  allocate (widget_node_t :: &
     crnt_list%next_widget_ptr , stat=alloc_stat)
  if (alloc_stat == 0) &
     crnt_list%next_widget_ptr%widget = flap
end associate
```

When deallocating, you need to proceed in the reverse order: First, you would deallocate all nodes in each element of the allocatable array widget_lists of object wing, and then deallocate the array itself.

If it was possible to construct this data structure using allocatable variables instead, one simple deallocation statement, of the most inclusive object, would deallocate all components throughout the hierarchy. If, therefore, the pointer components of types Widget_list_t and assembly_t can be changed to allocatable arrays, all components of variable wing would be deallocated by the last of the following statements:

```
type , public :: widget_list_t
   ...
   type (widget_t), allocatable :: widgets(:)
   ...
```

```
end type widget_list_t

type, public :: assembly_t
  ...
  type (widget_list_t), allocatable :: widget_lists(:)
  ...
end type assembly_t

deallocate (wing, stat=alloc_stat)
```

89. *Establish a convention for tracking the owner of a pointer target.*

Multiple pointers can be associated to a single pointer target. In the case where the pointer target was originally allocated via an **allocate** statement, the standard does not specify any "reference counting" or any other mechanism to ensure that when all of the pointers are disassociated, the target memory will be released. There is no "garbage collection" in Fortran. In order to avoid memory leakage, a programmer must establish a convention for which area of the code is responsible for deallocating the target.

In areas of code where the lifetime of the target is fairly short, for example, within a few lines, it may be very obvious that the target is both allocated and deallocated through the same pointer. The ownership is clear.

In contrast, a common situation is when a target is allocated in some subprogram, then passed up the call chain to a different routine. Ownership of the target might be considered the uppermost pointer with access to the target.

```
real, pointer :: input_data(:)
...
call read_routine (input_data)
call compute_routine (input_data)
deallocate (input_data, stat=alloc_stat)
```

One possibility of handling more complicated cases where there really are multiple pointers with simultaneous association with a target is to make the target a private module variable and to define an accompanying module variable that keeps track of the number of pointers associated with the target. User-written routines, used with discipline, can then be used to control association.

Listing 7.2: Module Global_target_mod

```
module Global_target_mod
  implicit none
  private
  public :: Deallocate, Nullify, Pnt_at_glob_targ

  ! target & association counter. Neither public.
```

```fortran
      integer , pointer   :: glob_targ (:) => null ()
      integer , protected :: i_ref_cnt = 0

   interface Deallocate
      module procedure Deallocate_pntr
   end interface

   interface Nullify
      module procedure Nullify_pntr
   end interface
contains
   subroutine Deallocate_pntr (pntr_to_targ , return_stat)
      integer (kind=kind (glob_targ )), intent (in out), &
         pointer :: pntr_to_targ (:)
      integer , intent (out) :: return_stat

      enum, bind(C)
         enumerator :: DEALLOC_ERR = 1, NO_ASSOC, BAD_ASSOC
      end enum
      integer :: alloc_stat , i_one_pass

      return_stat = 0
      !(Alternative: F2008, one_pass: block statement)
      one_pass: do i_one_pass = 1, 1

         ! check association
         if (i_ref_cnt == 0 .or. &
            .not. associated (glob_targ )) then
            return_stat = NO_ASSOC
            exit one_pass
         else if (.not. associated (pntr_to_targ , &
            glob_targ )) then
            return_stat = BAD_ASSOC
            exit one_pass
         end if
         if (i_ref_cnt > 1) then

            ! further associations remain, only nullify
            call Nullify (pntr_to_targ )
         else if (i_ref_cnt == 1) then

            ! final association
            call nullify (pntr_to_targ )
            deallocate (glob_targ , stat=alloc_stat )
            if (alloc_stat /= 0) return_stat = DEALLOC_ERR
         end if
      !(Alternative: F2008, end block one_pass statement)
```

```
    end do one_pass
  end subroutine Deallocate_pntr

  subroutine Nullify_pntr (pntr_to_targ)
    integer (kind=kind (glob_targ)), intent (in out), &
        pointer :: pntr_to_targ (:)

    nullify (pntr_to_targ)
    i_ref_cnt = i_ref_cnt − 1
  end subroutine Nullify_pntr

  function Pnt_at_glob_targ () result (pntr_to_targ)
    integer (kind=kind (glob_targ)), pointer :: &
        pntr_to_targ (:)

    i_ref_cnt = i_ref_cnt + 1
    pntr_to_targ => glob_targ
  end function Pnt_at_glob_targ
end module Global_target_mod
```

90. *Use procedure pointers to invoke different subprograms possessing identical interfaces.*

Beginning with Fortran 2003, programmers can use procedure pointers. You use them to choose between two or more subprograms that have identical interfaces. In this rule, we discuss general procedure pointers and reserve that for derived-type procedure pointer components to Rule 144.

The language has long possessed a restrictive and unchecked method for accomplishing this task: You could pass the name of subprogram as an actual argument and then invoke the dummy argument in the called procedure. In the following snippet of code, written in FORTRAN 77 style, SUB1 and SUB2 are two different subroutines with the same interface, a single **REAL** dummy argument. The name of the subroutine passed as an argument to subroutine CALPRC depends of the value of an integer variable ICALL. Subroutine CALPRC invokes the subroutine whose name was passed to it in dummy argument SUBARG.

```
    SUBROUTINE TOPPRC (ICALL)
    IMPLICIT NONE

    INTEGER ICALL
    EXTERNAL SUB1, SUB2

    IF (ICALL .LT. 0) THEN
      CALL CALPRC (SUB1)
    ELSE
      CALL CALPRC (SUB2)
    ENDIF
    END
```

```
SUBROUTINE CALPRC (SUBARG)
   IMPLICIT NONE
   EXTERNAL SUBARG

   REAL A
   . . .
   CALL SUBARG(A)
   . . .
END
```

In the following code, procedure pointers are used to choose between two possible versions of a subprogram based on the value of a state variable debug_on. The standard permits the use of optional arguments in the interface; hence, the calls can be different even though the interfaces must be identical, and this is demonstrated.

Listing 7.3:   Program Proc_point_test

```
module Calc_mod
  implicit none
  private
  public :: Calc_debug, Calc_normal, Calc_proc

    ! set up an interface to be used by the procedure
    ! statement that declares the procedure pointers.
  interface
    function Calc_proc (real_arg, opt_format) &
        result (ret_val)
      real, intent (in) :: real_arg
      character (*), intent (in), optional :: opt_format
      real :: ret_val
    end function Calc_proc
  end interface
contains

    ! two functions whose interfaces conform to the
    ! interface to Calc_proc.
  function Calc_debug (arg1, opt_format) &
      result (ret_val)
    real, intent (in) :: arg1
    character (*), intent (in), optional :: opt_format
    real :: ret_val
    ret_val = 0.0
    print *, "with debug"
    . . .
  end function Calc_debug
```

```
    function Calc_normal (arg1, opt_format) &
        result (ret_val)
      real, intent (in) :: arg1

        ! not used, but must be present.
      character (*), intent (in), optional :: opt_format
      real :: ret_val
      ret_val = 0.0
      print *, "normal"
      ...
    end function Calc_normal
end module Calc_mod

program Proc_point_test
  use Calc_mod, only : Calc_debug, Calc_normal, &
      Calc_proc
  implicit none

    ! declare procedure pointer that points to
    ! procedures whose interface conforms to the
    ! interface of Calc_proc.
  procedure (Calc_proc), pointer :: &
      calc_func_ptr => null ()
  real :: func_value = 0.0, real_arg = 0.0
  integer :: i_two_pass
  logical :: debug_on = .false.

  do i_two_pass = 1, 2
    if (debug_on) then
      calc_func_ptr => Calc_debug
    else
      calc_func_ptr => Calc_normal
    end if
    select case (i_two_pass)
    case (1)
      func_value = Calc_func_ptr (real_arg)
      debug_on   = .not. debug_on
    case (2)
      func_value = Calc_func_ptr (real_arg, "(G15.8)")
    end select
  end do
end program Proc_point_test
```

The program output is:

```
normal
with debug
```

7.3 Dynamic Data Attributes

91. *Where possible and appropriate, use the intrinsic function* kind *in conjuction with the instrinsic conversion functions* int, real, *and* cmplx *when converting types.*

Several situations exist where it may be useful to use the **kind** intrinsic function in conjunction with intrinsic functions such as **int**, **real**, and **cmplx**. This can help clarify potential portability, scalability, or accuracy problems inherent in the default type conversion rules.

In arithmetic expressions involving mixed data types, the basic rule is that less precise types, meaning those with less precision or those requiring fewer storage units, are converted to the more precise type; they are "promoted." The following code assumes that both the default integer kind and default real kind occupy four bytes of memory. The code defines two named constants using the intrinsic functions **selected_int_kind** and **selected_real_kind**. The integer kind corresponds to a single-byte integer; the real kind to double precision, requiring eight bytes of storage. The declaration of four variables, two integers, and two reals follow.

```fortran
! establish named constants for two non-default integers
! and one non-default real.

integer, parameter :: BYTE_1_INT = selected_int_kind (2)
integer, parameter :: D_PREC = &
   selected_real_kind (15, 307)

real :: x_def_real
real (D_PREC) :: y_doub
integer :: i_def_int
integer (BYTE_1_INT) :: j_byte_int
```

The next section of code presents four mixed arithmetic expressions, with comments describing the promotions.

```fortran
    ! Promote i_def_int to default real
x_def_real + i_def_int

    ! Promote j_byte_int to default integer
j_byte_int * i_def_int

    ! Two expressions, each in parentheses,
    ! Promote result of the second to default real.
(x_def_real + i_def_int) * (i_def_int - j_byte_int)

    ! Promote result from default real to D_PREC.
y_doub = x_def_real + i_def_int
```

When kind type parameters were introduced in Fortran 90, an optional kind argument was introduced to the intrinsic functions that convert data types. It is possible to think of the conversions the program is performing in the previous expressions as implicit use of these conversion functions. Using them, the last expression would be:

```
y_doub = real (x_def_real + &
    real (i_def_int , kind=kind (x_def_real) ), &
    kind=kind (y_doub))
```

You can override the default conversion behavior by using these conversion functions; when you do, use the **kind** function. Here, for example, the requirement is to add the truncated value of a real number to whole number m_int.

```
! No change required if kind of m_int is changed.
i_def_int = m_int + int (x_def_real , kind (m_int) )
```

There exists one type of conversion where you do not use the **kind** function: You may need to convert the type or the kind of an actual subprogram argument. In the following two lines, the real kinds WORK_PREC and SING_PREC are not the same:

```
real (WORK_PREC) :: temperature
...
call Sub_1 (real (temperature , kind=SING_PREC) )
```

Another opportunity for using the **kind** function occurs in the **case** construct. Here is an example where the execution branches based on the type of line being processed.

```
subroutine Process_line (this)
    ...
    type (line_t), intent (in) :: this
    ...
    select case (this%line_type)
    case (SOLID)
        ...
    case (DASHED)
        ...
    case default

    end select
    ...
end subroutine Process_line
```

Here, line_type is an integer component of type line_t, and SOLID and DASHED are named constants. The standard requires that all the *case-selector* entities, such as SOLID, be of the same type and kind as the *case-expression*, this%line_type. To ensure this, the case construct may be written:

```
select case (this%line_type , kind=kind (SOLID))
case (int (SOLID))
   . . .
case (int (DASHED))
   . . .
case default

end select
```

which allows for subsequent changes in the kind of the component line_type without requiring modification to the statements of the construct.

There are several situations where explicitly using the conversion functions, even though they are not required, are worthwhile because they mark potential problem spots.

The first occurs when the program converts from a higher precision number to a lower precision one, that is, the data is "narrowed." With floating-point numbers, the danger is, at best, a loss of precision; at worst, the generation of a floating-point overflow exception. Using the variables x_def_real and y_doub that were declared in the previous code, the following code will generate such an exception (see Section 13.3):

```
real (D_PREC), parameter :: HUGE_DP = huge &
   (1.0_D_PREC)
y_doub      = HUGE_DP
x_def_real = y_doub
```

It is best to signal to the reader that the program is executing a mixed-precision operation requiring converting a floating-point number, with the danger of raising an exception or losing precision, and to explicitly use the conversion function with the **kind** argument.

```
x_def_real = real (y_doub, kind (x_def_real) )
```

A more egregious problem can occur when converting integer values. Using the variable j_byte_int that uses one byte of storage, the following code will not work, meaning the expected assignment will not be correct because the number on the right-hand side is too large to be expressed by a single-byte integer.

```
i_def_int = 20000
   . . .
j_byte_int = i_def_int
```

Making the problem worse, Fortran is silent with integers; no warning will be issued or exception raised, but the number will not be correct. To point out the potential problem, write this using the conversion function using the **kind** argument.

```
j_byte_int = int (i_def_int , kind (j_byte_int) )
```

The second situation where the use of the conversion function with the optional **kind** argument clarifies the code is with all the intrinsic functions that return information about the size of an array or an index to an array element as a default integer. These functions include **size**, **ubound**, **maxloc**, and so on. If the size of the array exceeds the value that can be stored in a default integer, use of these functions can result in an incorrect value being returned. This is especially the case with large multi-dimensional arrays. So, if the size of the following array my_array exceeds the largest number that can be stored in a default integer, the first line of the following code produces an incorrect result; the second line at least points out the potential problem.

```
i_def_int = size (my_array)
...
i_def_int = int (size (my_array), kind (i_def_int) )
```

The final situation involves the numeric instrinsic functions **real**, which converts numbers to a real type, and **cmplx**, which converts one or two real numbers to a complex one. The problem here is that these functions always return a number of default kind, regardless of the kinds of the input arguments.

This can result in a silent loss of precision or a floating-point exception. To override this behavior, you must specify the kind of the result as shown in the second assignment in the following code:

```
! WORK_PREC is not default real.
integer, parameter :: WORK_PREC = &
    selected_real_kind (14, 300)
complex (kind=WORK_PREC) :: c_complex
real (kind=WORK_PREC)    :: x, y
...
c_complex = cmplx (x, y)
...
c_complex = cmplx (x, y, kind=WORK_PREC)
```

92. Use the Fortran intrinsic functions lbound *and* ubound *to determine both the lower and upper limits of iterations performed using the* do *construct and both the lower and upper limits of array assignments accomplished using both the* forall *and* where *statements and the* forall *and the* where *constructs.*

If this rule is followed, changes to both the dimensions and the bounds of arrays require only minor modifications to the code. It also helps avoid inadvertently referencing out-of-bound array elements and makes the loop more self-contained. In cases where the lower bound is known to be 1, the **size** intrinsic function may also be used for the upper bound.

In the first example next, a loop is performed over a three-dimensional array of volume elements, one of whose components (not all are shown) is the fluid flow velocity vector at the center of the element. The program calls a function that computes the Reynold's number of an element, and the section then is highlighted if its value exceeds a certain limit. The second example shows an assignment that employs a **forall** statement:

```
type, public :: vol_element_t
   real :: velocity(3)
   .. other components
contains
   procedure :: Comp_rey_no
   procedure :: Highlight_section
end type vol_element_t

integer :: jstrm, jxstrm, jdepth

   ! loop surface to bottom, left bank to right bank,
   ! upstream to downstream
do jdepth = lbound (vols, dim=3), ubound (vols, dim=3)
   do jxstrm = lbound (vols, dim=2), ubound (vols, dim=2)
      do jstrm = lbound (vols, dim=1), ubound (vols, dim=1)
         if (vols(jstrm, jxstrm, jdepth)%Comp_rey_no () &
            >= turb_lim) call vols(jstrm, jxstrm, &
            jdepth)%Highlight_section ()
      end do
   end do
end do

forall (i = lbound (amps, dim=1): ubound (amps, dim=1), &
        j = lbound (amps, dim=2): ubound (amps, dim=2), &
   amps(i, j) /= 0.0) &
   y(i, j) = 1.0 / amps(i, j)
```

93. *Use the intrinsic functions* shape *and* reshape *when initializing arrays of rank 2 or larger.*

The following example illustrates assigning a 2-by-2 array from a vector:

```
   real :: bounds(2, 2)
   bounds = reshape ([10.0, -10.0, 20.0, -20.0], &
      shape (bounds))
```

94. *When specifying the kind of both subprogram dummy arguments and function results, take advantage of the fact that Fortran knows the kind of a data type.*

The **kind** function permits you to determine the kind of data types. You can exploit this when declaring the kinds of dummy arguments and function results. This is especially useful when writing accessor subprograms that set and retrieve the values of components: You do not need to make any modification

to the following two subprograms if you need to change the kind of the real_a
to a real number with a different precision.

```
module Mod_a
  implicit none
  private

  type, public :: typea_t
    real (selected_real_kind (15, 307)), private :: &
      real_a
  contains
    procedure :: Get_real_a
    procedure :: Set_real_a
  end type typea_t

contains
  function Get_real_a (this), result (return_value)
    class (typea_t), intent (in) :: this
    real (kind (this%real_a)) :: return_value
    return_value = this%real_a
  end function Get_real_a

  subroutine Set_real_a (this, set_value)
    class (typea_t), intent (in out) :: this
    real (kind (this%real_a)), intent (in) :: set_value
    this%real_a = set_value
  end subroutine Set_real_a
end module Mod_a
```

7.4 Control Flow

95. *Always include the* stat= *option in all* allocate *and* deallocate *statements; always check its value.*

The standard specifies that a program will stop if it encounters a problem
allocating memory for a pointer or an allocatable data entity using the **allocate**
statement, or deallocating memory using the **deallocate** statement if the **stat**=
option is not included in the statements. From the point of view of the user,
this is the same as the program crashing. Use the **stat**= option to fail gracefully.
Starting with Fortran 2003, you can also use the **errmsg**= option with both
of these statements to obtain an explanatory message when an error occurs.

```
use iso_fortran_env, only : ERROR_UNIT

integer, parameter :: ERR_MSG_LEN = 200
character(*), parameter :: PROC_NAME = "Calc_temp: "
integer, allocatable :: int_ary(:)
character (ERR_MSG_LEN) :: alloc_err_msg
```

```
integer :: alloc_stat , ary_size
...
ary_size = 10
if (.not. allocated (int_ary)) then
  allocate (integer :: int_ary(ary_size), &
      stat=alloc_stat , errmsg=alloc_err_msg)
  if (alloc_stat /= 0) then
    write (ERROR_UNIT, "(A)") PROC_NAME // &
        trim (alloc_err_msg)
    .. code handling the failed allocation
  end if
end if
```

Handling error situations and returning control back to the caller with an indication of the error status also assists when writing unit tests, so that both normal and erroneous situations can be tested.

96. *Check the status of allocatable entities using the* allocated *intrinsic function before allocating or deallocating them.*

It is an error to allocate an allocatable entity that is already allocated or to deallocate an entity that is not allocated. Use of the **allocated** function permits you to avoid this error by testing the allocation status of the variable (see also Rules 79, 80, and 95).

```
integer , allocatable :: flow_grid (: , :)
integer :: alloc_stat
...
if (allocated (flow_grid)) then
  deallocate (flow_grid , stat=alloc_stat)
  ...
end if
```

97. *Write all loops that index arrays of rank 2 or greater such that the innermost (first) rank varies first, then the next most inner loop, and so on.*

To perform calculations, data is transferred between a computer's main memory and its central processing unit (CPU). The speed the processor works is far faster than the data transfer rate between memory and the CPU, by as much as two orders of magnitude or more. To mitigate this problem, cache memory units are placed in the data pipeline between the CPU and main memory. The data transfer rate between them and the CPU is faster than from main memory; if data can be kept in cache memory, the overall computing speed increases. One way to achieve this is to transfer data that is contiguous, meaning data that occupies consecutive memory addresses (see Rule 98).

Fortran stores arrays in memory such that the first subscript runs through all its possible values, then the second, the third, and so on. This is the opposite of C/C++. For rank 2 arrays this is column order. To avoid large jumps in memory references, which cause poor use of cache memory, and the accompanying increase in execution time, arrange loops to vary the indices in the appropriate order as shown in this example:

```
do j_col = 1, ubound (a, dim=2)
  do i_row = 1, ubound (a, dim=1)
    a(i_row, j_col) = i_row * a(i_row, j_col) + j_col
  end do
end do
```

98. *Where possible, assign the contiguous attribute to assumed-shape arrays and array pointers to improve performance.*

The **contiguous** attribute, new in Fortran 2008, allows the programmer to assist the compiler (see Reference [43]). Assumed-shape array dummy arguments assigned this attribute can be argument associated only with a contiguous actual argument and pointers thus assigned can be pointer associated with solely contiguous targets.

Contiguous arrays occupy consecutive locations in memory. If the compiler knows that an array is contiguous, it can generate optimized code and avoid unnecessary copying of data when invoking subprograms. So, whenever possible, assign this attribute as shown here:

```
real, intent (in), contiguous :: contig_array_arg (:)
integer, pointer, contiguous :: int_ptr (:)
```

You could, for example, create two subroutines, identical except for their interfaces: The first would use the argument contig_array_arg shown in the previous example; the second would use an argument not possessing the **contiguous** attribute.

```
subroutine Calc_vort_fast (vort, contig_array_arg)
  real, intent (in out) :: vort (:)
  real, intent (in), contiguous :: contig_array_arg (:)
end subroutine Calc_vort_fast

subroutine Calc_vort_slow (vort, non_contig_array_arg)
  real, intent (in out) :: vort (:)
  real, intent (in),    :: non_contig_array_arg (:)
end subroutine Calc_vort_slow
```

You would call the first subroutine with contiguous arrays and the second with noncontiguous ones. This can easily be determined using the new-to-Fortran 2008 intrinsic function **is_contiguous** that returns a logical scalar indicating if an array is contiguous:

```
if (is_contiguous (array_1)) then
  call Calc_vort_fast (vort_vals, array_1)
```

```
else
    call  Calc_vort_slow  ( array_1 ,  vort_vals )
end  if
```

99. *Code all logical tests that make up the scalar logical expressions of an* if *construct such that they can always be successfully executed.*

Unlike some other languages, such as C, Fortran is not required to "short circuit" when testing logical expressions in **if** constructs and statements. In some cases this requires nesting **if** blocks. A program containing the code below with the first block **if** construct will most likely crash when Sub_a is called without the optional argument. The **if** construct needs to be divided into two as shown in the nested blocks.

```
subroutine  Sub_a  ( arg_1 ,  switch )
    real ,      intent ( in  out )         ::  arg_1
    integer ,  intent ( in ),  optional  ::  switch

    ! Incorrect code:
    if  ( present ( switch ) .and. switch > 0) then
        ...
    end  if

    ! Correct code:
    if  ( present ( switch )) then
        if  ( switch > 0) then
            ...
        end  if
    end  if
```

In the next example, the square root of the difference of two numbers is tested in the same logical expression that the sign of the difference is tested to see if it is positive. This also needs to be separated into nested blocks:

```
real  ::  a,  b

    ! Incorrect
    if  (a > b .and. sqrt  (a − b) > 1.0) then

    ! Correct
    if  (a > b) then
        if  ( sqrt  (a − b) > 1.0) then
```

100. *Use a single-pass loop to avoid deeply nested constructs.*

Often a situation arises in which a series of checks must be performed. At each step, one of two conditions exist: There is no error and the execution may continue; or some type of error condition exists, and the execution flow of the program branches from the normal, error-free, flow. This can lead to code that looks, in skeleton form, like this:

```
if (error_flag1 /= 0) then
  call Log_error (error_table , error_flag1)
else
  . . .
  if (error_flag2 /= 0) then
    call Log_error (error_table , error_flag2)
  else
    . . .
    if (error_flag3 /= 0) then
      call Log_error (error_table , error_flag3)
    else
      ! normal error-free program flow
      . . .
    end if
  end if
end if
```

This leads to excessive indentation and the logic is convoluted. One possible alternative is to employ a labeled loop that only iterates once and to use **exit** statements to branch out of it:

```
this_block : do, i_multi_exit = 1, 1
  if (error_flag1 /= 0) then
    call Log_error (error_table , error_flag1)
    exit this_block
  end if
  . . .
  if (error_flag2 /= 0) then
    call Log_error (error_table , error_flag2)
    exit this_block
  end if
  . . .
  if (error_flag3 /= 0) then
    call Log_error (error_table , error_flag3)
    exit this_block
  end if

  ! normal program flow
  . . .
end do this_block
```

Fortran 2008 introduces the ideal solution, the **block** construct that provides the programmer with a more elegant alternative: Instead of enclosing the code above with the single-pass loop, use the **block** construct. Variables may also be declared within a **block** costruct, in which case their scope is limited to the construct.

```
this_block : block
  ! scope of i_stage limited to block
  integer :: i_stage
  ! ... code with multiple exit points
  exit this_block
  ! ... normal program flow
end block this_block
```

7.5 Character String Expressions

101. *For portability, use the lexical comparison functions* llt , lle , lge, *and* lgt *to compare character strings*.

If there is any chance your program will be used on more than one platform, where the default character set may be different than the one the program is developed on, write:

```
if ( llt ( string1 , string2 )) ...
```

and not the relational operator < as in

```
if ( string1 < string2 ) ...
```

The reason for this is that the "collating sequence," the ordering of the letters, digits, and special characters, differs between character sets, but "alphabetical order" is required by the standard, so A < B <... < Z. The relational operators use the ordering of the native character set. When that ordering changes, such as when a program that was developed on a machine using the ASCII character set is run on a machine that uses the EBCDIC character set, the results of the program may differ from the intended results.

The same issue occurs with the **char** and **ichar** intrinsic functions. These convert characters to the numeric ordinal of the machine's default character set and back. Since the ordinals can vary between character sets, it is usually best to specify them directly in terms of the ASCII character set. The **achar** and **iachar** intrinsic functions are used to internally convert between ASCII numerical values and whatever character set is in use.

The following is a simple function to convert a string to lowercase. It is written in terms of the ASCII character set. For portability, it uses **achar** and **iachar** to ensure it will work on other character sets.

Listing 7.4:   Function To_lower

```
elemental function To_lower (string) result &
    (return_string)
  character(len=*), intent (in) :: string
  character(len=len (string))     :: return_string
```

```fortran
integer, parameter :: UPPER_A = iachar ('A'), &
    UPPER_Z = iachar ('Z')
integer, parameter :: DELTA_LOWER_UPPER = &
    iachar ('a') - iachar ('A')

integer :: c
integer :: i

do, i=1, len (string)
  c = iachar (string(i:i))
  if (c >= UPPER_A .and. c <= UPPER_Z) &
      c = c + DELTA_LOWER_UPPER
  return_string(i:i) = achar (c)
end do
end function to_lower
```

It should be noted that while most computers at the time of this writing use the ASCII character set, newer encodings, such as Unicode, are being developed. Fortran allows for non-default character kinds. As with numeric kinds, the support for non-default kinds varies from compiler to compiler.

```fortran
character(kind=UNICODE_K, len=:), allocatable :: &
    unicode_string
```

8.

Input and Output

Reading data and writing results are fundamental operations that are common to almost all programs. Fortran provides a built-in set of input/output (I/O) statements. These statements generally operate on data files residing on disk drives, and with devices, such as keyboards and console displays, which can be presented to a program by the operating system in a file-like manner. Different devices have different capabilities, so not all operations are supported on each one. The executable I/O statements, divided into two groups, are shown in Table 8.1.

Fortran has always structured its I/O capabilities around the **read** and **write** statements. These statements operate on Fortran "units," which are represented by simple cardinal numbers called "unit numbers." A unit that is connected to a data file typically occupies system resources, such as buffers and file descriptors, from the time it is connected, when the file is opened, until the time it is disconnected using the **close** statement.

8.1 General I/O Operations

102. *Use the named constants in the intrinsic module* iso_fortran_env.

The intrinsic module **iso_fortran_env** provides named constants to help make applications portable. These named constants include values for standard input, output, and error unit numbers, such as **INPUT_UNIT**, **OUTPUT_UNIT**, and various values returned by the **iostat** specifier, such as **IOSTAT_END**, an argument common to many of the I/O statements that return an integer indicating the success or the failure of the I/O operation (see Rules 104 and 105).

These named constants should always be used instead of hard coding constants such as the numbers 5 and 6 for units.

```
use iso_fortran_env
. . .
read_points: do
  read (INPUT_UNIT, *, iostat=ioerror) x, y, z
  select case (ioerror)
  case (IOSTAT_END)
    exit
  case default
    write (ERROR_UNIT, *) "input error encountered"
```

Table 8.1. Executable I/O statements

Statement	Purpose
	Main Statements
close	Release a file from a unit number
inquire	Obtain information about files and units
open	Associate a file to a unit number
print	Write formatted data to the default output unit
read	Read formatted and unformatted data from a unit
write	Write formatted and unformatted data to a unit
	Auxlliary Statements
backspace	Position a sequential access unit back one record
endfile	Write a sequential "end-of-file" record (obsolete)
flush	Ensure coherency between any buffering and the unit
rewind	Position a sequential access unit to its beginning
wait	Wait for an asynchronous I/O operation to complete

```
      stop  1
    end  select

  . . .
end  do  read_points
```

103. *Manage unit numbers as a resource.*

All user-defined unit numbers should be centrally managed. A module is a convenient place for this purpose. At a minimum, named constants should be provided for each unit number, such as GRID_UNIT, TEMP_UNIT, and so forth, as shown at the beginning of the following module Lun_mod. Fortran processors typically predefine single digit unit numbers such as 5 and 6, and implementations vary. So the code starts with unit 10 to avoid them:

Listing 8.1: Module Lun_mod

```
module  Lun_mod
  implicit  none

  ! Use enumerators to provide unique ordinals.
  enum,  bind  (C)
     enumerator  ::  NO_UNIT  =  -1, &
        GRID_UNIT  =  10,  TEMP_UNIT,  PRESSURE_UNIT,  &
        LU_LOWER,  LU_UPPER  =  99
  end  enum
  private
  public  ::  GRID_UNIT,  Get_LUN,  PRESSURE_UNIT,  TEMP_UNIT

  integer,  parameter  ::  PRESET_ERROR  =  1
```

```
contains
  subroutine Get_LUN (lun, io_stat)
    integer, intent (out) :: lun
    integer, intent (out) :: io_stat

    integer :: i
    logical :: is_open

      ! Preset error condition.
    io_stat = PRESET_ERROR
    lun     = NO_UNIT
    do, i=LU_LOWER, LU_UPPER
      inquire (unit=i, opened=is_open)
      if (.not. is_open) exit
    end do

    if (i <= LU_UPPER) then

        ! Found an unused unit.
      io_stat = 0
      lun     = i
    end if
  end subroutine Get_LUN
end module Lun_mod
```

In applications where many unit numbers are opened and closed, or in the case of a library routine that might be mixed with any number of applications, it may be better to develop a routine to dole out unit numbers on an as-needed basis. Before an **open** statement, a routine can be called to search a range of unit numbers for one that is currently unused. The **inquire** statement may be used for this purpose. Subroutine Get_LUN in the previous module performs this task.

This code had two potential problems: The named constants may need to be adjusted for different processors; and the Get_LUN is not atomic and could fail in a concurrent programming environment such as OpenMP.

To at least partially fix the latter problem, the Get_LUN procedure would need to remember which unit numbers it has doled out, perhaps via a private array at module scope. A companion Free_LUN routine would need to be used to mark the unit number as unused after a **close** statement was used.

To avoid these problems altogether, Fortran 2008 allows an **open** statement to issue a unique unit number and return it for use in later I/O statements such as **read** and **write**. This capability is specified via the **newunit** specifier. The unit number returned has a negative value, so as to not conflict with user-defined unit numbers, which must, by the standard, be nonnegative integers.

```
open (newunit=elev_unit, file='elevation_data.txt',...)
read (unit=elev_unit, iostat=ioerr) elevations
```

104. *Use the optional* iostat= *specifier in all input/output statements to verify that the operation was successful and to control the program flow.*

Always consider checking the success or failure of input/output (I/O) operations. The statements **read**, **write**, **open**, **close**, **backspace**, **endfile**, **rewind**, and **inquire** all accept the optional specifier **iostat** =. The alternative, letting the program abort on an error, can prevent proper unit testing. It also does not lead to "user-friendly" applications (see Rule 118).

Generally **open** statements and the first **read** or **write** statements on a unit are the most susceptible to file access errors. **Read** statements are especially vulnerable to bad input files created by other programs. On output, checking **iostat** may not be very important on small files. However, when writing voluminous output, the operation can be affected by available disk space or other device restrictions, so it should be checked.

The **iso_fortran_env** intrinsic module contains two named constants that can be used in conjunction with the **iostat** = specifier. These are **IOSTAT_END**, the value returned by **iostat** when an end-of-file condition is encountered, and **IOSTAT_EOR**, the value when an end-of-record condition is encountered. (**IOSTAT_EOR** is used when performing partial record processing with **advance**='no'.) Also, the **iomsg**= specifier may be used to obtain the error message associated with the **iostat** =*value* (see Rule 102).

Here is an example demonstrating the use of these named constants and **iomsg**= with the **read** statement when reading from a file that contains an unknown number of records. You can use the value returned by the **iostat** = specifier to terminate reading (see Rule 80).

```
use iso_fortran_env , only :: IOSTAT_END, IOSTAT_EOR

integer , parameter :: READ_UNIT = 10, IOMSG_LEN = 200, &
    NAME_LEN = 50
character (IOMSG_LEN) :: io_mess
character (NAME_LEN)  :: emp_name
integer :: io_stat , emp_id , no_recs
real    :: salary

! read and count input records.
no_recs = 0
read_input: do

    ! try to read a record.
    read (unit=READ_UNIT, fmt="(i9 , a, f10.3)" , &
        iostat=io_stat , iomsg=io_mess) emp_id , &
        emp_name, salary

    ! process read: (end-of-record constitutes an error)
    select case (io_stat)
    case (:-1, IOSTAT_EOR)
```

```
      call Process_err (read_unit, io_stat, io_mess)
   case (IOSTAT_END)
      call Process_end_of_input (no_recs)
   case default
   end select

      ! have a record, so count it and process it.
      no_recs = no_recs + 1
      call Process_name (emp_id, trim (emp_name), salary, &
         no_recs)
   end do read_input
```

105. *Use* **open** *and* **close** *statements for all data files.*

All data files should have associated **open** statements to dynamically open the file. The **open** statement also serves to document the file, its access, and usage. Preconnected unit numbers, with the exception of **INPUT_UNIT**, **OUTPUT_UNIT**, and **ERROR_UNIT** should be avoided for two reasons: They are not self-documenting, and implementation varies considerably between Fortran environments. Although the only required specifier in an **open** statement is **unit** for the unit number, more specifiers should be used for their documentation value. Especially recommended for all files are the following specifiers:

- **file** (the file name)
- **access** ("sequential," "direct," "stream")
- **status** ("new," "old," "unknown," "replace," "scratch")
- **action** ("read," "write," "readwrite")
- **iostat** (to handle errors)
- **iomsg** (to provide error message text)

The **status** and **action** specifiers allow the runtime library to check for the expected state of the file as early as possible.

Here is code that demonstrates opening and reading from a file. It uses the **iomsg** and the F2008 **newunit** specifiers as well as some of the familiar ones previously described.

Listing 8.2: Subroutine Process_elev_file

```
subroutine Process_elev_file ()
   use iso_fortran_env, only : ERROR_UNIT
   integer, parameter :: IOMSG_LEN = 200
   character(*), parameter :: ELEV_FILE = 'elev_data.txt'
   character(len=IOMSG_LEN) :: iotxt
   integer :: ioerr, elev_unit

   open (newunit=elev_unit, file=ELEV_FILE, &
```

```
      status='old', action='read', iostat=ioerr, &
      iomsg=iotxt)
  if (ioerr /= 0) then
    write (ERROR_UNIT, *) 'problem opening: ', &
        ELEV_FILE, 'for reading.'
    write (ERROR_UNIT, *) ' message        : ', &
        trim (iotxt)
    stop 1 ! Or return an error to the caller.
  end if

  do
    read (elev_unit, *, iostat=ioerr, iomsg=iotxt) &
        height, temperature, pressure
    if (ioerr /= 0) exit
  end do

  if (ioerr /= IOSTAT_END) then
    write (ERROR_UNIT, *) 'problem reading: ', ELEV_FILE
    write (ERROR_UNIT, *) ' message        : ', &
        trim (iotxt)
    stop 2 ! Or return an error to the caller.
  end if
end subroutine Process_elev_file
```

106. *Use the* inquire *statement for computing direct-access record length.*

Direct access files have fixed-length records. The record size must be specified in the **open** statement with the **recl** specifier. The units used in the **recl** specifier are called *file storage units* or FSUs. It is implementation defined as to how a FSU is measured. Generally it is either the size of a character (e.g., 8-bit bytes), or in *numeric storage unit*, NSU, size (e.g., often 32-bits for many modern computers). It is also often difficult to reliably calculate the total record size when the I/O list is composed of different data types, each with specific alignment requirements. Compilers will also vary as to padding requirements specific to the machine and environment.

To be able to compute the size of the record in a portable manner, the **inquire** statement should be used. In this mode, the **inquire** statement is written very much like a **read** or **write** statement for the file, because it has an I/O list. The record length for the given I/O list is returned via the **recl** value:

```
character(len=DESCRIPTION_LEN) :: fil_txt
real       :: x_pos, y_pos, z_pos
integer :: point_recl, i_rec, ioerr, point_unit
character (len=IOMSG_LEN) :: msgtxt
...
inquire (recl=point_recl) fil_txt, x_pos, y_pos, z_pos
open (unit=point_unit, file='points_file', &
```

```
            access='direct ', recl=point_recl, status='old ', &
            action='read ', iostat=ioerr, iomsg=msgtxt)
    ...
read (point_unit, rec=i_rec, iostat=ioerr, &
    iomsg=msgtxt) fil_txt, x_pos, y_pos, z_pos
```

107. When reading or writing arrays, use implied loops only when the storage order needs to be changed from the default.

Use the array name rather than implied **do** loops in the I/O list when reading or writing an entire array. Implied **do** loops can be hard to read. Moreover, some compilers have been known to call their internal I/O library on an element-by-element basis, which may cause a hidden performance problem on large files. By simply stating the name of the array, the code is clear and it executes quickly. Here are two examples, one showing a complete matrix, the second an array section (see Rule 31):

```
integer :: my_data(:,:)
integer :: io_err
character (len=IOMSG_LEN) :: msg_txt
    ...
write (unit=data_unit, iostat=io_err, &
    iomsg=msg_txt) my_data

integer :: my_data(:,:)
integer :: i1, i2, j1, j2
    ...
write (unit=data_unit) my_data(i1:i2, j1:j2)
```

The implied **do** should be reserved for cases where the normal Fortran column-wise storage order is not wanted. The following code builds a run-time format and then writes out a matrix by rows:

```
real :: result_table(:,:)
character(FRMT_LEN) :: frmt
integer :: i, j
    ! Print the table in human readable form.
write (frmt, '(a, i0, a)') '(', &
    ubound (result_table, dim=2), 'f8.4)'
do, i=1, ubound (result_table, dim=1)
  write (*, frmt) (result_table(i,j), &
    j=1, ubound (result_table, dim=2) )
end do
```

108. Use the same formats and I/O lists when writing, and reading back, a data file.

It is common for a program to write intermediate data to a file and then, at some later time, read the results back in. The reading program could be the same program that wrote the file, or perhaps a different program written by a different author.

The I/O lists in the **write** statements should be identical to the I/O lists on the corresponding **read** statements. This ensures that the data items and the record lengths written out are the same as those expected when reading the data back. For example:

```
write (temp_unit, iostat=io_error) i, j, k, r, s, t
...
read  (temp_unit, iostat=io_error) i, j, k, r, s, t
```

Sometimes the I/O lists will differ in small ways but can still be arranged so that they are as close as possible to the eye. This example writes out the sizes of arrays before writing the arrays themselves. The reader is expected to read the size of the arrays, allocate space for them, and then read the arrays.

```
write (temp_unit, iostat=io_error)   size (arr_1), &
    size (arr_2)
write (temp_unit, iostat=io_error)   arr_1, arr_2
...
rewind (temp_unit, iostat=io_error)
read  (temp_unit,  iostat=io_error) arr_1_len, arr_2_len
allocate (arr_1(arr_1_len), stat=alloc_error)
allocate (arr_2(arr_2_len), stat=alloc_error)
read  (temp_unit, iostat=io_error) arr_1, arr_2
```

With formatted I/O, named character constants, and character strings in general, may be an alternative to the traditional format statements. An advantage of these is that they can be located at module scope, so that a common definition may be used between procedures. When written as named constants, compilers will often check the formats for errors as thoroughly as they do format statements.

109. *Read and write only a single data record in each data transfer statement*.

In formatted I/O, the format specifications can become fairly complex if more than a single operation is carried out in one **write** statement. It is recommended that only a single record be written or read per data transfer statement to make the code easier to comprehend. An exception might be made during reading where records need to be skipped. Where this occurs, a comment should be inserted describing what is being skipped as shown here (*Cmnt-1):

```
write (rep_unit, *, iostat=io_err) 'Output table:'
write (rep_unit, *, iostat=io_err) &
    'index   description   values'
write (rep_unit, *, iostat=io_err) &
    '_____'
do, i=1, ubound (objects)
```

```
   write ( rep_unit , fmt='(i0 , a , f10.4)' , &
        iostat=io_err ) i , objects ( i )%description , &
        objects ( i )%num_value
end do
. . .
rewind ( rep_unit , iostat=io_err )

   ! *Cmnt-1: comment skipping
read ( rep_unit , * , iostat=io_err ) ! skip title
read ( rep_unit , * , iostat=io_err ) ! skip col. title
read ( rep_unit , * , iostat=io_err ) ! skip hyphens
do, i=1, ubound ( objects )
   read ( rep_unit ,'( i0 , a , f10.4 )' , iostat=io_err ) &
        i , objects ( i )%description , objects ( i )%num_value
   if ( io_err /= 0) exit
end do
```

110. *When writing I/O routines for each derived type, consider using defined derived-type I/O.*

Derived types are commonly packaged in modules with procedures that process fundamental operations pertaining to that type. All derived types should have I/O routines for an object of that type, at least one to print debugging information (see Rule 133).

Routines for writing to files and reading from input files can also be implemented. Prior to Fortran 2003, a limited set of default rules governed I/O on derived types. Starting with Fortran 2003, the derived-type I/O (DTIO) facility may be used to override the default rules by specifying user-provided routines for performing I/O on a type.

User-provided DTIO routines are specified in the type-bound procedure section of a type declaration. They have a specific dummy argument list that is defined by the Fortran standard. With formatted I/O, the DTIO facility is invoked by using the "DT" edit descriptor in the format of **read** and **write** statements. List-directed and namelist forms of formatted I/O are also supported (see Rule 112). Here is an example:

Listing 8.3:   Program DTIO_demo

```
module My_type_mod
   implicit none
   private

   type, public :: my_type_t
      integer :: i , j , k
      real    :: r , s , t
```

```fortran
   contains
     procedure :: Debug_print
     generic :: Print => Debug_print

       ! DTIO routine
     generic :: write (formatted) => Debug_print
   end type my_type_t
contains

   subroutine Debug_print (this, unit, iotype, v_list, &
       iostat, iomsg)
     use iso_fortran_env, only : ERROR_UNIT
     class(my_type_t), intent(in) :: this
     integer, intent(in) :: unit

     ! iotype is either 'DT' with a user-supplied suffix,
     ! 'NAMELIST', or 'LISTDIRECTED'.
     ! v_list(1)... v_list(6) contain field widths for
     ! each of the six derived type components,
     ! Not used in this example.

     character(len=*), intent (in) :: iotype
     integer, intent (in) :: v_list(:)
     integer, intent (out) :: iostat
     character(len=*), intent (in out) :: iomsg
     integer :: i_pass

     iostat = 0
     iomsg = ""
       ! single-pass loop provides exit point.
       ! (F2008 Alternative: this_block: block)
     this_block: do i_pass = 1, 1
       write (unit, *, iostat=iostat, iomsg=iomsg) &
           'my_type_t:'
       if (iostat /= 0) exit this_block
       if (iotype(1:2) == 'DT' .and. len (iotype) > 2) &
           write (unit, *, iostat=iostat, iomsg=iomsg) &
               iotype(3:)
       if (iostat /= 0) exit this_block
       write (unit, *, iostat=iostat, iomsg=iomsg) &
           ' components i, j, k:', this%i, this%j, this%k
       if (iostat /= 0) exit this_block
       write (unit, *, iostat=iostat, iomsg=iomsg) &
           '          r, s, t:', this%r, this%s, this%t
       ! (F2008 Alternative: end block this_block)
     end do this_block
```

```fortran
    if (iostat /= 0) then
      write (ERROR_UNIT, "(A)") "print error: " // &
        trim (iomsg)
      write (ERROR_UNIT, "(A, 10)") "       iostat: ", &
        iostat
    end if
  end subroutine Debug_print
end module My_type_mod

program DTIO_demo
  use My_type_mod
  implicit none

  type(my_type_t) :: my_object

  my_object = my_type_t (i=4, j=5, k=6, r=42.0, &
    s=43.0, t=44.0)
  write (*,'(dt "my_object")') my_object
  write (*,'(dt)') my_object
end program DTIO_demo
```

The unformatted version of DTIO is similar the formatted version. The main difference is that the **iotype** and **v_list** dummy arguments are elided (see Reference [38] and Rule 117).

111. *Consider using asynchronous I/O to increase the speed of data transfer.*

I/O operations generally involve the intervention of the operating system. In some cases, these I/O operations can take a great deal of time to complete. In the case of an electromechanical device such as a disk drive, the time to access data may be measured in milliseconds, compared to central processor operations that may be measured in fractions of a nanosecond. With a device such as a keyboard, where human intervention is required, or perhaps a lab experiment, where a result is periodically produced, even longer time periods are involved.

Operating systems and runtime libraries use a variety of techniques to mitigate problems caused by the relative slowness of I/O devices. For example, a technique called "read ahead," where more data is obtained from the device than is actually needed, places the unused data in a "buffer" in the hope that the additional data will be eventually needed. This allows data for succeeding requests to be obtained directly from memory, rather than having to wait for the slow device to operate again. Likewise, on writes, a technique called "write behind" is used with buffering to delay placing data on the device until a large request can be formed. These techniques are normally invisible to the programmer.

However, sometimes it is more efficient to program the I/O operations explicitly. The idea is to issue a time-consuming read or write operation and gain control back before it has completed. Other useful work can then proceed in parallel. At some point, the program can poll the I/O operation using the **inquire** statement to probe to see if it has completed. Alternatively, both the **wait** and the **inquire** statements can block execution of the program until the operation has completed. File positioning statements, such as **rewind**, can also block the program execution until the I/O operation terminates.

Several key areas need to be addressed by any program that uses asynchronous I/O:

- Ensure asynchronous I/O is supported by the operating system for the file.
- Ensure that requests will be large enough that the additional coding complexity will be beneficial.
- Document and account for side effects by using the **asynchronous** attribute.
- Check for errors upon issuing the I/O request.
- Ensure completion to the extent possible.
- Check for errors upon completion of the I/O request.

When you open a file for asynchronous I/O, by using the *asynchronous='yes'* specifier in the **open** statement, you should check the result returned by the **iostat** argument. If the file cannot be properly connected in asynchronous mode, it may be necessary to provide alternative code to perform normal synchronous requests.

Two key performance parameters for a device are its latency, which is the time it takes for a typical minimal request to begin, and its bandwidth, which is the speed additional data can be transferred between the device and the computer's memory once the operation has begun. These specifications can be determined by looking at manufacturer's data sheets and by using benchmarking tools such as *lmdd* (see Reference [48]).

A typical disk drive at the time of this writing spins at 7200 RPM, giving a maximum rotational latency of about 8 milliseconds. Ignoring operating system and hardware buffering, large data transfers run at about 150 megabytes per second. To checkpoint a large three-dimensional array, say 1000x1000x128 data points at 8 bytes per point, the time required is easily computed. It would take:

$$0.008 + 1.024e9/1.50e8 = 6.835 \text{ seconds}$$

If this operation needs to be performed many times, it could be beneficial to split the data across multiple disk drives by using asynchronous I/O.

When declaring variables, the **asynchronous** attribute is used to indicate data objects that are in the I/O list of asynchronous operations. The attribute indicates that side-effects on the objects can occur, so that compilers will be conservative in how they optimize code. In this sense, the attribute is similar to the **volatile** attribute. However, **asynchronous** is weaker than **volatile** because the compiler only has to take into account code between the issuance of a **read** or **write** operation and the corresponding **wait**, or other blocking operation. The compiler is then free to fully optimize data access outside these boundaries (see Rule 71).

In program units where **read** and **write** statements have an *asynchronous='yes'* specifier, the I/O list variables automatically have the **asynchronous** attribute. However, in a procedure that might be called with an argument that may have an asynchronous operation active on it, the dummy argument must have the **asynchronous** attribute as well. Otherwise the compiler could improperly optimize code involving the variable. Even in the procedures where the asynchronous I/O operations are performed, it is useful to use the **asynchronous** attribute explicitly to document its use.

Once the asynchronous operation has been initiated, the **inquire** statement may be used to probe to see if the operation is still active, in "pending" state, or has completed. At some point, the **wait** statement can be used to block further execution of the program until the operation has completed.

Generally, the **inquire** and **wait** statements operate on the unit as a whole – rather than with individual requests. Because multiple asynchronous operations may be issued on a unit, an **id** specifier may be used in the **read** and **write** statements. The specifier provides a variable that is filled in by the Fortran runtime library with a unique value to identify each I/O operation. Later, this variable can be used in an **id** specifier with the **inquire** and **wait** statements to either probe or wait on individual requests.

```
real , asynchronous :: buf_io ( : , : , : )
integer :: io_id
. . .
read (AIO_UNIT, asynchronous='yes ' , id=io_id , &
    iomsg=io_msg , iostat=ioerr ) buf_io
. . .
inquire (AIO_UNIT, id=io_id , pending=io_pending )
. . .
wait (AIO_UNIT, id=io_id , iomsg=io_msg , &
    iostat=ioerr )
```

Here is an example of double buffering. The idea is to sequentially read ahead in the file, while processing is overlapped with the the data in the current buffer. Two buffers are defined, and a pointer used to point to the one with coherent data for processing. Once an end of file situation is encountered and the loop is exited, the final buffer is processed.

Listing 8.4:   Program Dbuf_example

```
module Compute_mod
  implicit none
```

```fortran
  private
  public  ::  Compute

contains
  subroutine  Compute  (buf)
    real ,  intent(in)  ::  buf(:)

    print  *,  'buf(1)  =',  buf(1)
  end  subroutine  Compute
end  module  Compute_mod

program  Dbuf_example

  ! Demonstrate double buffer I/O with overlapping
  ! computations.

  use  Compute_mod ,  only :  Compute
  use  ISO_Fortran_env ,  only:  IOSTAT_END
  implicit  none

  character(*),  parameter  ::  AIO_FILE='datafile1 '
  integer ,  parameter  ::  AIO_UNIT=11, IO_MSG_LEN=128, &
      BUF_SIZE=1000

  real ,  dimension(BUF_SIZE) ,  target ,  asynchronous  ::  &
      buf1 ,  buf2
  real ,  pointer  ::  buf_compute(:)
  integer  ::  id1 ,  id2 ,  ios11 ,  ios12 ,  ios21 ,  ios22 ,  &
      io_err
  character(IO_MSG_LEN)  ::  iomsg11 ,  iomsg12
  character(IO_MSG_LEN)  ::  iomsg21 ,  iomsg22
  integer  ::  read_number
  logical  ::  pending1 ,  pending2

  iomsg11  =  ''
  open  (AIO_UNIT ,  file=AIO_FILE ,  action='read ',  &
      status='old ',  asynchronous='yes ',  &
      form='unformatted ',  iostat=ios11 ,  iomsg=iomsg11)
  if  (ios11  /= 0)  then
    print  *,  'cannot  open  file :  ',  AIO_FILE
    print  *,  '    msg =  ',  trim  (iomsg11)
    stop  1
  end  if

  ! Initial read on buffer 1 to get things going.
  read_number  = 1
  print  *,  'issuing  read_no ',  read_number
```

```fortran
read (AIO_UNIT, asynchronous='yes', id=id1, &
    iomsg=iomsg11, iostat=ios11) buf1

IO_loop: do

    ! Issue read on buffer 2, then compute with
    ! buffer 1.
    read_number = read_number + 1
    print *, 'issuing read_no', read_number
    read (AIO_UNIT, asynchronous='yes', id=id2, &
        iomsg=iomsg21, iostat=ios21) buf2

    iomsg11 = ''
    inquire (AIO_UNIT, id=id1, pending=pending1, &
        iomsg=iomsg11)
    if (.not. pending1 .and. ios11 == IOSTAT_END) then
      print *, 'inquiry 1 msg = ', trim (iomsg11)
      buf_compute => null ()
      exit IO_loop
    end if

    iomsg12 = ''
    wait (AIO_UNIT, id=id1, iomsg=iomsg12, iostat=ios12)
    if (ios12 == IOSTAT_END) then
      print *, 'waiting 1 msg = ', trim (iomsg12)
      buf_compute => buf2
      exit IO_loop
    end if

    buf_compute => buf1
    call compute (buf_compute)

    ! Issue read on buffer 1, then compute with
    ! buffer 2.
    read_number = read_number + 1
    print *, 'issuing read_no', read_number
    read (AIO_UNIT, asynchronous='yes', id=id1, &
        iomsg=iomsg11, iostat=ios11) buf1

    inquire (AIO_UNIT, id=id2, pending=pending2, &
        iomsg=iomsg21)
    iomsg21 = ''
    if (.not. pending2 .and. ios21 == IOSTAT_END) then
      print *, 'inquiry 2 msg = ', trim (iomsg21)
      buf_compute => null ()
      exit IO_loop
    end if
```

```
    iomsg22 = ""
    wait (AIO_UNIT, id=id2, iomsg=iomsg22, iostat=ios22)
    iomsg22 = ''
    if (ios22 == IOSTAT_END) then
      print *, 'waiting 2 msg = ', trim (iomsg22)
      buf_compute => buf1
      exit IO_loop
    end if

    buf_compute => buf2
    call compute (buf_compute)
  end do IO_loop

  ! Final compute portion.
  if (associated (buf_compute)) &
      call Compute (buf_compute)

  iomsg11 = ''
  close (AIO_UNIT, iostat=io_err, iomsg=iomsg11)
  if (io_err /= 0) &
      print *, 'problem closing' // trim (iomsg11)
end program Dbuf_example
```

A limitation in the Fortran implementation of asynchronous I/O is that there is no way to program a "time-out" or otherwise cancel the request once a request is issued.

8.2 Formatted, Unformatted, and Stream I/O

112. *Use formatted I/O for human-readable files.*

Formatted I/O involves the reading and writing of files containing text and character data that can be read and are understandable in the context in which they are used in the program. They can be created with a text editor, viewed and manipulated with various operating system tools such as a sort utility, and printed on printers.

In all formatted I/O transfers, when numeric variables are read and written, a conversion process must be performed. There are two steps to the process: First, the specified format must be interpreted in order to define how each I/O list item will be converted. The second step is to process each I/O list item according to the desired conversion. These steps require work by the central processor, and so may be time-consuming when used with large data files.

Because of the conversion process, floating-point data can suffer loss of precision when used with formatted I/O. For example, a 64-bit IEEE floating-point variable can represent about 17 decimal digits. If the formats specify fewer digits on an output file, accuracy could be lost when the file is read back in.

For such data, when storing intermediate results for future reuse, it may be better to use unformatted I/O (see Rule 117).

Formatted I/O comes in several forms: The most common is specified by a format string or **format** statement in conjunction with the **fmt** specifier in **read** or **write** statements (see Rules 113 and 114).

```
read (point_data_unit, fmt='(3i0)') i, j, k
...
write (output_unit, fmt=100) x, y, z
100 format ('The answers are: ', 3f8.3)
```

A second form, called "list-directed" I/O, is specified by using an asterisk with the **fmt** specifier. List-directed I/O uses Fortran-defined rules for performing a reasonable, but not always desirable set of conversions. This is especially the case with floating-point variable output. The full conversion of each numeric item may involve dozens of digits, quickly leading to output that is difficult to read.

```
write (unit=*, fmt=*) 'x, y, z = ', x, y, z
```

A third form is called "namelist" I/O. As with list-directed I/O, namelist I/O uses a predefined set of rules for performing conversions. It also moves the I/O list away from the individual **read** and **write** statements, and into special **namelist** statements that define namelist group names. These namelist group names are then used as needed. If derived types are to be printed with namelist, consider using the **sequence** statement in the derived-type definition so the namelist output will not be rearranged (see Rule 110).

```
namelist /elev/ height, temperature, pressure
...
read (ELEV_UNIT, nml=elev, iostat=ioerr, iomsg=msgtxt)
```

Data records within a namelist file contain the namelist group name, the individual variable names and their values in name=value form. Each record is terminated with a slash character. Because of the name=value form, on input, the variable names may be in any order. A value may even be omitted, which leaves the original value of the variable unchanged.

```
&elev height=500,
  temperature=65,79 !pressure is unchanged
/
&elev height=1000, pressure=12.4, temperature=60.5
/
```

113. *Use named character constants for frequently used format specifications.*

If a format specification is used in I/O statements throughout a module, create a named character constant whose scope is the entire module, and if the specification is used throughout your program, consider placing it in a separate module (see Rules 47, 48, 108, and 114). Traditional format statements are not allowed at module scope. So, for example, you could use the following named character constant:

```
character (*), parameter :: &
    NOD_REC_FMT = "(a, i0, a, g14.7, a)"
...
write (unit = *, fmt=NOD_REC_FMT) &
    "Node ", node_id, ", Temp.: ", node_temp, " deg."
```

114. For infrequently used format specifications, use character literals directly in I/O statements.

If a particular format specification is used in only a few locations, the clearest manner to specify it is to embed a character literal in the I/O statement that employs it. In this example, the frequency, response, and phase shift of a transfer function are printed in tabular form (see Rule 113).

```
write (unit=WRITE_UNIT, &
    fmt="(t2, f12.5, t20, g14.4, t40, g14.7)") &
    freq, response, shift
```

115. Use internal read and write statement for converting between character strings and numeric items.

A very common requirement when building or interpreting character strings is to convert between decimal digits and their numeric equivalents. Since the formatted I/O statements must perform this task for file I/O, the same statements and conversion capabilities are also available for character strings. The syntax is identical except that the unit number is replaced by a character string (see Rule 199).

```
integer, parameter :: STRING_LEN = 32
character(STRING_LEN) :: string
real :: temperature
...
read (string, fmt='(f8.3)') temperature
```

This example reads character string records from a data file. Based on the first few characters of each record, different conversions are made depending on record type:

Listing 8.5: Program Read_sensor_file

```
module Pres_mod
  implicit none
  private
  public :: Pressure_process
contains
  subroutine Pressure_process (pres, time_stamp)
```

```fortran
    real , intent (in out) ::  pres
    character (*), intent (in) :: time_stamp

    print *, "Pressure process " // trim (time_stamp)
  end subroutine Pressure_process
end module Pres_mod

module Temp_mod
  implicit none
  private
  public :: Temperature_process

contains
  subroutine Temperature_process (temp, time_stamp)
    integer, intent (in out) :: temp
    character (*), intent (in) :: time_stamp

    print *, "Temperature process " // trim (time_stamp)
  end subroutine Temperature_process
end module Temp_mod

program Read_sensor_file
  use iso_fortran_env , only : ERROR_UNIT
  use Pres_mod , only: Pressure_process
  use Temp_mod , only: Temperature_process
  implicit none

  integer , parameter :: RECORD_LEN = 128, &
      MSG_LEN = 200, TIMESTAMP_LEN = 8, &
      SEN_UNIT = 10
  character(*) , parameter :: &
    SENSOR_FILE='sensor_data.txt '

  character(MSG_LEN) :: io_msg
  character(RECORD_LEN)    :: record
  character(TIMESTAMP_LEN) :: timestamp
  real     :: pressure
  integer :: temperature , ioerr , indx_pressure , &
      indx_temp

  open (unit=SEN_UNIT, file=SENSOR_FILE, &
      status='old ', action='read ', &
      iomsg=io_msg , iostat=ioerr)
  open_ok: if (ioerr == 0) then
    read_record : do
      read (SEN_UNIT, fmt='(a)', &
          iostat=ioerr , iomsg=io_msg) record
```

```
      if (ioerr /= 0) exit read_record
      record = adjustl (record)

      action_switch: select case (record(1:8))
      case ('comment')

         ! Do nothing.
      case ('pressure') action_switch
         indx_pressure = indx_pressure + 1
         read (record(9:), fmt='(a8, f8.3)', &
             iostat=ioerr, iomsg=io_msg) &
             timestamp, pressure
         call Pressure_process (pressure, timestamp)
      case ('temp') action_switch
         indx_temp = indx_temp + 1
         read (record(9:), fmt='(a8, i5)', &
             iostat=ioerr, iomsg=io_msg) &
             timestamp, temperature
         call Temperature_process (temperature, &
             timestamp)

      case default action_switch
         write (ERROR_UNIT, *, iostat=ioerr) &
             'unknown record ignored: ', trim (record)
      end select action_switch
    end do read_record
    close (SEN_UNIT, iostat=ioerr, iomsg=io_msg)
  else open_ok
    write (ERROR_UNIT, *) 'problem opening ', &
        SENSOR_FILE
  end if open_ok
end program Read_sensor_file
```

116. *Use format reversion where possible to simplify format statements.*

Fortran provides a method whereby simple format statements can serve for I/O lists containing more elements than there are edit descriptors in the format list. This is called format reversion, and a few examples best illustrate its use. Here an array of shape [4, 4] is printed one row per line:

```
real :: rot_array(4, 4)
print "(4f12.5)", (rot_array (i_row, j_col), &
                  j_col = 1, 4, i_row = 1, 4)
```

Even though there are 16 array elements to print, you need only specify the format for one record; it will be reused for the remaining three.

The following example shows the same technique used for reading records. Say you have a file containing both historical and real-time information about equities. Each record contains the stock symbol, the current price, the current volume, the price-to-earnings ratio, and the stock's market capitalization. A record may look like this:

NCC 16.1114025776.6410.03E9

For a real-time display you might need only the first three pieces of information. If you know ahead of time the exact number of records to be read, you can achieve this by using the following single I/O statement:

```
read (unit = READ_UNIT, fmt = "(a, f6.2, 19)", &
      iostat = ios) (symbol(i), price(i), &
      i = 1, NO_OF_RECORDS)
```

When edit descriptors are nested with parentheses, and format reversion takes place, the innermost parenthesized edit descriptors are repeated. The following demonstrates how a title and some column data are printed in a single **print** statement:

```
print "(a/ (i5, f8.3))", " index   value", &
      (i, values(i), i=1, size (values))
```

In Fortran 2008, an asterisk can be used to indicate an edit descriptor that repeats indefinitely. With this feature, the previous code can be more clearly stated as:

```
print "(a, *(/i5, f8.3))", " index   value", &
      (i, values(i), i=1, size (values))
```

117. *Use unformatted I/O when full numerical accuracy needs to be maintained.*

Unformatted files have a number of advantages over formatted ones. The data is copied directly between internal buffers and the I/O list items with no conversion taking place. The data can be moved at a very high speed because of this. And, because there is no conversion, numeric data does not suffer any loss of precision.

Unformatted I/O is indicated by using **form="unformatted"** in the **open** statement, and by omitting the **fmt** specifier in **read** and **write** statements.

```
complex, allocatable :: sigs, sigs_inverted (:)
. . .
open (newunit=sig_unit, file='signal_file.dat', &
      form='unformatted', &
      iostat=io_err, iomsg=io_msg)
write (sig_unit, iostat=io_err) sigs, sigs_inverted
. . .
rewind (sig_unit, iostat=io_err)
read (sig_unit, iostat=io_err) sigs, sigs_inverted
```

Each unformatted **write** statement writes a record composed of values of the I/O list variables out to the file. On a sequential file, the records may be of variable length, that is, each **write** statement may have different I/O list items with different types of data, different shapes of arrays, and so on. In order to distinguish one record from the next, the Fortran runtime library will typically place a record mark of some sort in the file between each record. The record mark generally contains a count of the length of the record. This count supports skipping records on sequential files without transferring their data into I/O list items, via a **read** statement with no I/O list. Likewise, the counts also support the **backspace** statement, which allows positioning to the previous record so that it can be reread, or overwritten. Note that the record marks are implementation-defined, and, therefore, unformatted files may not be portable between environments. Also, floating-point and endian issues may further complicate portability.

When skipping and backspacing are not required, a streaming option is allowed. The streaming is specified in the **open** statement with the **access**='stream' specifier. Streaming does not organize data into records. Data is transferred based on the I/O list given. This removes the need for record marks within a file, thereby removing an implementation-dependent issue when interfacing with non-Fortran files, such as those written by other languages or hardware devices. In the following program, four data entities are written to file METER_FILE. It will simulate a device that provides this as a continuous stream of data. To control the device, only the pressure is needed; all the data is read in as a stream, and only the pressure is used.

Listing 8.6:   Program Stream_demo

```fortran
program Stream_demo
  implicit none

  integer, parameter :: TIME_MARK_LEN = 5, &
      NO_OF_SAMPLES = 3, METER_UNIT = 20, &
      IO_MSG_LEN = 100
  character (len=*), parameter :: &
      METER_FILE = "meter_dat"

  character (len=TIME_MARK_LEN) :: &
      time_marks(NO_OF_SAMPLES) = ["14:01", "14:02", &
      "14:03"]
  character (len=IO_MSG_LEN) :: msg_text
  real, dimension(NO_OF_SAMPLES) :: pres, temp, vel
  integer :: i_samp, io_err, j_one_pass

  do i_samp = 1, NO_OF_SAMPLES
    pres(i_samp) = i_samp * 10.0
    temp(i_samp) = i_samp + 20.0
    vel(i_samp)  = i_samp * 50.0 + 600.0
  end do
```

```fortran
      ! open for steam I/O.
  open (unit=METER_UNIT, file=METER_FILE, &
       status="replace", access="stream", &
       iostat=io_err, iomsg=msg_text)

      ! single-pass loop for error exit.
      ! (F2008 Alternative: io_block1: block)
  io_block1: do j_one_pass = 1, 1
    if (io_err /= 0) exit io_block1

      ! establish data source, stream I/O.
    do i_samp = 1, NO_OF_SAMPLES
      write (METER_UNIT, iostat=io_err, iomsg=msg_text) &
          time_marks(i_samp)
      if (io_err /= 0) exit io_block1
      write (METER_UNIT, iostat=io_err, iomsg=msg_text) &
          pres(i_samp), temp(i_samp), vel(i_samp)
      if (io_err /= 0) exit io_block1
    end do
    rewind (METER_UNIT, iostat=io_err, iomsg=msg_text)
    if (io_err /= 0) exit io_block1

      ! read data back in, stream I/O.
    do i_samp = 1, NO_OF_SAMPLES
      read (METER_UNIT, iostat=io_err, iomsg=msg_text) &
          time_marks(i_samp)
      if (io_err /= 0) exit io_block1
      read (METER_UNIT, iostat=io_err, iomsg=msg_text) &
          pres(i_samp), temp(i_samp), vel(i_samp)
      if (io_err /= 0) then
        exit io_block1
      else

          ! use pressure (only) for feedback.
        write (*, "(A, I0)") "sample no: ", i_samp
        write (*, "(A, G8.3)") "pressure: ", &
            pres(i_samp)
      end if
      if (io_err /= 0) exit io_block1
    end do
    if (io_err /= 0) &
        write (*, "(A, I0, A)") "Error no.: ", io_err, &
        msg_text
    close (METER_UNIT, iostat = io_err)
      ! (F2008 Alternative: end block io_block1)
  end do io_block1
end program Stream_demo
```

The program output is:

```
sample no: 1
pressure: 10.0
sample no: 2
pressure: 20.0
sample no: 3
pressure: 30.0
```

8.3 Messages

118. *Issue meaningful error messages.*

The purpose of an error message is to inform the user of a situation that the program is not able to handle. Good error messages will aid the user in correcting the inputs in order to conform to whatever requirements are needed.

The best error messages for an end-user are related to items that are under the user's control. They are also written in terms that the user is familiar with. For example:

```
ERROR: Attempted to connect element 73 edge 2 to unknown
       element 7463. Please correct geometry in file:
          problem_23/widget_geometry.dat
```

This error message describes the situation encountered and points in the direction of a fix. It even tells where the problem might be found.

Error messages may also be directed to those who maintain the program. The program may, for instance, log all program messages to a file. For these types of messages, to locate the source of the problem in the code, you should indicate the location of the error, including the module name and the contained procedure within the file:

```
Angular_formulae_mod::XYZ_Computation:
  ERROR: Input value was 76.5, but must be
         greater than 0.0 and less than pi.
```

119. *Use meaningful* **stop** *statements for error termination.*

The normal method of terminating a Fortran program is either by executing the **stop** statement, or by encountering the **end** statement of the main program unit. In cases where processing must end prematurely, such as in an error situation, you should indicate the reason this occurred.

The Fortran 2008 standard has adopted the POSIX standard of issuing an "exit status" on program termination. This is accomplished by specifying a series of between one to five digits with the **stop** statement. The default exit status for successful termination is the digit "0." This allows for a shell script to detect different cases of termination and take appropriate actions.

The following is a segment of code showing an error termination. It is followed by a POSIX compliant shell script showing access to the exit status of a process by using the question mark (?) environment variable:

```
use ISO_fortran_env , only : ERROR_UNIT
    . . .
open (MYDATA_UNIT, file=DATA_FILE_NAME, status='old ',    &
    access='read ', iostat=ioerr , iomsg=msgtxt)
if ( ioerr /= 0) then
    write (ERROR_UNIT,*) &
        'Error encountered opening: ', DATA_FILE_NAME
    write (ERROR_UNIT,*) '  message: ', trim (msgtxt)
    stop 1
end if
```

```
# sh shell script to run the program
meltdown_sim
if [ $? = 0 ]; then
    echo Successful execution ;
else
    echo exit status was: $?;
fi
```

It is generally better to return an error status to the caller of a procedure than to abort the program. This allows the caller to decide upon an appropriate action to take. It also allows the precedure to be more readily unit tested. Example:

```
if (present (error_status )) then
    error_status = ERROR_CODE
    return
else
    write (ERROR_UNIT, *) "Procedure xyz: Error ..."
    stop 1
end if
```

9.

Packaging Conventions

9.1 Files

120. *Place each program unit in a separate file.*

Program units in Fortran are the main program, external subroutines, modules, and submodules. Placing each unit in a separate file makes the program easier to maintain. Shorter files tend to compile faster. You can locate different program components in files more easily. When a team of programmers is collaborating on a project, smaller files make it less likely that the work of one programmer will conflict with that of others.

It is crucial that you place submodules in files separate from their parent modules. Doing so prevents "compilation cascade," a phenomena where a change in the implementation of a subprogram needlessly causes the recompilation of other program units (see Rule 124).

121. *Whenever possible, use the module name, the type name, the subprogram name, or the program name as the file name.*

This rule makes it easier to maintain programs. This is especially true if you code in conformance to Rule 133 and place each derived type in its own module, and you also choose to use either a prefix or suffix attached to a common base name when naming derived types and the modules that contain them. In that case, name the file according to the base name. For instance, you might have a type called pixel_t defined in module pixel_mod, and you can name the file `pixel.f03` (see Section 4.2).

9.2 External Procedures

External procedures are those that do not reside in a module or are an internal procedure within a main program. An explicit interface is not defined unless one is created by using interface blocks. Examples of external procedures are older FORTRAN 77 code, and code written in other languages, such as C.

122. *Group the interface blocks for all user-defined external procedures in one or more modules. Use these modules in all procedures where these external procedures are referenced.*

Using this rule allows an interface to be easily changed. Say you have an external subroutine contained in its own file:

```
subroutine Sub_a (argi, argr)
   implicit none
   integer, intent (in)      :: argi
   real,     intent (in out) :: argr
   ... code to calculate argr
end subroutine Sub_a
```

In every location in the program from which Sub_a is called, be it from a module subprogram or from another external procedure, an interface should be provided. One method of doing so is to include an interface block in the specification section of the calling unit.

```
subroutine Sub_b
   implicit none
   integer :: int1
   real    :: real1
   interface
      subroutine Sub_a (argi, argr)
         integer, intent (in)      :: argi
         real,     intent (in out) :: argr
      end subroutine Sub_a
   end interface
   ...
   call Sub_a (int1, real1)
   ...
end subroutine Sub_b
```

If the interface changes, all such interface blocks must be changed accordingly. A better method is to gather all such interface blocks into modules and use the modules where needed. The module would appear as shown in the following code. This method is the preferred manner in which to package a library of external procedures. The source code is placed in one or more files, and a module containing the interfaces to all the procedures is provided.

```
module Interface_mod
   implicit none
   interface
      subroutine Sub_a (argi, argr)
         integer, intent (in)      :: argi
         real,     intent (in out) :: argr
      end subroutine Sub_a
      ... additional blocks for other procedures
   end interface
end module Interface_mod

subroutine Sub_b
   implicit none
   integer :: int1
```

```
real      ::  real1
use Interface_mod
 . . .
call Sub_a (int1 , real1)
 . . .
end subroutine Sub_b
```

123. *Place the declaration of the dummy arguments of external procedures in a separate file and then include it using an* include *line in the file containing the procedure and every file containing its interface block.*

Conforming to this rule will prevent you from inadvertently forgetting to change the interface block to an external procedure after you have modified the interface to the procedure itself.

Here's an external procedure, contained in its own file, sub_a_args.f90, followed by the contents of the included file:

```
subroutine Sub_a (arg_1 , arg_2)
  implicit none
  include "sub_a_args.f90"
 . . .
end subroutine Sub_a

! contents of file sub_a_args.f90
complex, intent (in out) :: arg_1
real ,    intent (in), optional :: arg_2
```

The module making the interface available would look like this:

```
module Interface_mod
  implicit none
  interface
    subroutine Sub_a (arg_1 , arg_2)
      include "sub_a_args.f90"
    end subroutine Sub_a
    ... additional blocks for other procedures
  end interface
end module Interface_mod
```

9.3 Submodules

Modules are the fundamental feature of modern Fortran for grouping highly related definitions, globally available variables, and procedures. However, problems occur in large applications because there is not a clean split between the interface the module defines for the outside world, and the internal implementation of that interface.

One problem is that of "compilation cascade," whereby changes in a low-level module that did not affect the interfaces to its procedures trigger an unnecessary recompilation of many program units that depend on that module's interface. The change could be as small as fixing a typographical error in a comment line, yet massive recompilation could occur.

A second problem is that it is sometimes desirable to distribute the interface in source form, yet maintain the actual procedural code separately as external procedures. In this case, interface blocks are defined for the procedures. The problem here is that there is no linkage between the interface blocks and the actual procedures. The interface is therefore defined in at least two places. The developers must vigilantly keep multiple files in sync, or possibly use **include** files in some manner (see Section 9.2).

The ISO/IEC Technical Report TR 19767, *Enhanced Module Facilities* (see Reference [32]) addressed the issue by developing "submodules." This TR is incorporated as part of Fortran 2008. Submodules provide a method for cleanly separating the interfaces of module procedures from their implementation.

124. *Use submodules to separate the interfaces of module procedures from their implementations. Specify the interface in the parent module only.*

Here is a module that defines a data type vector_t, and an interface block to define a function for that type: It is followed by a submodule that contains the actual implementation of the function Comp_components:

```fortran
module Vector_mod
  implicit none
  private
  public :: Comp_components, UNIT_VECTORS, vector_t

  type, public :: vector_t
    real, dimension(3) :: origin = 0.0, &
        dir_cos = [1.0, 0.0, 0.0], vec_len = 0.0
  end type vector_t

  interface
    function Comp_components (this) result (ret_vals)
      import :: vector_t
      implicit none
      type (vector_t), intent (in) :: this
      real :: ret_vals(3)
    end function Comp_components
  end interface

  type (vector_t), parameter, dimension(3) :: &
      UNIT_VECTORS = &
      [vector_t (vec_len =1.0), &
       vector_t (dir_cos =[0.0, 1.0, 0.0], vec_len =1.0), &
       vector_t (dir_cos =[0.0, 0.0, 1.0], vec_len =1.0)]
end module Vector_mod
```

```
submodule (Vector_mod) Vector_submod
  implicit none
contains
  module procedure Comp_components
    ret_vals = this%vec_len * this%dir_cos
  end procedure Comp_components
end submodule Vector_submod
```

The **submodule** statement specifies the module that the submodule is associated with. Here it is module Vector_mod. The **module procedure** statement states that the interface from the parent module is to be used. In this case, it is function Comp_components. The argument list and various declarations do not need to be repeated, so there is no opportunity for error. The submodule code for this can, and, in fact, should, reside in a separate file from the parent module, so that it can be developed independently of the interface.

A drawback of this manner of writing the procedure code in submodules is that you do not see the interface when you are looking at the source code listing; you need to refer to the listing of the parent module as well. The submodule that follows, however, would also work. Its use removes this disadvantage by repeating the interface. The compiler is required to compare the two interfaces and issue an error if they differ. However, the previous form is still preferable because the code specifying the interface exists solely in one place, the parent module. If you need to change the interface, you can make all changes to the interface code in it alone.

```
submodule (Vector_mod) Vector_submod

contains
  function Comp_components (this) result (ret_vals)
    type (vector_t), intent (in) :: this
    real :: ret_vals(3)
    ret_vals = this%vec_len * this%dir_cos
  end function Comp_components

end submodule Vector_submod
```

The parent module is the one specified in **use** statements in other program units to obtain access both to the module procedure interfaces and to objects whose scope is the module.

```
module ModA_mod
  use Vector_mod, only : Comp_components, vector_t

  implicit none
  private
  public :: ! ... list of public entities
```

```
contains
    ! ... procedures that reference the function
    ! ... Comp_Components in submodule Vector_submod.
end module ModA_mod
```

If you modify the implementation of Comp_components in submodule Vector_submod, but do not modify the interface, module ModA_mod need not be recompiled because it does not use Vector_submod.

When using an application building tool, such as *make*, in the specification used to build the application, compilation of the parent module is the prerequisite for compilation of the submodules. It should also be the prerequisite for all program units that need access to the public entities and interfaces of the module; compilation of the submodules should not be the prerequisite to these units. For this reason, you should define all public objects, not just the interfaces, in the parent module. The named constant UNIT_VECTORS in module Vector_mod in the previous example is an example as is the type vector_t. With most make programs, you will need to place the parent module and each of its submodules in a separate file to prevent the unneeded compilation (see Rule 120).

10.

Generic Programming

A common requirement when writing code is the ability to use the identical, or nearly identical, code for different data types. In the case of the public domain LAPACK linear algebra library (see Reference [5]), for instance, procedures support much the same set of operations for each of **real**, **double precision**, and **complex** data types. For example, the **real** version of a matrix operation routine might be identical to the **complex** version, except for a few details, primarily:

- The data type of the dummy arguments.
- The data type of function return values.
- The data type of localized temporary variables.
- Numeric constants (e.g., 1.0 vs (1.0,0.0)).

In addition to the data type, the kind and rank of arguments may also differ. A routine that processes **real** data may be identical to its **double precision** counterpart, thereby making the kinds different. And often routines accepting scalar arguments may need to be expanded to accept array arguments.

A number of techniques are used to make the job of generic programming easier and less error prone than simply replicating and hand-editing code. These techniques can be divided into three general methodologies: reducing the need to replicate code, reducing the number of code changes required to replicate code, and finally, automating the replication of code. The specific techniques we discuss are:

- Use parameterized derived types to avoid replication based on **kind** and **len**.
- Create and use generic names for procedures with **interface** blocks.
- Use **optional** arguments to avoid the need for additional replication.
- Use **elemental** procedures for rank independence.
- Use the **result** clause for function result names.
- Use generic names for intrinsic procedures.
- Use a preprocessor for automated replication of code and handling conditional operations.
- Create and use generic specifications for two or more type-bound procedures using the **generic** keyword.
- Use polymorphic dummy arguments.

The guidelines in this chapter cover all these points except the final two: They more naturally belong in Chapter 11, Object Orientation, where you can find the guidelines that explain them (see Rules 143 and 154).

10.1 Generic Code Techniques

125. *Use parameterized derived types to create generic code.*

Parameterized derived types, new in Fortran 2003, add a generic capability to derived types. They enable the programmer to use a single derived-type definition to serve as the derived type for components of various kinds and lengths. Here is an example definition; it is based on a type used in Rule 170. The kind type parameters are pixel_kind and color_kind. They set the kinds, respectively, of components pixel_intensity and i_colors, and they are identified by the keyword **kind**. The length type parameter is color_len; it sets the dimension of the rank 1 array i_colors and is identified by the keyword **len**. The length parameter may also be used for character string lengths (see Rule 137). All type parameters are integers.

```
type pixel_t ( pixel_kind , color_kind , color_len )
   integer , kind :: pixel_kind , color_kind
   integer , len :: color_len
   real ( real_kind ) :: pixel_intensity = 0.0
   integer ( color_kind ) :: i_colors ( color_len ) = NO_COLOR
end type pixel_t
```

You must specify the kind type parameters such that they can be determined during compilation. The length type parameters can vary. Here is a sample declaration of an assumed-shape array of pixels, where SMALL_INT is a named constant, and number_of_colors is a variable:

```
type ( pixel_t ( pixel_kind=selected_real_kind ( 6 , 37 ) , &
   color_kind=SMALL_INT , &
   color_len=number_of_colors )) :: pixels ( : , : )
```

Liberal use of parameterized derived types can eliminate the necessity of writing separate code to handle different kinds of intrinsic data types. Here is the code, for example, for a simple linked list of default integers:

```
module Int_Linked_List_mod
   implicit none
   private

   type , public :: int_node_t
      integer :: int_value
      type ( int_node_t ), pointer :: next_node => null ()
   contains
      procedure :: Get_next_node
```

```
    procedure :: Insert_node
    ! other type-bound procedures
  end type int_node_t
```

```
contains
    ... code implementing procedures Get_next_node,
    ... Insert_node, etc.
end module Int_Linked_List_mod
```

The code declaring a linked list would be:

```
type (int_node_t), pointer :: def_int_list
```

If the need exists for a linked list for a second kind of integer, you could create a separate module and duplicate the code for the default kind for the second kind. The procedures could then be made generic using the techniques described in Rule 126. An alternative method is to make this type a parameterized derived type as shown here:

```
    type, public :: int_node_t (int_kind)
      integer, kind :: int_kind = kind (1)
      integer (int_kind) :: int_value
      type (int_node_t), pointer :: next_node => null ()
    contains
      procedure :: Get_next_node
      procedure :: Insert_node
      ! other type-bound procedures
    end type int_node_t
```

The following is a declaration for a list containing integer values of extended magnitude:

```
type (Int_node_t (int_kind = selected_int_kind (15))), &
    pointer :: ext_int_list
```

126. *Create generic names for related specific procedures.*

When multiple procedures exist that perform identical, or nearly identical, operations, **interface** blocks can be used to create a single generic name for them. At compile time, when the compiler encounters a call to a generic name, it will examine each of the actual arguments in the call and attempt to match it to one of the specific procedures based on the type, kind, and rank of the arguments. Fortran 2008 also differentiates between the **allocatable** and **pointer** attributes. Each of the procedures will be coded to handle its own specific arguments. The advantage to the caller of a generic named procedure is that the specific routine name is irrelevant, provided the compiler can find a suitable specific version of the routine to call. This manner of creating a generic procedure for two or more distinct derived types is referred to in object-oriented terminology as "overloading." The method shown here was the one you could use in Fortran 95. In Fortran 2003, the preferred way is to write type-bound procedures (see Chapter 11).

```fortran
module Polysort_mod
  use Kinds_module

  implicit none
  private
  public :: Polysort

  interface Polysort
    module procedure Polysort_real
    module procedure Polysort_dp
    module procedure Polysort_char
  end interface Polysort
contains

  subroutine Polysort_real (input, direction, output, &
      return_stat)
    real, intent (in)  :: input(:)
    character(*), intent (in) :: direction
    real, intent (out) :: output(:)
    integer, intent (out), optional :: return_stat
    ...
  end subroutine Polysort_real

  subroutine Polysort_dp (input, direction, output, &
      return_stat)
    real (DP_K), intent (in)  :: input(:)
    character(*), intent (in)  :: direction
    real (DP_K), intent (out) :: output(:)
    integer, intent (out), optional :: return_stat
    ...
  end subroutine Polysort_dp

  subroutine Polysort_char (input, direction, output, &
      return_stat)
    character(*), intent (in)  :: input(:)
    character(*), intent (in)  :: direction
    character(*), intent (out) :: output(:)
    integer,     intent (out), optional :: return_stat
    ...
  end subroutine Polysort_char
end module Polysort_mod
```

For functions, only the argument lists are matched to find the correct specific procedure. The function result type is not to be used for matching. For example, the following code is incorrect; the compiler will not differentiate between the two functions:

```
interface Calc_value
  module procedure Calc_value_real
  module procedure Calc_value_int
end interface

function Calc_value_real (this) result (return_value)
  type (object_t), intent (in) :: this
  real :: return_value
end function Calc_value_real

function Calc_value_int (this) result (return_value)
  type (object_t), intent (in) :: this
  integer :: return_value
end function Calc_value_int
```

One way to overcome this problem is to pass an additional argument that will allow the compiler to distinguish between the two routines.

```
function Calc_value_real (this, type_mold) &
    result (return_value)
  type (object_t), intent (in) :: this
  real, intent (in) :: type_mold
  real :: return_value
end function Calc_value_real

function Calc_value_int (this, type_mold) &
    result (return_value)
  type (object_t), intent (in) :: this
  integer, intent (in) :: type_mold
  integer :: return_value
end function Calc_value_int
```

More than one module can possess the same generic procedure name. Here's an example using two derived types:

```
module Node_mod
  implicit none
  private
  public :: node_t, Print_data

  type node_t
    real :: points(3)
  end type node_t

  interface Print_data
    module procedure Print_node
  end interface Print_data
contains
```

```fortran
  subroutine Print_node (this)
    type (node_t), intent (in) :: this
    ! ... code to print the components of a type
    ! ... node_t object
  end subroutine Print_node
end module Node_mod

module Element_mod
  use Node_mod, only : node_t, Print_data
  implicit none
  private
  public :: element_t, Print_data

  type element_t
    integer :: id
    type (node_t), allocatable :: nodes(:)
  end type element_t

  interface Print_data
    module procedure Print_element
  end interface Print_data
contains

  subroutine Print_element (this)
    type (element_t), intent (in) :: this
    integer :: i_node

    ! ... code to print this%id
    if (allocated (this%nodes)) then
      do i_node = 1, size (this%nodes)
        call Print_data (this%nodes(i_node))
      end do
    end if
  end subroutine Print_element
end module Element_mod
```

127. *Use* **optional** *arguments to avoid replication.*

The use of optional arguments allows a procedure to be called with a basic set of arguments, and then, as additional capabilities are needed, the procedure can grow to accommodate them (see Rules 57 and 58).

In the following example, two optional arguments provide the capability of specifying that the printing of either of the components may be disabled. Otherwise all are.

Listing 10.1: Module My_type_mod

```fortran
module My_type_mod
  implicit none
```

```
private
public :: my_type_print

integer, parameter :: NAME_LEN = 50

type, public :: my_type_t
  character(NAME_LEN) :: name_comp
  real,       allocatable :: vals(:)
  integer, allocatable :: locs(:)
end type my_type_t

contains
  subroutine My_type_print (this, prt_vals, prt_locs)
    type (my_type_t), intent(in) :: this
    logical, intent(in), optional :: prt_vals, prt_locs

    logical :: local_prt_vals, local_prt_locs

    ! default: print both components vals and locs
    local_prt_vals = .true.
    local_prt_locs = .true.
    print *, 'my_type_t dump: ', this%name_comp
    if (present (prt_vals)) local_prt_vals = prt_vals
    if (local_prt_vals) print *, '  vals = ', this%vals

    if (present (prt_locs)) local_prt_locs = prt_locs
    if (local_prt_locs) print *, '  locs = ', this%locs
  end subroutine My_type_print
end module My_type_mod
```

128. *Use* elemental *procedures to create rank-insensitive code*.
When using arrays, it is often the case that procedures may need to be replicated for each rank. Because Fortran supports arrays of up to 15 dimensions, plus scalars, there could be as many as 16 rank combinations for each argument. The number of procedures needed to support, say, two real kinds and two complex kinds would be 64. By using **elemental** procedures, you may be able to reduce this example to only four (see Rule 59).

Elemental procedures are written with all scalar dummy arguments. When called with array actual arguments, the compiler will automatically call the procedure for each array element. Elemental procedures are a special case of pure procedures. So when evaluating candidates, keep in mind that they must not introduce side effects (see Rule 52).

A typical example of such a subprogram is an accessor function that retrieves the value of a component of a derived type.

```
type obj_t
  real :: r_comp
end type obj_t
```

```
elemental function Get_comp (this) result (ret_val)
   type (obj_t), intent (in) :: this
   real (kind (this%r_comp)) :: ret_val
   ret_val = this%r_comp
end function Get_comp
```

All three of the references to Get_comp in the following code will work. The
function will return either a scalar or an array that conforms to the actual
argument.

```
integer, parameter :: MAX_1 = 10, MAX_2 = 20, MAX_3 = 5
type (obj_t) :: obj_s, obj_1(MAX_1), obj_2(MAX_2, MAX_3)
real :: r_s, r_1(MAX_1), r_2(MAX_2, MAX_3)

r_s = Get_comp (obj_s)
r_1 = Get_comp (obj_1)
r_2 = Get_comp (obj_2)
```

Elemental functions present one problem: All the actual arguments of elemental functions must be scalars. The compiler will reject the following function
interface because arguments x_lim and y_lim are arrays:

```
elemental function Is_out_of_bounds (this, &
      x_lim, y_lim) result (return_value)
   type (point_t),      intent (in) :: this
   real, dimension(2), intent (in) :: x_lim, y_lim
   logical :: return_value
   ...
end function Is_out_of_bounds
```

One way to make this an elemental function is to organize the two arrays into
a derived type and to recast the interface:

```
type, public :: limit_t
   real, dimension(2) :: x_lim, y_lim
end type limit_t
   ...
elemental function Is_out_of_bounds (this, limit_pair) &
      result (return_value)
   type (point_t), intent (in) :: this
   type (limit_t), intent (in) :: limit_pair
   logical :: return_value
end function Is_out_of_bounds
```

129. *Use the* result *clause for function return values.*

Fortran requires a symbolic name be used for function return values. By
default, the name is the same as the function itself. In complicated functions,

Table 10.1. Specific and generic names for the intrinsic square root functions

Specific Name	Generic Name	Argument Type
csqrt	sqrt	default **complex**
dsqrt	sqrt	**double precision real**
sqrt	sqrt	default **real**

the name may be both assigned to and used in many places. When replicating the function to create specific versions, each and every one of these places needs to be modified. To eliminate the need for simply changing the name of the return value, the **result** clause may be used to define a non-default name.

```
function Distance_real (a, b) result (return_val)
  real, intent(in) :: a, b

  ! Generic name for result
  real :: return_val

  ! This line need not be changed during replication.
  return_val = abs (a-b)
end function Distance_real
```

130. *Use the generic form of intrinsic functions.*

For many generic intrinsic functions, Fortran has historically provided programmers with sets of specific function names. Each function has a specific name, corresponding to both the type and kind of arguments that are passed to it and to the type and kind of result that is returned. For example, the Fortran standard specifies the set of functions in Table 10.1 to calculate the square root of a number. The generic versions of the intrinsic functions will work in the same manner as the specific procedures and should always be used.

```
complex :: hypot
real    :: comp_len
...
comp_len = sqrt (real (hypot)**2.0 + aimag (hypot)**2.0)
```

Over the years, compiler vendors have also added their own functions and extensions. Their use increases the likelihood that you will not be able to port your code from one computing platform to another. For this reason you should refrain from using them.

10.2 Preprocessor Replication

A preprocessor is a tool that reads the file that is to be compiled, performs a set of transformations on it, then outputs the result to the compiler for compilation. Preprocessing Fortran is *not* a standard stage of the compilation process; it is typically specified in the specification file used by a tool, such as the *make* utility, to automate the build process.

Although some uses of preprocessors have been made obsolete by improvements in Fortran itself, replicating code with them is still widely done. Preprocessing reduces the possibility of errors that can occur when code is replicated by manual editing. On the minus side, the code can be harder to comprehend at first glance. A more serious problem is that error messages and diagnostics will sometimes point to locations in the preprocessed code and not the original. Preprocessing also presents the challenge of anticipating all required specific procedures and creating them. With large combinations of dummy arguments of different types, kinds, and ranks, this could create an explosion of specific routines. Care must be used to design routines that minimize this problem.

Two preprocessors are commonly used: the C language and the Fortran CoCo (Conditional Compilation) preprocessors. We describe the latter, and present an example of the former.

131. *Use a preprocessor to automate generation of generic code via CoCo.*

Beginning with the Fortran 95 Standard, a specification for an optional preprocessor has been available. The preprocessor specification was primarily designed for *conditional compilation*, that is, for code with sections that need to be compiled differently for different environments. Machine-dependent code, for example, handling differences between Unix and Windows file naming conventions, can be written in a Fortran-like syntax. At compile time, the preprocessor can then be instructed to present the appropriate version of the code to the compiler. The preprocessor defined by the Standard is commonly known as CoCo (pronounced "cocoa").

An enhanced version of CoCo is publicly available (see Reference [19]). This extended version allows substitution of text via a macro facility, which makes it usable for performing generic code replication. Its use is similar to the C processor, described in the following rule, and we refer you to the reference for details.

132. *Use a preprocessor to automate generation of generic code via the C language preprocessor.*

The C language preprocessor is commonly used for conditional compilation, name substitution, and replication of code (see Reference [46]). A Fortran-specific variation is sometimes provided by the compiler vendor because some of the syntax common to both Fortran and C conflict in their meaning. For example, // is the operator for character string concatenation in Fortran, but it begins an in-line comment in C99. The variant limits the preprocessor slightly to make itself more friendly to Fortran code. Some C preprocessors accept a "traditional" option, which is also friendlier to Fortran code than in strict ANSI C mode.

The C preprocessor operates on the basis of macro substitution. It is case-sensitive. The convention is to use UPPERCASE for words that the pre-processor needs to substitute via macro substitution. First, the code to be replicated is placed in its own file. The following is an example. The file is called scan_generic.inc:

```
function SPECIFIC_NAME (array) result (res)
  SPECIFIC_TYPEKIND, intent(in) :: array(:)
  SPECIFIC_TYPEKIND :: res(size (array, dim=1))

  SPECIFIC_TYPEKIND, parameter :: zero = 0

  integer :: i
  SPECIFIC_TYPEKIND :: carry
  logical :: flip

  carry = array(1)
  res(1) = carry
  do, i = 2, size (array, dim=1)
    carry = SPECIFIC_OPERATOR(array(i), carry)
    res(i) = carry
  end do
end function SPECIFIC_NAME
```

A module is then created, which can be run through the preprocessor. It uses the #**define** directive to create a macro for setting the correct name, type and kind, and operation for each specific procedure. The generic code is inserted for each specific routine via the #**include** directive. Then the #**undef** directive is used to clear the name so that it can be redefined for the next specific routine. Generic interface declarations allow the compiler to choose the correct specific version at compile time.

<u>Listing 10.2: Module Scan_mod</u>

```
module Kinds_mod
  implicit none
  integer, parameter :: DP = selected_real_kind (15,300)
end module Kinds_mod

module Scan_mod
  use Kinds_mod
  implicit none

  interface Scan_plus
    module procedure Scan_plus_real
    module procedure Scan_plus_dp
  end interface
```

```
    interface Scan_product
      module procedure Scan_product_real
      module procedure Scan_product_dp
    end interface Scan_product
contains

    ! Plus scan
#define SPECIFIC_OPERATOR(a,b) (a + b)

#define SPECIFIC_NAME Scan_plus_real
#define SPECIFIC_TYPEKIND real
#include "scan_generic.inc"
#undef SPECIFIC_NAME
#undef SPECIFIC_TYPEKIND

#define SPECIFIC_NAME Scan_plus_dp
#define SPECIFIC_TYPEKIND real(DP)
#include "scan_generic.inc"
#undef SPECIFIC_NAME
#undef SPECIFIC_TYPEKIND

    ! Product scan
#define SPECIFIC_OPERATOR(a,b) (a * b)

#define SPECIFIC_NAME Scan_product_real
#define SPECIFIC_TYPEKIND real
#include "scan_generic.inc"
#undef SPECIFIC_NAME
#undef SPECIFIC_TYPEKIND

#define SPECIFIC_NAME Scan_product_dp
#define SPECIFIC_TYPEKIND real(DP)
#include "scan_generic.inc"
#undef SPECIFIC_NAME
#undef SPECIFIC_TYPEKIND
end module Scan_mod
```

11.

Object Orientation

Until the advent of modern Fortran, the language could be classified as a strictly procedural one, built from subroutines and functions. A procedural program could be thought of as a series of calls to these procedures in which the desired computations are performed. Object-oriented programming, on the other hand, can be thought of as the interaction of independent entities, whereby the computations are carried out by means of messages sent and received by procedures (methods) bound to the entities (see Reference [8]).

Object-oriented programming (OOP) is a paradigm for programming that emphasizes the construction of objects that group related data. The objects are grouped with associated procedures and placed into a program unit, the module beginning with Fortran 90. Fortran 90 provided a limited capability for OOP, often referred to as "object-based" programming. Fortran 2003 provides the additional features that allow a programmer to program using object-oriented techniques. Some of the key features of OOP are (a) entities are constructed as objects. All objects are "instances" of what is commonly referred to as a "class," which Fortran 90 introduced as "derived types." These types define templates for the type data and its procedures. The placing of data in derived types is called "encapsulation." (b) The procedures are referred to as "methods." Execution of a program is carried out by objects communicating with each other by invoking the methods of other objects. This process is called "sending and receiving messages." In Fortran 90, methods were created by writing module procedures. Fortran 2003 expanded this capability by introducing type-bound procedures and procedure components, methods that are bound to a particular derived type.

Two additional OOP techniques that Fortran 2003 has brought to the language, and that now allow the programmer to write code that conforms to the OOP paradigm are "inheritance" and "polymorphism." With inheritance, derived types can be organized into a hierarchy of types. This is done in Fortran by creating an "extended derived type" or "descendant" from an existing one, which is referred to as the "parent type," or "ancestor." This new type inherits the existing type's data and methods, to which it can add its own. Polymorphism is accomplished by declaring an object as a "class." Such an object can take on the characteristics of its declared type or any of the descendants of that type.

Object-oriented programming increases the possibility for creating reusable code. Fortran programmers are accustomed to placing commonly used algorithms into procedures, and then grouping the procedures in libraries, so that the code can be reused. In Chapter 10 we have seen tools by which we can write generic code that is written in a single way, yet can be expanded by the compiler or preprocessor to handle a variety of input argument ranks, data types, kinds, and so on. Now, with the full capability for object-oriented programming that Fortran 2003 puts at his disposal, the programmer's ability to create reusable code that is easily maintained and expanded is further enhanced.

The remainder of this chapter comprises five sections: The first presents some basic rules for designing derived types; the rules apply equally well to derived types written solely to the Fortran 95 standard as well as to types written for Fortran 2003. The second section contains guidelines for the creation, construction, initialization, and assignment of derived types. Here, the concentration is on aspects of types not involved with object orientation.

The last three sections make up a group: The third section introduces type-bound procedures and the fourth inheritance. In the first of these two, the use of these procedures is explained. The section again discusses creation, construction, and so on, zeroing in on features and capabilities that require type-bound procedures. In this section, **final** procedures, which must be written as type-bound procedures, are presented. In the section on inheritance, the remaining guidelines explain how type-bound procedures enable the inheritance of object-oriented methods. Polymorphism, both regular and unlimited, is explained in the final section (see Reference [12]).

11.1 Type and Class Design

The rules in this section are general ones that apply to all derived types equally well; they would be applicable to code written in conformance to the Fortran 95 standard.

133. *Define every derived type in its own module, along with its type-specific procedures.*

For ease of maintenance, each major derived type should be defined in a distinct module. In this manner, a data object of one type can easily be made a component of another type or several types (see Rule 120).

Commonly required type-specific procedures, including type-bound procedures, should also be packaged along with their type definitions. A minimal set of procedures to be considered are:

- Initialization procedure – beyond what is possible with default initialization (see Section 7.1)
- Final procedure – when a derived-type object controls resources that require special processing when the object ceases to exist (see Rule 147)
- Accessor procedures – to allow other program units access, as required, to individual private components of derived-type objects (see Rule 135)

- Defined operators – such as assignment, equality and inequality
- Print procedure – for debugging the type (see Rules 110 and 145)
- Module-specific error handler – for unified handling of errors

134. *Use a unique name for every derived type.*

Always choose a unique name for a derived type. A standard-conforming compiler should *not* compile the following code because two distinct modules, Name1_mod and Name2_mod, both define a type called same_name_t, each distinct, and both are used in the main program, thereby creating an ambiguity.

```
module  Name1_mod
  implicit  none
  private
  public  ::  same_name_t

  type  same_name_t
    integer  ::  int_a   = 0
    real     ::  real_a  = 1.0
  end type  same_name_t
  ...
contains
  ... module  procedures
end module  Name1_mod

module  Name2_mod
  implicit  none
  private
  public  ::  same_name_t

  type  same_name_t
    integer  ::  int_a   = 0
    real     ::  real_a  = 1.0
  end type  same_name_t
  ...
contains
  ... module  procedures
end module  Name2_mod

program  Same_name
  use  Name1_mod,  only  :  same_name_t
  use  Name2_mod,  only  :  same_name_t
  implicit  none

  type  (same_name_t)  ::  name_var

  name_var%int_a  =  1.0
  ...
end  program  Same_name
```

An exception applies if both type definitions include a **sequence** statement, thereby making them sequence types. The physical storage and order of these types are fixed, thereby allowing storage association of blocks of data. They serve their purpose, for example, accessing external telemetry data, where the data is arranged in a particular order, but their use is restricted (see Reference [38] and Rule 112). Here type same_name_t is a sequence type:

```
type same_name_t
  sequence
  integer :: int_a = 0
  real    :: real_a = 1.0
end type same_name_t
```

135. *Declare any data component of a derived type that is not required for computation-intensive calculations to be* private. *Provide access to its components so declared using type-bound accessor procedures.*

Good programming practice using object-oriented programming techniques recommends hiding the components of derived types. The program accomplishes all interactions with the concrete objects through their methods. The term for this is "encapsulation." In Fortran, the unit of encapsulation is the module. Almost all entities in a module are publicly available within the module regardless of whether they possess the **public** or the **private** attribute. Other modules gain access to the public entities of modules by use of the **use** statement. This grants them use access. They can further restrict and modify access using the **only** option and the renaming capability (see Rules 48 and 49). This rule applies to modules accessing other modules by use association.

By default, all derived-type components possess the **public** attribute. You can assign the **private** attribute to all the components, or, alternatively, beginning with Fortran 2003, you can assign one of these two attributes on a component-by-component basis. For public access to private components, you need to write accessor routines. In the example that immediately follows, subroutine Set_rgb is the accessor procedure, written as a type-bound procedure, for the private component array rgb.

```
module Pixel_mod
  implicit none
  private
  public :: NO_OF_PRIM_COLS

  integer, parameter :: NO_OF_PRIM_COLS = 3

  type, public :: pixel_t
    private
    integer :: rgb(NO_OF_PRIM_COLS) = 0
    ... other components
  contains
```

```
      procedure :: Set_colors => Set_rgb
      ... other procedures
   end type pixel_t

contains
   subroutine Set_rgb (this, colors)
      class (pixel_t), intent (in out) :: this
      integer (kind (this%rgb)), intent (in) :: &
         colors (NO_OF_PRIM_COLS)
      this%rgb = colors
   end subroutine Set_rgb
   ...
end module Pixel_mod
```

Here is a section of code that calls Set_colors.

```
type (pixel_t) :: pixel_grid (GRID_SIZE, GRID_SIZE)

call pixel_grid (ir, ic)%Set_colors ( &
   [(WHITE, i = 1, NO_OF_PRIM_COLS )])
```

If, however, a component is used repeatedly in a time-consuming calculation, it could be left **public** and used directly in the calculation. In the next example, a plate is divided into a grid of elements, each at a different initial temperature. The elements are of derived type grid_t , defined in the following Grid_mod module. The final temperatures are determined by repeatedly calling the code that follows the module to iterate to a solution by averaging the temperatures of neighboring elements. If there are many calls, this could be time-consuming because there would be repeated calls to a function to retrieve each element's temperature.

```
module Grid_mod
   implicit none
   private

   type, public :: grid_t
      real :: temp = 0.0
      ... other components
   end type grid_t
   ...
end module Grid_mod

use grid_mod, only : grid_t

integer, parameter :: GRID_SIZE = 10000
integer :: ir, ic
type(grid_t), dimension(GRID_SIZE, GRID_SIZE) :: &
   plate_elems, new_plate_elems
```

```
... code to initialize temperatures
loop_rows: do ic = 2, size(plate_elems, dim=2) − 1
  loop_cols: do ir = 2, size(plate_elems, dim=1) − 1

    !.. interior elements
    !.. compute temperature from surrounding elements.
    new_plate_elems(ir, ic)%temp = 0.25 * &
      (plate_elems(ir −1, ic)%temp + &
       plate_elems(ir +1, ic)%temp + &
       plate_elems(ir , ic −1)%temp + &
       plate_elems(ir , ic +1)%temp)
  end do loop_cols
end do loop_rows
... similar code for boundary elements
```

As an alternative to this direct access, quickly access its value using an accessor that returns a pointer. In the current example, type grid_t would be written like this:

```
module Grid_mod
  implicit none
  private

  type, public :: grid_t
    real, private :: temp = 0.0
    ... other components
  contains
    procedure :: Get_temp_ptr
    ! ... other type−bound procedures
  end type grid_t
  ...
contains
  function Get_temp_ptr (this) result (return_ptr)
    class (grid_t), intent (in), target :: this
    real, pointer :: return_ptr

      ! quick; no copy involved
    return_ptr => this%temp
  end function Get_temp_ptr
end module Grid_mod
```

With this modification in place, the body of the loop in the previous code would be:

```
new_plate_elems (ir, ic)%temp = 0.25 * &
      (plate_elems (ir −1, ic)%Get_temp_ptr () + &
       plate_elems (ir +1, ic)%Get_temp_ptr () + &
       plate_elems (ir , ic −1)%Get_temp_ptr () + &
       plate_elems (ir , ic +1)%Get_temp_ptr ())
```

This is one of the few cases where a function can safely return a pointer. There are no ownership issues that can lead to memory issues.

11.2 Creation, Construction, Initialization, and Assignment

Creation   Objects are created in numerous ways. Section 7.1 contains rules that pertain equally well to both intrinsic and derived-type objects. In this section we narrow our focus to derived-type objects. The most basic method of creating an object is a simple scalar or array declaration.

```
type(object_t)  ::  object1 ,  obj_vector1 (100)
type(object_t),  target    ::  obj_tar ,  obj_mat3_tar (: ,: ,: )

  ! object is created by an assigment or an allocation
type(object_t),  allocatable  ::  object2 ,  obj_mat2 (: ,: )

  ! object may be created by an allocation (but may
  ! be associated with a previously created object)
type(object_t),  pointer  ::  obj_p ,  obj_mat_row_p (: )
```

Objects may also be created in nonobvious ways. The return value of a function may be a derived type. Procedure arguments with **intent (out)** also create objects. Likewise, expressions involving objects can also create temporary objects.

Construction   Unlike other object-oriented languages, Fortran does not support a user-defined constructor, a procedure that executes *automatically* whenever a derived-type object is created in any manner. The optional default initialization of components in the derived-type specification is the only vehicle for automatically initializing an object. Fortran does have what are called "structure constructors." These are explained in the next section on initialization. Even though they are called constructors, they are not, from a strict object-oriented sense, truly constructors because they do not execute automatically whenever an object is created; instead, they must be explicitly written into the code in every spot you need them to be executed.

Initialization, Part 1: Component Initialization   The following rules apply to initializing the components of derived types in their definition:

136. *Whenever possible, initialize the components of derived types in their definition. Always initialize pointer components to* null ().

Whenever a variable of derived type comes into scope, that is, is created, its components take on the values optionally specified in its definition (see Rule 137). For example, if a subroutine has a dummy argument of derived type whose intent is **intent (out)**, and any of the type's components are initialized in its definition, the program will initialize them to the specified values when execution enters the routine. The value of any component not so specified is undefined. Providing a default initialization in this manner will prevent accidentally referencing an undefined variable. Here is an example of a derived type that is a three-dimensional vector defined by its origin, direction cosines, and length:

```fortran
type vector_t
   ! set all components of origin = 0.0
   real, dimension(3) :: origin = 0.0, &
        dir_cosines = [1.0, 0.0, 0.0]
   real :: vec_len= 0.0
end type vector_t
```

On entry to a program with the following interface, the value of the components of dummy argument ret_value will be initialized as specified in the definition:

```fortran
subroutine Init_vector (origin, components, ret_value)
   real, dimension(3), intent (in) :: origin, components
   type (vector_t),    intent (out) :: ret_value
end subroutine Init_vector
```

137. *Initialize all derived-type parameters in the definition of parameterized derived types.*

Initialize the length and kind type parameters in parameterized derived types when they are defined. Here is an example of a type containing a text label. Both the type parameters and the components are initialized (see Rule 136).

```fortran
integer, parameter :: MAX_LENGTH = 80

type, public :: label_t (text_l, text_k, loc_k)
   integer, len  :: text_l = MAX_LENGTH
   integer, kind :: text_k = kind ("a"), &
                    loc_k  = selected_int_kind (3)
   character (len=text_l, kind=text_k) :: text = ""
   integer (kind=loc_k) :: location (2) = 0
end type label_t
```

Initialization, Part 2: Structure Constructors Structure constructors may be used to initialize variables in their declarations and to create unnamed objects within expressions. However, unlike the behavior described in Part 1, structure constructors initialize derived-type components only when they, the constructors, are specified explicitly in the code.

Here are two examples of structure constructors being used to initialize data: in the first, an array called blood_cells of type cell_t, in the second, a variable of type colors_t called us_flag_colors. Each of the nameless expressions such as cell_t ("red") and colors_t ("red") on the right-hand side of the assignment statements are also structure constructors.

```
! initialization in a declaration.
type( cell_t )  ::  blood_cells(2) = &
    [cell_t ("red"), cell_t ("white")]

! initialization in an assignment.
type( colors_t ), allocatable ::  us_flag_colors (:)
...
us_flag_colors = [colors_t ("red"), &
    colors_t ("white"), colors_t ("blue")]
```

138. *Always use keywords in structure constructors.*

The use of keywords in derived-type structure constructors permits you to override the initial values given to a component in the type definition. It allows the derived type definition to vary as the program is developed and maintained, both in its contents (components) and their order without affecting existing code. Here is a short program that includes a polymorphic derived type (see Section 11.5). First, two types are defined, each in its own module. A short program that uses a structure constructor follows:

Listing 11.1: Program Comp_name

```
module Position_mod
  implicit none
  private

  type, public :: pos_t
    real :: xy_coords(2) = 0.0
  contains
    procedure :: Get_coords
  end type pos_t

contains
  function Get_coords (this) result (ret_vals)
    class (pos_t), intent (in) :: this
    real (kind (this%xy_coords)) :: ret_vals(2)

    ret_vals = this%xy_coords
  end function Get_coords
end module Position_mod

module Pixel_mod
  use Position_mod, only : pos_t
  implicit none
  private
  public :: BLACK, GRAY, WHITE
```

```fortran
      integer , parameter :: &
         MAX_LEVEL = 256, GRAY_LEVEL = MAX_LEVEL / 2
      integer , parameter :: &
         BLACK = 0, GRAY = GRAY_LEVEL, WHITE = MAX_LEVEL

      type , public , extends (pos_t) :: pixel_t
         integer :: rgb(3) = BLACK
      contains
         procedure :: Get_rgb
      end type pixel_t

   contains
      function Get_rgb (this) result (ret_vals)
         class (pixel_t), intent (in) :: this
         integer (kind=kind (this%rgb)) :: &
            ret_vals(size (this%rgb))
            ret_vals = this%rgb
      end function Get_rgb
   end module Pixel_mod

   program Comp_name
      use Position_mod , only : pos_t
      use Pixel_mod ,    only : GRAY, pixel_t
      implicit none

      integer , parameter :: I_ROWS = 10, I_COLS = 10
      type (pixel_t), allocatable :: pixels (:, :)
      type (pos_t) :: loc
      integer :: alloc_stat

      allocate (pixel_t :: pixels(I_ROWS, I_COLS), &
         stat=alloc_stat )
      if (alloc_stat == 0) then

         ! two structure constructors with keywords:
         ! use name of the parent type in pixel_t.
         ! override default rgb component.
         loc     = pos_t (xy_coords=[5.3, -4.2])
         pixels = pixel_t (rgb=GRAY, pos_t=loc )

         print *, "rgb: ", pixels(1, 1)%rgb
         print *, "xy_coords: ", pixels (1, 1)%xy_coords
      else
         print *, "allocation problem"
         stop
      end if
   end program Comp_name
```

139. *Always use keywords to specify the values of type parameters when declaring parameterized derived types and when initializing them using structure constructors.*

The Fortran 2003 standard specifies an order for type parameters for use when declaring a derived type. For a nonextended type, it is the order of the type parameters in the definition. For extended types, the order is first the type parameters of the parent type followed by those of the child type, both in the order they were specified in their respective definitions. To avoid confusion, use keywords to specify the values. Here is the definition of such a type, temp_grid_t:

```
integer, parameter :: SP = selected_real_kind (6, 37)
integer, parameter :: DP = selected_real_kind (15, 307)
integer, parameter :: DEF_COLS = 20, DEF_ROWS = 20

type temp_grid_t (prec, cols, rows)
  integer, kind :: prec = SP
  integer, len  :: cols = DEF_COLS, rows = DEF_ROWS
  real (kind=PREC) :: temperatures(rows, cols) = 1.0
end type temp_grid_t
```

When a data object of type temp_grid_t is initialized by coming into scope, its components and type parameters will take on the default values specified in the type definition. It is possible to override the default values of the length type parameters (only), either in the declaration or by using a structure constructor as in these two examples here:

```
  ! declaration
type (temp_grid_t (cols=40, rows=40)) :: temp_grid_1
...
  ! structure constructor
type (temp_grid_t) :: temp_grid_2
temp_grid_2 = temp_grid_t (cols=40, rows=40) &
    (temperatures = 100.0)
```

140. *For derived types requiring extensive initialization, consider using user-defined structure constructors.*

Fortran 2003 introduced the capability of overriding the default structure constructor for objects that need more extensive initialization. For example, an object may need to have some of its elements read in from a data file, so a procedure can be written and explicitly called after it is created. This is done by creating a generic function whose name is the same as the derived type but whose interface differs unambiguously from the interface of the default constructor.

As an example, here is a segment of code. It contains a type that needs to be initialized by a subprogram. Instead of explicitly calling a routine, a logical component indicates if a variable of the type has been initialized, and an override of the structure constructor causes the initialization to occur.

```fortran
module Mesh_mod
  implicit none
  private

  type, public :: mesh_t
    character(:), allocatable :: filename
    integer, allocatable :: pts(:,:)
    integer, allocatable :: connects(:,:)
    logical :: init = .false.
  end type mesh_t

    ! create structure constructor override by interface
    ! whose name is the type.
  interface mesh_t
    module procedure Mesh_t_const
  end interface

contains
    ! procedure called when using constructor override.
  function Mesh_t_const (mesh_file) &
      result (return_value)
    character(*), intent(in) :: mesh_file
    type (mesh_t) :: return_value

    call Mesh_init (return_value, mesh_file)
  end function Mesh_t_const

  subroutine Mesh_init (this, mesh_file)
    type(mesh_t), intent (in out) :: this
    character(*), intent (in)     :: mesh_file

    integer :: io_stat

        ! ... code to open, read, and close the file,
        ! ... setting io_stat at each stage.
    if (io_stat == 0) this%init = .true.
  end subroutine Mesh_init
    ...
end module Mesh_mod
```

The following constructor will trigger a call to the user-defined constructor:

```fortran
type (mesh_t), intent (in out) :: mesh
...
if (.not. mesh%init) &
    mesh = mesh_t (mesh_file="data_dir/mesh_def")
```

Here, the interface of the constructor override differs unambiguously from the default constructor. Therefore, the following constructor would trigger the normal structure constructor, not the user-defined one:

```
mesh = mesh_t (filename=" data_dir/mesh_def" , &
     pts=null (), connects=null (), init=.false.)
```

In cases where there might be an ambiguity, you can ensure that only a user-written override constructor, and not the default constructor, be called from outside a module by specifying the accessibility of the components to be private. If this is not possible, always specify argument names in the override that differ from the component names, and then invoke either the default constructor or the override, as necessary, by employing keywords. If the function statement interface to the override had been

```
function Mesh_t_const (mesh_file , pnts , con) &
        result (return_value)
```

the first of the following two statements invokes the default constructor, the second the override:

```
! dummy argument keyword is component name: default
! constructor
mesh_t (filename = " data_dir/mesh_def", &
    pts = null (), connects = null () )
...
! dummy argument keyword is argument name of override:
! override constructor
mesh_t (mesh_file = " data_dir/mesh_def", &
    pnts = null (), cons = null () )
```

A significant restriction of user-defined structure constructors is that they cannot be used in initialization expressions in variable declarations.

Assignment   In this section we discuss using a defined assignment for extensive derived-type initialization.

141. *For derived types requiring extensive initialization, consider using a defined assignment.*

An alternative method of accomplishing the extended initialization described in Rule 140 is to use a defined assignment. Defined assignment operations are carried out by user-written subroutines that are assigned to the generic specifier **assignment**(=). This is an overload of the assignment operator. Here is the code to accomplish this:

```
module Mesh_mod
  implicit none
  private
  public :: assignment (=)
```

```fortran
type, public :: mesh_t
  character(:), allocatable :: filename
  integer, allocatable :: pts(:,:)
  integer, allocatable :: connects(:,:)
  logical :: init = .false.
end type mesh_t

interface assignment (=)
  module procedure Mesh_t_assign
end interface

contains
  subroutine Mesh_t_assign (a, b)
    type (mesh_t), intent (out) :: a
    type (mesh_t), intent (in) :: b

    ! assign on a component-by-component basis.
    ! (a = b, itself an assignment, generates an
    ! illegal and endless recursive call.)
    if (b%init) then
      a%filename = b%filename
      a%pts      = b%pts
      a%connects = b%connects
      a%init     = b%init
    else
      call Mesh_init (a, mesh_file=b%filename)
    end if
  end subroutine Mesh_t_assign

  subroutine Mesh_init (this, mesh_file)
    type (mesh_t), intent (in out) :: this
    character(*), intent (in) :: mesh_file

    integer :: io_stat

    ! ... code to open, read, and close the file,
    ! ... setting io_stat at each stage.
    if (io_stat == 0) this%init = .true.
  end subroutine Mesh_init
  ...
end module Mesh_mod
```

Contrasting this with the code in Rule 140, with this code in place, a mesh_t object can be created by simply using the structure constructor in an assignment to trigger the initialization:

```fortran
! Assignment invokes call to Mest_t_assign
! with default constructor on r.h.s. of =.
mesh = mesh_t (filename=" data_dir/mesh_def")
```

Make further note that because allocatable array components are used, and therefore cannot have their default initialization specified in the type definitions, they will be initialized to an unallocated state in the structure constructor. This is a Fortran 2008 feature. For Fortran 2003 compilers, the intrinsic function **null** () needs to be explicitly used to achieve the same end:

```
mesh = mesh_t (filename="data_dir/mesh.def",  &
    pts=null (), connects=null () )
```

A caveat applies to this: The assumption in writing this particular assignment is that the data components of mesh_t are public; otherwise, you cannot access them from outside the module. If the data components are private, as Rule 135 recommends for most situations, a defined assignment can still be used. One way would be to write a public module function that returns a variable of the target type, mesh_t in the example, whose dummy argument corresponds to the filename component:

```
function Build_mesh_t (filename) result (return_mest_t)
  character (*), intent (in)  ::  filename
  type (mesh_t) :: return_mesh_t

  return_mesh_t%filename = filename
end function Build_mesh_t
```

The defined assignment would then work if it was written like this:

```
mesh_object=Build_mesh_t (filename="data_dir/mesh_def")
```

11.3 Type-Bound Procedures and Procedure Pointer Components

Type-bound procedures, introduced in Fortran 2003, are intricately involved in type design and object orientation. This section discusses their general capabilities. The first rule explains their syntax, accessibility, and invocation; the second explains how to use the **generic** statement to create generic names from two or more of these procedures. The third moves to a related and similar feature, procedure pointer components, also referred to simply as procedure components.

142. *Write type-bound procedures to implement inheritance and polymorphism.*

In object-oriented terminology, procedures bound to objects of a specific type are called methods; invoking the procedure is called "sending the object a message." The creation of the object is termed "instantiation." In Fortran 2003, you create methods by writing type-bound procedures.

Type-bound procedures are an indispensable tool in inheritance. Their use greatly reduces the need to rewrite code, but you need not restrict their use to types that are extended; you can use them for all derived types.

What follows in this guideline is a basic description of type-bound procedures: the syntax used to declare them, and the attributes that fix the manner in which they are both accessible to and invoked in program units other than the one in which they are defined.

Basic Syntax Type-bound procedures are specified within the derived-type definition in a separate section marked by the keyword **contains**.

```
module Pt2d_mod
  implicit none
  private

  type, public :: pt2d_t
    private
    real :: x = 0.0, y = 0.0
  contains

      ! binding-name => [procedure-name]
      ! no procedure name if it is the same as the
      !  binding name
    procedure :: Add_points
    procedure :: Get_length => Comp_dist
    ... more process binding statements.
  end type pt2d_t
    . . .
contains
  ! ... code for procedure Add_points

  function Comp_dist (pt_1, pt_2) result (ret_val)

      ! class must be used for the passed argument.
    class (pt2d_t), intent (in) :: pt_1, pt_2
    real ( kind (pt_1%x) ) :: ret_val
    real ( kind (pt_1%x) ) :: x_dist, y_dist
    ... executable code
  end function Comp_dist
    . . .
end module Pt2d_mod
```

Accessibility: public and private An important feature in the previous code is the fact that the type-bound procedures are not listed in a module-scope **public** statement. Their accessibility differs from module procedures and other entities having module scope.

Here are specific characteristics about type-bound procedure accessibility:

- Unless specifically declared to be private using the **private** keyword in the definition of a derived type, type-bound procedures are public. Moreover, even if the specific procedures are assigned the **private** attribute, the generic procedure, assignment, or user-defined operator to which they are bound can be given the **public** attribute when it is specified as being **generic.**
- To have public accessibility, type-bound procedures need not be specifically assigned the public attribute in a **public** statement even if the default accessibility of a module is **private**. The type, however, must be public.
- Type-bound procedures are accessible via use association of a module even if the binding name is not listed among the entities following the **only** option of a **use** statement. The type it is bound to, though, must be accessible. A **use** statement to obtain this access could be as follows:

```
use Pt2d_mod , only : pt2d_t
```

Invocation: pass and nopass   Here is code that invokes binding Get_length, which causes a reference to specific procedure Comp_dist.

```
type (pt2d_t) :: point_a , point_b
real :: distance

! Invoke binding name
distance = point_a%Get_length (point_b)
```

Each type-bound procedure and procedure component possesses by default the **pass** attribute. This means that the object is passed as an actual argument, and that argument, again by default, corresponds to the first dummy argument of the specific procedure interface. In the case of subroutine Comp_dist, the data reference is point_a.

Alternatives to the **pass** attribute are **pass** (*arg-name*) and **nopass**. The first provides a method of designating a dummy argument other than the first as the one to pass as the object. Here, the second argument of procedure Comp_dist is the one passed:

```
procedure , pass (point_2) :: Get_length => Comp_dist

distance = point_b%Get_length (point_a)
```

If you assign the **nopass** attribute, the object is not passed at all. This capability is useful for procedures that operate on the class as a whole, rather than on a specific object. Note, though, that the same syntax is used to invoke the procedure as that for procedures having the **pass** attribute (see Rule 144).

```
procedure , nopass :: Calc
...
call obj%Calc ()
```

143. *Create generic specifications for type-bound bindings that perform similar tasks but have distinct dummy arguments.*

Employing the **generic** keyword to create a generic binding, you can make two or more type-bound procedures generic, that is, you can invoke them using a common name. This makes the **generic** specifier, the common name, generic in the same sense as the generic interface block explained in Rule 126, and the same rules that applied there apply with generic bindings. The following type definition shows how this works:

```fortran
module Simple_mod
   type, public :: simple_t
      integer :: int_comp
      real    :: real_comp
   contains

      ! no public access to procedures
      private
      procedure :: Set_int_comp
      procedure :: Set_real_comp

      ! public access to generic binding
      generic, public :: Set => Set_int_comp
      generic, public :: Set => Set_real_comp
   end type simple_t
contains
   ...

   subroutine Set_int_comp (this, passed_int)
      class (simple_t), intent (in out) :: this
      integer, intent (in) :: passed_int

      this%int_comp = passed_int
   end subroutine Set_int_comp

   ... similar code for set_real_comp.
end module Simple_mod
```

The generic specifier is Set. Here are two calls to it – the first to set the value of the integer component, the second to set the real component:

```fortran
type (simple_t) :: simple_obj
integer :: int_val
...
call simple_obj%Set (int_val)
call simple_obj%Set (4.52)
```

144. *Use procedure pointer components to invoke different subprograms possessing identical interfaces.*

In Rule 90 we presented procedure pointers. Here, we introduce procedure pointer components, which are also such pointers. They share much in common with type-bound procedures: the attributes you can assign to them, the syntax you use to invoke them, and the rules you use to govern their behavior.

This next example is a complete program called Transaction demonstrating these types of components. Where necessary, comments in the code point out some of the characteristics of procedure components. The term following the keyword **procedure** in parentheses is designated the *interface-spec*. It can be the name of either an abstract interface or of a specific procedure having an explicit interface. Procedure components share both the **pass** and **nopass** attribute with type-bound procedures, and the characteristics of the attribute are indentical for both.

<u>Listing 11.2:</u> <u>Program Transaction</u>

```fortran
module Transaction_mod
  implicit none
  private
  public :: BUY, Execute_op, Print_report, SELL

  enum, bind(C)
    enumerator :: NO_OP = 0, BUY, SELL
    enumerator :: BRIEF = 1, DETAIL
  end enum

  type, public :: transaction_t
    integer :: trans_id, i_op
    character(len=:), allocatable :: trans_name, comment
    real :: amount, price

    ! procedure component declared with data components,
    ! not with type-bound procedures.
    procedure (Print_type), pointer, private :: &
        Print_ptr => null ()
  end type transaction_t

  abstract interface
    subroutine Print_type (this)
      import :: transaction_t
      class (transaction_t), intent (in) :: this
    end subroutine Print_type
  end interface
```

```fortran
integer, parameter :: NO_OF_OPS = 3, MAX_TRANS = 1000
integer :: id_op = 0, index_current = 0, &
    j_report_level = BRIEF
character(len=*), parameter :: &
    OP_NAMES(0: NO_OF_OPS - 1) = &
    [character(len=5) :: "NO_OP", "BUY", "SELL" ]
type (transaction_t), save :: transactions(MAX_TRANS)

contains
    function Execute_op (op_name, i_op, op_amount, &
        op_price, op_comment) result (return_id)
    character (len=*), intent (in) :: op_name
    integer, intent (in) :: i_op
    real,      intent (in) :: op_amount, op_price
    character (len=*), intent (in), optional :: &
        op_comment
    integer :: return_id
    type (transaction_t) :: transaction

    return_id = 0
    id_op     = id_op + 1

    transaction = transaction_t (trans_id=id_op, &
        i_op=i_op, trans_name=trim (op_name), &
        comment=null (), &
        amount=op_amount, price=op_price)

    if (present (op_comment)) &
        transaction%comment = trim (op_comment)
    index_current = index_current + 1
    transactions(index_current) = transaction
    return_id = id_op
    end function Execute_op

    subroutine Print_brief (this)
    class (transaction_t), intent (in) :: this

    write (*, "(A, I0, A)") "id: ", this%trans_id, &
        " name: " // trim (this%trans_name), &
        " operation: " // OP_NAMES(this%i_op)
    write (*, "(2(A, F0.3))") "shares: ", this%amount, &
        " price: ", this%price
    end subroutine Print_brief

    subroutine Print_detail (this)
    class (transaction_t), intent (in) :: this
    write (*, "(A, I0, A)") "id: ", this%trans_id, &
        " name: " // trim (this%trans_name), &
        " operation: " // OP_NAMES(this%i_op)
```

```
      write  (*,  "(2(A,  F0.3))")  "shares:  ",  this%amount,  &
        "  price:  ",  this%price
    if  (allocated  (this%comment))  &
      write  (*,  "(A)")  "comment:  "  //  trim  (this%comment)
  end  subroutine  Print_detail

  subroutine  Print_report
    integer  ::  j_op

      ! point procedure component to the appropriate
      ! procedure.
    select  case  (j_report_level)
    case  (BRIEF)
      forall  (j_op=1:  index_current)  &
          transactions(j_op)%Print_ptr  =>  Print_brief
    case  (DETAIL)
      forall  (j_op=1:  index_current)  &
          transactions(j_op)%Print_ptr  =>  Print_detail
    case  default
    end  select

    do  j_op  =  1,  index_current
      call  transactions(j_op)%Print_ptr  ()
    end  do
  end  subroutine  Print_report
end  module  Transaction_mod

program  Transaction_demo
  use  Transaction_mod,  only  :  BUY,  Execute_op,  &
      Print_report,  transaction_t,  SELL
  implicit  none

  integer  ::  id_op

  id_op  =  Execute_op  ("AJAX",  BUY,  25.2,  3.53)
  id_op  =  Execute_op  ("ACME",  SELL,  33.3,  8.54,  &
      "short  sale")
  call  Print_report
end  program  Transaction_demo
```

The following is the program output:

```
id: 1 name: AJAX
 operation: BUY
shares: 25.200 price: 3.530
id: 2 name: ACME
 operation: SELL
shares: 33.300 price: 8.540
```

A new feature of Fortran 2008 applies to procedure component initialization that Fortran 2003 limits to the **null** () intrinsic function. With Fortran 2008 you may initialize the binding by writing the derived-type definition for transaction_t like this:

```
procedure (Print_type), pointer, private :: &
    Print_ptr => Print_brief
```

145. *For debugging purposes, for every derived type, write a type-bound procedure that prints its components.*

You should write a procedure for every derived type that prints the value of its components. Fortran 2003 has introduced defined derived-type input/output (DTIO), which can be used to write output routines for printing the components of derived type (see Rule 110).

146. *Write type-bound subroutines for defined assignments.*

The accessibility characteristics of type-bound procedures, and of generic operators or assignments bound to them (see Rule 142) make them especially useful, and safer, for defined assignments. They should be used in place of the user-defined structure constructors written using module procedures (see Rule 140). These characteristics imply that a defined assignment will always be carried out if it is a type-bound procedure; there is almost no possibility of an intrinsic assignment of a variable to an expression if both are of the same derived type.

This rule returns to Rule 141. In that rule, the defined assignment was created using a module procedure. Now it's created using a type-bound procedure. The definition of type mesh_t is now:

```
module Mesh_mod
  implicit none
  private

  type, public :: mesh_t
    character(:), allocatable :: filename
    integer, dimension (:,:), allocatable :: &
        pts, connects
    logical :: init = .false.
  contains
      ! no public access to the procedure.
    private
    procedure :: Mesh_t_assign
      ! public access to the assignment
    generic, public :: assignment (=) => Mesh_t_assign
  end type mesh_t
```

With this code in place, an assignment such as this can be written:

```
type (mesh_t) :: mesh_a, mesh_b
...
mesh_a = mesh_b
```

147. *Provide a final subroutine for all derived types that have pointer components or that require special handling when they cease to exist.*

As mentioned in the section introduction, while Fortran does not support automatic constructors; it does support user-defined finalization procedures, often called destructors in other languages. These are type-bound procedures that the program will invoke whenever a derived-type object ceases to exist. Final procedures allow you to cleanly handle both objects with non-simple components such as pointers to other objects, reference counts, and objects that have reserved resources such as open data files.

A program will automatically invoke a type-bound final subroutine when an object of a derived type ceases to exist. To prevent memory leaks and dangling pointers, you should write one that processes the pointer components of all derived types. In addition, components requiring special processing, such as a file unit number representing an open file that needs to be closed, should be processed to properly release their resources.

Referring to the code in Rule 146 that presents module mesh_mod and derived type mesh_t, we add a unit number component for file objects.

```
type, public :: mesh_t
   integer :: unit_number = INVALID_UNIT
   character(:), allocatable :: filename
   integer, dimension(:,:), pointer :: pts, connects
   logical :: init = .false.
contains
     private
   ...
end type mesh_t
```

Now, when a variable of type mesh_t goes out of scope and no longer exists, the file needs to be properly closed. Furthermore, there are two pointer components to account for. If a type mesh_t object is allocatable, only filename is automatically deallocated when the object is. The following code will cause deallocation of filename in addition to mesh_1: The file, however, will not be automatically closed nor the pointers automatically deallocated.

```
type, allocatable :: mesh_1
...
deallocate (mesh_1, stat=alloc_stat)
```

And in the following subroutine Mesh_generate, none of the components of temp_mesh are deallocated when variable temp_mesh goes out of scope on subroutine exit because no deallocation process is initiated.

```fortran
subroutine Mesh_generate (this)
  type (mesh_t), intent (in out) :: this
  type (mesh_t) :: temp_mesh
!... code that allocates all components of variable
!... temp_mesh and copies it on exit to argument this if
! ... there are no errors.
end subroutine Mesh_generate
```

To ensure that the file is always closed and that the components are deallocated, you need to write a finalizer as shown here:

```fortran
type, public :: mesh_t
  integer :: unit_number = INVALID_UNIT
  character(:), allocatable :: filename
  integer, dimension(:,:), pointer :: pts, connects
  logical :: init = .false.
contains
    private
    procedure :: Mesh_t_assign
    generic, public :: assignment (=) => Mesh_t_assign
    final, public :: Finalize => Final_mesh
  end type mesh_t

contains
  . . .
    ! finalizer
  subroutine Final_mesh (this)
    type (mesh_t), intent(in out) :: this

    integer, parameter :: IO_MESSAGE_LEN = 80
    logical :: file_opened
    integer :: io_stat , dealloc_stat
    character(IO_MESSAGE_LEN) :: io_message

    if (associated (this%pts) ) &
        deallocate (this%pts, stat=dealloc_stat)
    if (associated (this%connects) ) &
        deallocate (this%connects, stat=dealloc_stat)

    inquire (unit=this%unit_number, opened=file_opened ,&
            iostat=io_stat , iomsg=io_message)
    if (file_opened) close (this%unit_number, &
        iostat=io_stat , iomsg=io_message)
  end subroutine Final_mesh
```

148. *Be aware of the situations where finalization occurs.*

Just as objects can be created in ways that may not be obvious, the finalizer can be invoked in less than obvious ways. The standard lists seven situations where finalization occurs and two additional situations where its occurrence is processor-dependent (see Reference [39]).

To avoid unexpected behavior, three of the more unusual situations where finalization occurs are important for the programmer to be aware of:

- If the target of a pointer has a finalizer, the target is finalized when the pointer is deallocated.

```
type (mesh_t), target  :: obj_mesh_t
type (mesh_t), pointer :: mesh_ptr
...
mesh_ptr => obj_mesh_t
...
deallocate (mesh_ptr, stat=alloc_stat)
```

- If an object of a derived type has a finalizer and if it is the actual argument corresponding to a dummy argument of a subprocedure that has the **intent** (**out**) attribute, the object is finalized on entry into the subprocedure.

  Here, the intent of argument this in subroutine mesh_generate in Rule 147 is changed to **intent** (**out**). The call to mesh_generate will cause a reference to the finalizer of object mesh_1, closing file mesh_1%unit_number if it is open:

```
subroutine Mesh_generate (this)
  type (mesh_t), intent (out) :: this
end subroutine Mesh_generate
...
type (mest_t) :: mesh_1
...
call mesh_generate (mesh_1)
```

- Another situation is an intrinsic assignment. In the following code snippet, variable obj_mesh_t is of type mesh_t. The dummy argument will be finalized before the assignment:

```
subroutine Mesh_generate (this)
  type (mesh_t), intent (in out) :: this
  ...
  type (mesh_t) :: obj_mesh_t
  ...
  this = obj_mesh_t
end subroutine Mesh_generate
```

It is important to note that finalization of active objects does not occur when the end of a program is encountered by either executing a **stop** statement, or the end of the main program unit is encountered. So if an object requires it, the **final** procedure should be called explicitly.

11.4 Inheritance

149. *Use type inclusion for Has-A relationships and type extension for Is-A relationships.*

When building objects from other objects, there are two basic techniques: type inclusion and type extension. The first, type inclusion, has been available in Fortran since Fortran 90 and is a feature of its "object-based" programming model. The second, type extension, is a more powerful feature that was introduced in Fortran 2003.

Type Inclusion   Type inclusion occurs when objects are nested within derived types. Type inclusion represents a "has a" relationship from the point of view of the containing object. The included objects are the components of the derived types. The two types defined in the next code, photograph_t and organism_t, demonstrate this:

```fortran
module Photograph_mod
  implicit none
  private

  type, public :: photograph_t
    private
    character(:), allocatable :: mesh_file
  contains
    procedure, private :: Photograph_t_print
    generic :: Print => Photograph_t_print
  end type photograph_t

contains
  subroutine Photograph_t_print (this)
    class (photograph_t), intent (in) :: this

    print *, "Photo in file:" // trim (this%mesh_file)
  end subroutine Photograph_t_print
end module Photograph_mod

module Organism_mod
  use Photograph_mod , only : photograph_t
  implicit none
  private
```

```
type, public :: organism_t
  private
  real :: average_life = 0.0
  real :: average_mass = 0.0
  character(:), allocatable :: latin_name
  ! has a photograph of the object
  type(photograph_t), pointer :: image => null ()
contains
  procedure :: Organism_t_print
  generic   :: Print => Organism_t_print
end type organism_t

contains
  subroutine Organism_t_print (this)
    class(organism_t), intent(in) :: this

    print *, 'organism:', trim (this%latin_name)
    print *, 'avg life:', this%average_life
    print *, 'avg mass:', this%average_mass
    if (associated (this%image)) call this%image%Print
  end subroutine Organism_t_print
    . . .
end module Organism_mod
```

Type Extension Type extension represents an "is a" relationship. In Fortran 2003 this is done using the **extends** attribute. This relationship is used when an existing object needs to be extended to be a more specialized type. The extended object still has all the properties of the original base object, including reuse of the base object's data components, procedure components, and type-bound procedures. The new object can add additional components and type-bound procedures that may not be relevant to the parent object.

Type extension is a very powerful technique because it allows reuse of all of the parent's type-bound procedures. This can dramatically reduce the amount of replicated code when defining multiple, specialized, yet related types. The parent type contains components and type-bound procedures that are common to the various specialized types. The specialized types are then free to implement new components and procedures as needed. Here is an extended derived type, based on the original derived type organism_t. It contains specialized information on animals:

```
type, extends(organism_t) :: animal_t
  integer :: no_of_eyes  = 2
  integer :: no_of_legs  = 4
  logical :: warm_blooded = .true.
end type animal_t
```

An application that uses an extended type refers to the components in the original type as if no extension had taken place. That is, if we have an array called animal_array of type animal_t, with parent organism_t, there are two syntactically correct ways we can refer to the average mass of one of its elements:

```
animal_array(j_ind)%average_mass
...
animal_array(j_ind)%organism_t%average_mass
```

150. *Provide an abstract base object type for the application.*

An application-wide base object type for an application is one that is a parent to all other types, that is, one that all other objects are extended from. In some object-oriented languages all objects automatically have a predefined base object. For example, in Java there is a base type called Object. To accomplish this in Fortran, you must define your own base type and then extend all your types from it. Such a base object type can be very simple and contain only a minimal number of highly used components and type-bound procedures. It may even be empty. For this purpose, the abstract derived type containing deferred type-bound procedures is useful. Abstract types are just that. You cannot declare a data object to be of an abstract type, although a polymorphic variable may be one (see Rule 152). You can use it solely as the parent of other types. The keyword **abstract** in the interface, combined with the keyword **deferred**, means that the interface is a template and that specific procedures whose interface exactly match the deferred ones *must* be written for specific data types that are immediate descendants of the abstract type. Here is a module for a sample base object:

module Base_object_mod

```
! Purpose: A module defining an abstract type that every
! derived type is extended from.

    implicit none
    private

    type, abstract, public :: base_object_t
    contains
        procedure (Print_type), deferred :: Print
    end type base_object_t

    abstract interface
        subroutine Print_type (this)

! Purpose: Interface for type—bound procedure to print
! type components. All immediate descendants must
! possess this procedure with the identical interface.
```

```
      implicit none
      import :: base_object_t
      class (base_object_t), intent (in) :: this
    end subroutine Print_type
  end interface
end module Base_object_mod
```

151. *Provide a concrete base object type for the application.*

This guideline continues Rule 150. The starting point is abstract derived type base_object_t . Type base_object_t is a simple type; it comprises no data or procedure pointer components and a solitary deferred type-bound procedure, **Print**. If this is adequate for an application, it is most likely sufficient as the base object, from which all other types are extended. If the abstract type is even slightly more populated by components and deferred procedures, then it can be advantageous to immediately extend this object to a nonabstract, that is, a concrete, one, and from it extend all the other types. The following code and explanation show the reasons why this is the case.

Say just two components are added to the type along with a set of accompanying deferred type-bound procedures.

```
type, abstract, public :: base_object_t
  character (:), allocatable :: name
  integer :: err_flg
contains
  procedure (Print_type),    deferred :: Print
  procedure (Clear_err_flg), deferred :: Clear_error
  procedure (Get_err_flg),   deferred :: Get_error
  procedure (Get_name),      deferred :: Get_object_name
  procedure (Set_err_flg),   deferred :: Set_error
  procedure (Set_name),      deferred :: Set_object_name
end type base_object_t
```

Here is the abstract interface for the procedure interface Get_err_flg . The others perform similar tasks. They are accessor procedures that either set or retrieve the appropriate component.

```
abstract interface
  function Get_err_flg (this) result (return_err_flg)
    import :: base_object_t
    class (base_object_t), intent (in out) :: this
    integer (kind (this%err_flg)) :: return_err_flg
  end function Get_err_flg
end interface
```

Every derived type extended directly from abstract type base_object_t must supply specific type-bound procedures corresponding to every one in the abstract type. If the application has many derived types extended directly from base_object_t, you will have to replicate the code repeatedly. To avoid this, you should first extend the abstract base object to one that is not abstract:

```
module Concrete_base_object_mod
    . . .
    type, public, extends (base_object_t) :: &
        concrete_base_object_t
    contains

        ! non_overridable: always execute this module's
        ! procedure.
        procedure, non_overridable :: &
            Clear_error => Clear_flg
        procedure, non_overridable :: &
            Get_error => Get_flag
        procedure, non_overridable :: &
            Get_object_name => Get_obj_name

        ! overridable: each child object may provide its
        ! own procedure.
        procedure :: Print => Print_flag
        procedure, non_overridable :: Set_error => Set_flag
        procedure, non_overridable :: Set_object_name &
            => Set_obj_name
    end type concrete_base_object_t
    . . .
contains
    . . .
    function Get_flag (this) result (return_err_flg)
        class (concrete_base_object_t), intent (in out) :: &
            this
        integer :: return_err_flg

        return_err_flg = this%err_flg
    end function Get_flag
    . . .
end module Concrete_base_object_mod
```

where, as an example, one of the five needed specific procedures is shown. Using concrete_base_object_t as the launching point for all further derived-type extensions, there is no need to write the code for the five nonoverridable procedures.

11.5 Polymorphism

In discussing the term "polymorphism" in object-oriented programming, Reference [8] lists four different programming capabilities and techniques that programmers refer to. One of those, *ad hoc* overloading, the ability to assign a single name to many functions, has already been discussed in the section on generic coding techniques (see Rule 126). Another, templates, is a capability not available in Fortran except in the sense of parameterized derived types. These types are also explained in the section on generic coding techniques (see Rule 125).

In this section we turn our attention to the two other capabilities of polymorphism: the ability to have a single variable assigned dynamically to be one of various types, which may be user-defined derived types or intrinsic types, and the ability to call, within the context of inheritance, different procedures (methods) based on the type of the variable used in the procedure invocation.

Several guidelines in the subsections following this one refer to the two modules, Pt2d_mod and Pt3d_mod, and a program, Type_bound_demo, whose source can be found in Appendix A.1. The main program is divided into two major sections: the first comprises two sets of tests and demonstrates inheritance; the second comprises four test sets and demonstrates polymorphism.

152. *Do not confuse the meaning of a derived data type, keyword* type, *with the meaning of a polymorphic variable, keyword* class.

Many object-oriented languages refer to inheritable objects as classes. This is the keyword used in C++, Java, Python, C#, and the object Pascal language used in Borland's Delphi™ product. Fortran uses the keyword **type**. In Fortran, an entity declared using the keyword **class** is polymorphic, one that can be a derived data type or any of its descendants. A class entity must be a dummy argument, an allocatable variable, or a pointer.

```
class (base_t), intent(in)    :: this
class (base_t), allocatable   :: class_var
class (base_t), pointer       :: class_ptr (:)
```

153. *Use sourced allocation to allocate polymorphic variables.*

In Rule 79 sourced allocation was discussed under the category of the advantages of using allocatable variables, and it was mentioned that this type of allocation could be used equally well with pointers as it could with allocatable variables. However, sourced allocation is critical for polymorphic variables because such variables cannot appear on the left side of an intrinsic assignment statement.

Given the next declaration of array temp_pts of extensible type pt2d_t, the assignment statement that follows it is not correct; the sourced allocation, as shown, must be used.

```
class (pt2d_t), allocatable  :: temp_pts (:)

! INCORRECT CODE.
temp_pts = passed_pts

! Correct sourced allocation.
allocate (temp_pts, source=passed_pts, stat=alloc_stat )
```

Fortran 2008 has removed this restriction; the following code from the previous code is correct:

```
temp_pts = passed_pts
```

Program Type_bound_demo has several examples of sourced allocation (*Cmnt-6, *Cmnt-7) (see also *Cmnt-3 in program Unlimited_demo in Appendix A.2). The final two sets of output, for example, show the sourced allocation of a polymorphic allocatable variable. The output from this set is the following:

```
Callee: Module pt2d_mod: Print_pt: x: 1.00    y: 2.00

Callee: Module pt3d_mod: Print_pt
Callee: Module pt2d_mod: Print_pt: x: 11.0   y: 12.0
Callee: Module pt3d_mod: Print_pt: z: 13.0
```

154. *Exploit inheritance and polymorphic dummy arguments to write generic code.*

The passed-object dummy argument of type-bound procedures of derived types must be declared as polymorphic using the keyword **class**, and its declared type must be the type to which it is bound. This allows polymorphic calls to the routine. That is, when a derived type is extended, users of the extended derived type can use the procedures defined in the parent type. In this manner the procedure becomes a generic one (see Chapter 10 and Rule 142).

As an example, in module Pt3d_mod, there is no type-bound procedure corresponding to Get_xy_coordinate_pair in module Pt2d_mod. In the main program there is a call to this function, whose generic binding is Get, passing a variable of type Pt3d_t (see *Cmnt-8).

```
point_pair = pt_3d%Get ()
```

The program output for this particular test, which shows that Get_xy_coord_pair in module Pt2d_mod is called, is:

```
Callee: Module pt2d_mod: Get_xy_coord_pair
Result: point_pair (pt_2d) x/y:   11.00000      12.00000
```

155. *Use the* select type *construct to dynamically dispatch polymorphic data objects to the appropriate type-bound procedure.*

When you do need to override a type-bound procedure, you will often be required to use the Fortran 2003 **select type** construct to correctly dispatch the call. The type-bound binding Get_coord in both module Pt2d_mod and Pt3d_mod demonstrates this. Their task is to return the value of the x, y, or z component as indicated by the value of component coord in the second dummy argument, **mold**.

In module Pt3d_mod, the code for Get_coord contains a **select type** construct (*Cmnt-2). This construct branches to the appropriate code based on either the type or the class of a data object (see Rule 156). Part I of the main program contains several invocations to this routine. The relevant program output is next:

```
Callee: Module pt2d_mod: Get_coord
Result: coordinate_value  2.000000

Callee: Module pt2d_mod: Get_coord
Result: coordinate_value  0.000000

Callee: Module pt3d_mod: Get_coord
Callee: Module pt2d_mod: Get_coord
Result: coordinate_value  12.00000

Callee: Module pt3d_mod: Get_coord
Result: coordinate_value  13.00000

Callee: Module pt2d_mod: Get_coord
Result: coordinate_value  12.00000
```

156. Use unlimited polymorphic variables to create data structures containing heterogeneous data types.

In addition to polymorphic variables of a declared type, it is possible to declare entities to be unlimited polymorphic using the notation **class** (*) (see *Cmnt-2 in module Base_node_mod in program Unlimited_demo in Appendix A.2). Such variables can be dynamically associated with any intrinsic or user-defined derived type.

Many applications define what are called "container procedures," those that aggregate objects into data structures such as stacks and linked lists. It is often useful to write the container procedures to operate on an application-wide base type. The ability to associate with every type makes unlimited polynomial variables ideal for creating container data structures that hold sets of heterogeneous data. Because all of the derived types within the application can be extensions of the base type, only one set of container routines needs to be written to handle all objects. Appendix A.2 contains a complete program demonstrating such a structure.

12.

Parallel Processing

In the world of scientific and engineering computing, applications must often take advantage of all the processing power the system is capable of providing. With the advent of low-cost computers with multiple processing cores, writing programs that employ parallel processing has become common.

Modern computers operate in the digital domain, yet users wish to simulate or control physical processes, which are usually continuous, or analog, in nature. The conversion between the two domains is necessarily imprecise. The closer the digital process can model the real-world one, the better the result.

A numerical model must be fine-grained enough to accurately model the process, yet it must not be too fine, or resource requirements such as CPU utilization and main memory space will be exceeded. A practical choice must often be made between precision of results and the ability to produce results in a reasonable time frame, if at all.

When faced with the requirement to speed up a computation, it is natural to consider parallel processing as a solution. At its inception, Fortran was designed in terms of a scalar processor model. That is, only a single thread of control is present, and code is executed in a serial fashion. However, as computers have evolved, many features have been added to the language that can be executed in parallel. These parallel capabilities are built in. Their use depends on the hardware available and the compiler. To the programmer, their use is part of the language, regardless of the hardware and software environment. Moreover, Fortran has often been used as a base for parallel computations using either language extensions, or library-based approaches.

Three sections compose this chapter: The first concentrates on the characteristics of the target application and those of the hardware and software environment that should be considered before converting a program to run in parallel. The second moves on to the program and discusses in its three subsections, "Data Parallelism," the built-in features of the language that can be executed in parallel, and two of the widely used technologies used with Fortran to create applications that execute in parallel: the OpenMP application programming interface (API) and the message-passing interface (MPI) library. The final section presents two new features of Fortran 2008 designed specifically for parallel processing: the **do concurrent** construct and coarrays.

12.1 Preliminary Considerations

157. *Tune programs to run correctly and as quickly and efficiently as possible as a single thread program running on a single processor before rewriting them for parallel processing.*

Two essential steps should be accomplished before turning your attention to ways to parallelize an application: The first is to thoroughly verify that the program is running correctly and producing the correct results when it is not optimized. The second is to tune it to run as fast as possible as a single-thread program running on a single processor. In doing so, you establish a benchmark, a reference point, from which to measure the improvement later achieved by converting code to run in parallel. And, because one of the preliminary steps in tuning is to pinpoint the most time-consuming code, tuning aids in determining where to focus your attention when converting. Tuning encompasses, among other tasks, algorithm design and code optimization using the compiler (see References [22], [53], and [61]). Frequently, tuning also includes choosing the most suitable publicly available libraries for computation.

A common tool used to analyze code performance is a profiler. This is a program that provides an indication of the time an application in spending in each section of code. Many compiler vendors provide some form of profiler; on Unix and Linux, the common profilers are the programs *prof* and *gprof* (see Reference [76]). Commercial compiler vendors often provide profilers that extend the capabilities of *gprof*, and they also offer additional tools for optimizing code. Here is an example shell script:

```
$ gfortran -pg my-program.f90
$ a.out
$ gprof
```

158. *Estimate the performance improvement that can be realized using parallel programming methods.*

One of the first questions to ask is "how much performance improvement can I expect from parallel processing"? (Estimating the expected improvement may lead to the conclusion that it is not worth the effort, and that the improvements in speed that can be obtained using the built-in Fortran data parallel capabilities and the compiler optimizations will suffice.) To model the expected speedup of an application, Dr. Gene Amdahl published his famous equation known as Amdahl's Law (see Reference [6]):

speedup $= 1/((1 - P) + P/Np)$

where:

P = Fraction of computations that can run in parallel

Np = Number of parallel processing units

The $(1 - P)$ term represents the scalar portion of a computation, and the P/Np term is the parallel portion.

If, for example, 50 percent (P = 0.5) of the calculations are parallelizable, the maximum possible speedup with an infinite number of processors is twice the serial speed. On a machine with, say, sixteen processors (Np = 16), the expected speedup would be:

$$= 1/((1 - 0.5) + 0.5/16)$$
$$= 1/(0.5 + 0.031)$$
$$= 1.89$$

Likewise, if 95 percent of the time spent in computations can be done in parallel, the maximum is twenty times the serial speed. The estimated speedup with sixteen processors becomes:

$$= 1/((1 - 0.95) + 0.95/16)$$
$$= 1/(0.05 + 0.059)$$
$$= 9.14$$

Clearly, as the number of processors increases, the scalar term becomes dominant. This indicates that a large percentage of the computations must be parallizable in order to effectively utilize large numbers of processors.

Amdahl's Law, as originally devised, ignores an important problem in parallel processing, communications overhead. Communications overhead comprises two major components: synchronization overhead, the overhead needed to keep the processors working in unison with one another; and data motion, or data communications, overhead, the overhead caused when one parallel task needs access to data associated with a different task.

Depending on the parallel processing model and the actual hardware in use, communications overhead can cause degradations to the expected speedups calculated from Amdahl's Law. When evaluating a computation, it is important to know how the communications scale with the size of the problem and with the number of parallel tasks. For example, with so-called "embarrassingly parallel" problems, communications might be limited to distributing a small amount of initial input data and, as a result, the communications overhead may scale along with the number of processors. In this case, communications may not be an issue.

An alternative example might be a case where data objects are distributed across processing threads, as with a weather model that divides the processes along boundaries of latitude and longitude. Boundary information between neighbors must be communicated. So, as the size of the problem increases, relatively more communication will be needed.

Finally, in some cases, parallel computations have been known to exhibit "super-linear" speedup. These are cases where a computation involving a distributed object runs faster than expected on a larger number of processors than the increase in processor count alone would explain. Typically, the reason is that as the number of processors increases, and the problem size is held constant, the individual portions of the distributed objects begin to fit better within the various levels of memory caching hierarchy (see Rule 97 and Reference [51]).

159. *Determine the hardware configuration on which the application will run.*

A common classification of parallel architectures (see Reference [51]) divides them into four categories, three of which apply to our discussion:

Single Instruction, Single Data (SISD) This is what is referred to as the classic von Neumann model of a program with a single stream of instructions processing a single stream of data.

Single Instruction, Multiple Data (SIMD) In SIMD computing, a single program is run, with parallel instructions "fanned out" to the various parallel computing elements. This architecture carries out a single instruction on multiple pieces of data. It is usually the compiler that parallelizes the code. Many of the Fortran data parallel capabilities are SIMD (see Section 12.2.1).

Multiple Instruction, Multiple Data (MIMD) In MIMD computing, there may be either multiple threads of control executing within a single program, or multiple programs executing concurrently. Most modern parallel architectures fall into this category. Each processing unit processes its own stream of instructions on its own data.

Before continuing, we introduce two terms used in parallel computing: The first is a Processing Environment (PE). This is a hardware term for a combination of a processor, its memory, communications interface, and possibly I/O devices. The second term is the thread, which is a software term used when there are multiple processors running within a single program image, but not necessarily in lockstep with each other as in SIMD code.

The final category, MIMD, can be further divided into shared memory and distributed memory architectures. There are also hybrid systems that combine the two.

Shared memory machines support multiple processors sharing a single memory system. Each processor, taken individually, has equal and high-speed access to data in the memory. This style of programming is easy to comprehend since normal Fortran constructs are used to lay out data and access it. However, with multiple processors running at the same time, the memory system must be designed to be robust enough to handle the aggregate of all processors requests, or degradation will occur. Per processor cache memory can help mitigate the performance issues, but at some point serious degradation can occur, limiting the scalability of the program.

Distributed memory machines are built in a modular fashion. The basic component is a node. Each node contains a local memory system, and one or a small number of processors. Each processor in the node is a PE. These nodes are then interconnected with a special communications fabric or network. The communications fabric has a topology, or order to it that allows parallel communications between nodes. Topologies can vary from simple, such as rings, with two connections on each node for the left and right neighbors, to grids, with four connections (up, down, left, and right), to cubes and beyond.

Hybrid systems are distributed memory machines where each node has several processing units, either multiple processors, multicore processors, or both.

When evaluating various parallel processing architectures, communications costs can be extremely important. It is always beneficial to select techniques and machines with the lowest overhead possible in order to provide maximum scalability. However, when scaling from moderate to very high processor counts, it is difficult and costly to provide a shared memory solution.

12.2 Parallel Program Patterns

Three common patterns used in Fortran to structure source code for parallel computation are loop parallelism, fork/join, and multiple instruction, multiple data (MIMD) (see Reference [51]). The first concentrates on converting the iterations of time-consuming loops that execute one after another in serial fashion into iterations that execute in parallel. With the fork/join pattern, a unit of execution spawns a set of units of execution (UE) that execute in parallel and then rejoin and continue as a single UE. When structured for MIMD, each parallel UE processes a set of instructions, each with its own set of data.

Data Parallelism   Many computer vendors introduced array syntax extensions into their Fortran compilers for use with various parallel processing schemes, in a style known as data parallel computing (see Reference 71). Array syntax often allows the replacement of a small loop with a single assignment statement. Array syntax was successful enough that it was incorporated into Fortran 90, and has been extended since then. Array syntax is generally used in a shared memory environment, and is especially useful with SIMD computers, though SIMD instructions are not required. With extensions for data placement, it can also be used in a distributed memory environment.

In the mid-1990s, the High Performance Fortran (HPF) specification was developed. HPF extended the data parallel concept by adding directives for data placement, additional parallel constructs over Fortran 90, and a useful set of intrinsic procedures. However, some aspects of HPF were more difficult to implement than anticipated, so HPF was not widely adopted. Nonetheless, some HPF concepts were incorporated into Fortran 95. And others are useful to keep in mind while writing code in a data parallel style (see Reference [48]).

Fork/Join   Many compilers have supported "directive-based" syntax to specify areas of code that could be parallelized, in particular, **do** loops. The problem for application developers was that different compilers used different directives to represent similar concepts. In response, in the mid-1990s, a consortium of compiler vendors decided to publish a common specification. This became known as OpenMP. It is a fork/join method for parallel computation.

OpenMP has been widely implemented on shared memory machines. But since it allows shared data access between threads, implementation in distributed memory environments is a challenge (see References [62], [11], and [13]).

MIMD Message passing is a style of computing where multiple programs are executing in a team to solve a problem. When they need to pass data between themselves, they use explicit calls to special message passing subroutines. It represents a form of MIMD parallel computing.

Because all communication between the programs is accomplished using explicit calls, each program has access to only its own private, low-level memory. This allows the programs to be run in either a shared memory environment, where the blocks of data may be moved between programs via simple shared memory copies, and also in a distributed memory environment where the blocks of data are moved by special communications hardware.

The most common message passing library in current use is the aptly named Message Passing Interface MPI. MPI is an extensive library with over 100 calls for passing data, performing certain low-level computations that require message passing, synchronization, and even parallel I/O (see References [58], [50], and [26]).

In the three following subsections, we expand our discussion of these patterns.

12.2.1 Data Parallel Programming

160. Use built-in Fortran data parallelism to replace simple loops that can execute in parallel.

Many processors, from some of the earliest parallel machines of the 1960s, to the latest microprocessors, offer SIMD capability, the ability to execute a single instruction on multiple array elements simultaneously. With this capability, the serial nature of Fortran execution is maintained, yet each instruction causes multiple data items to be processed. This scheme of parallel processing is often known as "data parallel" computing (see Reference [72]).

In a data parallel environment, it is often useful to think of each element of a data array being associated with its own processing element and private memory. In this model, data communication occurs when data associated with one processor is needed for a computation on a different processor. Because the array elements are placed for optimal access for the "owning" processor, it may be likely that this is at the price of suboptimal access by other processors. For example, while processing the **matmul** intrinsic, each processor may need to read data in the row and column it is associated with. If we imagine the processors as being placed in a two-dimensional grid, each processor will need to ask its neighbors to the right and left, and those above and below, for data.

The following sections describe the tools that are part of the language that will execute in parallel if the appropriate hardware and compiler is used. In each, we bring forth any issues involving communications.

Broadcasting A broadcast operation is a one-to-many operation where a single scalar value is assigned to an entire array or an array section. The scalar value is fanned out to each processor, and then each processor initializes its portion of the data array. Although broadcasting is a form of communication, broadcasts of a scalar such as this will generally be very fast. A trivial example is:

```
real, dimension (MAX_ELEMS) :: b
b = 0.0
```

Parallel Assignments Fortran offers array expressions that allow programmers to directly state parallel computations in data parallel fashion. In the following code, three arrays all having the same shape, a, b, and d, are defined. Array syntax is used to indicate that a parallel operation be used in the addition and assignment:

```
real, dimension(128, 128, 128) :: a, b, d
...
a = b + d
```

These operations are known as "elemental operations." Each array element is operated on with other associated array elements in the equation on a one-for-one basis with no interplay with its neighbors. Importantly, there is also no order implied as to which elements are processed in which order.

The use of array syntax often leads to the use of arrays of temporary data, compared to **do** loop code, which might use scalar temporary variables instead. Compilers can often merge multiple statements together and eliminate the use of a temporary array, even though the programmer was forced to include it in the code. However, the statements usually need to be grouped together so that it is easy for a compiler to analyze the usages.

An alternative may be to use the Fortran 2008 **do concurrent** loop capability. The temporary variable may be written as a scalar. The compiler then has less to analyze to produce optimal code (see Rule 168).

In addition to entire arrays, array sections could be processed using array section notation. Say, for three arrays a, b, and d, a $20 \times 20 \times 20$ array section is to be processed. The following maintains the relationships between the elements of the arrays to one another. No communication takes place:

```
a(:20,:20,:20) = b(:20,:20,:20) + d(:20,:20,:20)
```

Communication issues come up, however, when the data elements are moved from their original position:

```
a(11:30,  11:30,  11:30) = b(:20,:20,:20) &
                         + d(6:25,6:25,:20)
```

Arrays a, b, and d may all be aligned such that the first elements of each are associated with the same processor. As the relationship changes between the different variables within the array expression, at some point the data may not be optimally placed for fastest access by the processor that needs to access it.

The forall Statement and Construct The **forall** statement and construct are used to write array-based code, which is difficult to state in normal array syntax. This statement and construct specifies, on an element-by-element basis, which elements are to be processed in parallel in an assignment statement, or group of assignments that are written in scalar form.

An example of **forall** is the processing of a sparse matrix. This example assumes that each of the elements in the indices array is unique and that the expression may be evaluated in any order.

```
forall (i=1:size (indices))
   a(indices(i)) = a(indices(i)) + b(i)
end forall
```

Code similar to this is often used for building histograms. With a histogram, the indices array would likely have many repeated values, and this would make parallel processing difficult. For this case, a scalar **do** loop should be used. This is a case where the programmer must know his data usage to ascertain which way the assignment statement should be written. Here is a case where **forall** is used to unpack a character string into individual characters:

```
character(len=:), allocatable  ::  string
character(len=1), allocatable  ::  char_array(:)
. . .
allocate (char_array(len (string)), stat = alloc_stat)
forall (i=1:size (indices))  &
       char_array(i) = string(i:i)
```

Unfortunately, the **forall** construct has proved in practice to be difficult for compilers to optimize. Therefore, if profiling shows that a specific **forall** statement is a "hot spot," it may be better to use an explicit loop with either an OpenMP directive or the Fortran 2008 **do concurrent** construct. (see Sections 12.3 and 12.2.2).

Intrinsic Elemental Functions Besides the usual arithmetic and logical operators, many of the intrinsic functions are categorized as "elemental functions." These functions accept arguments of any rank and shape, and return array results of the same rank and shape, again on a one-for-one basis with no order implied. These functions include the usual math intrinsic functions such as **sin**, **sqrt**, and **mod**.

```
b = cos (sqrt (a))
```

Transformational Intrinsic Procedures The transformational intrinsic functions either process their input arrays in a nonelemental fashion, or create a result where the shape may differ from the input array. We have previously discussed reasons why column-wise access of array elements is faster than row-wise access (see Rule 97). The compiler is generally given the responsibility to arrange the data motion in an optimal fashion.

The **cshift** and **eoshift** intrinsic functions shift data through their neighbors in either a circular, or an "end off" manner. On distributed memory SIMD memory machines of the past, these intrinsic functions directly mapped into communications instructions between the nodes in order to place the array elements into more optimal locations. The following example moves a two-dimensional array section to the origin of the matrix. It uses **eoshift** so that the data motion can be clearly seen:

<u>Listing 12.1:   Program Shift_demo</u>

```fortran
program Shift_demo
  implicit none

  integer :: a(4, 4) = reshape ( source = [ &
    11, 12, 13, 14, &
    21, 22, 23, 24, &
    31, 32, 33, 34, &
    41, 42, 43, 44  &
  ], shape = shape (a), order = [2, 1])

  call Print_matrix (a, 'initial configuration')

  a = eoshift (array=a, shift=2, dim=1)
  call Print_matrix (a, 'after dimension 1 shift')

  a = eoshift (array = a, shift = 2, dim=2)
  call Print_matrix (a, 'after dimension 2 shift')

contains
  subroutine Print_matrix (matrix, text)
    integer, intent(in) :: matrix(:,:)
    character(*), intent(in) :: text

    integer :: i
    logical :: first_time = .true.

    if (.not. first_time) &
      print *
    first_time = .false.
```

```
      print *, text
      do, i = 1, size (a, dim=1)
        print *, a(i,:)
      end do
  end subroutine Print_matrix

end program Shift_demo
```

When run, this program prints:

```
initial configuration
11 12 13 14
21 22 23 24
31 32 33 34
41 42 43 44

after dimension 1 shift
31 32 33 34
41 42 43 44
0 0 0 0
0 0 0 0

after dimension 2 shift
33 34 0 0
43 44 0 0
0 0 0 0
0 0 0 0
```

The **transpose** intrinsic flips a two-dimensional matrix across its diagonal. Since a transpose must process array elements in both column-wise and row-wise patterns, it can represent an extreme case to the computer's memory and communications system. The term "bisection bandwidth" relates to how well one-half of a machine can interchange data with the other half. The bisectional bandwidth is often a key indicator of how well a machine can scale.

The **reshape** intrinsic function is used to rearrange array elements from one dimensionality to another. We saw earlier where **reshape** is used to turn a one-dimensional array into a two-dimensional array in an initialization expression. The one-dimensional array was laid out row-wise to look like a textbook representation of a matrix for ease of reading. The **reshape** intrinsic function is used to perform the task of properly creating a two-dimensional matrix from it (see Rule 93).

The **dot_product** and **matmul** intrinsic functions are transformations, because for every point in the input matrices both row-wise and column-wise access are used.

User-Defined Elemental Functions   User-defined **elemental** procedures also
fit into the data parallel model (see Rule 128). Such procedures are written as
if they accept scalar arguments and return a scalar result. The compiler can
then use the function in array expressions of any rank and shape. For example,
here is a simple elemental function that returns the volume of a cone, followed
by a call to it:

```
elemental function Compute_cone_volume (radius, height) &
    return (volume)
  real, intent(in) :: radius, height
  real :: volume

  volume = 1.0/3.0 * PI * radius**2 * height
end function Compute_cone_volume


real, dimension(NO_OF_CONES) :: volumes, radii, heights
...
volumes = Compute_cone_volume (radii, heights)
```

Conditional Operations   The **merge** intrinsic function is very useful for
implementing "branch-less" conditional code. The first two arguments are the
two expressions with values to choose from. The third argument is a logical
expression that indicates which of the two choices to use. Because **merge** is
elemental, the selection process is performed on an element-by-element basis.
The input arguments must have identical shapes, and the result will have
the same shape as the inputs. All three arguments in the **merge** intrinsic are
evaluated prior to the selection process; when carried out in this manner, the
resulting branch-less code can be very highly optimized by most compilers.

```
a = merge (b, d, b > PI)
```

The **where** statement and construct also provide a way to conditionally process array data. The conditional expression is evaluated. The remaining array
expression is evaluated for the elements that are true. In its statement form, a
single assignment is performed. In the construct form, there can be multiple
blocks as shown in the two examples here:

```
where (abs (b) > 0.0) d = a / b


where (0.0 <= b .and. b <= PI)
  a = b
else where (PI < b .and. b <= PI_TIMES_TWO)
  a = -(PI_TIMES_TWO - b)
else where
  a = d
end where
```

These conditional operations are often implemented by processing all of the calculations, whether needed or not, then assigning the desired results and throwing away the rest. For high levels of parallelism and relatively small expressions, this style of programming can be very fast.

However, when there are complicated expressions that take some time to compute, it seems wasteful to calculate results and then discard them. So an alternative is to compress the desired input data elements into shorter arrays, run the expressions using this subset of data, and then restore the data back to its original shape. The **pack** and **unpack** intrinsic functions are used for this task.

```
real      ::  raw_data (:)
logical  ::  non_zeros ( size ( raw_data ))
real , allocatable  ::  short_data (:)
integer  ::  alloc_stat
. . .
non_zeros = abs ( raw_data ) > 0.0
allocate ( real  ::  short_data ( count ( non_zeros )) , &
      stat=alloc_stat )
short_data = pack ( array=raw_data , mask=non_zeros )
. . .
raw_data = unpack ( vector=short_data , mask=non_zeros , &
      field=raw_data )
```

The elemental approach to conditionals tends to be best when the ratio of trues to falses is high and the conditional expressions are fairly simple. When the data becomes sparse, or the conditional expressions are complicated, the compression technique is usually best.

Reductions A reduction operation is a many-to-one operation. Most commonly, these are summations, which are represented by the **sum** and **count** intrinsic functions. Other associative operations, represented by the **product**, **minval, maxval, all**, and **any** intrinsic functions, also carry out reduction operations.

```
real , allocatable  ::  a (:)
real  ::  total
logical , allocatable  ::  valid_cases (:)
integer  ::  n_valid
. . .
total   = sum ( a )
n_valid = count ( valid_cases )
```

Like broadcasting, reduction is a communications operation. However, fast algorithms exist for performing reduction operations in parallel. One such is to perform Np partial reductions in parallel and then to combine the partial reductions in $\log(Np)$ steps to obtain a single result.

With floating-point summations in particular, the parallel result may slightly differ numerically from the result obtained by equivalent scalar **do** loop code. This is due to the differing rounding of the intermediate computations that is the result of the differing order of computations. Often this difference can be ignored because, due to the nature of floating-point arithmetic, it is hard to say which result is "more correct" without having some knowledge of the data being reduced, and its ordering within the array.

12.2.2 OpenMP

161. Use the OpenMP API to create sections of code that execute in parallel.

The OpenMP application programming interface (API) is a set of directives and procedures that permit the programmer to target sections of code to execute in parallel. When a parallel section of code is encountered, as defined by an OpenMP compiler directive, a team of parallel threads are created during the parallel region. As such, it is an example of the fork/join model; a single thread forks into a team of parallel threads for a portion of the execution. Each thread can execute on a different processing element. When completed, the threads rejoin to again form a single execution thread. Each thread may access both shared data, which is visible to all of the OpenMP threads, and private data, which is replicated for each thread. OpenMP's ability to target specific sections of code differs from the message passing model, which normally requires extensive planning before any code is written or rewritten.

When using free source form, the directives are prefixed using the sentinel "!$omp." When you compile code containing such directives, the compiler will normally read these as comment statements because of the leading exclamation mark. To activate the directives, a compiler flag is set or specified, and the compiler will process the directives and generate the program for execution in parallel. To indicate a parallel region of the code, the **parallel** directive is used:

```
    !  ...  serial region of code
!$omp parallel
    !  ...  parallel region of code
!$omp end parallel
    !  ...  serial region of code
```

Clauses on the parallel region indicate whether variables within the region are either shared, that is, there is a single copy of each variable that all of the threads share, or private, variables that are replicated so that each thread has its own copy. As a special case, variables used as part of a reduction operation can also be indicated.

Loops can be processed in parallel within a parallel region using the **do** "workshare" directive. The iterations of the loop are then divided among the parallel threads:

```
!$omp  parallel
    ... code runs Np times − once per thread
!$omp  do
   do,  i =1, N
          ... code runs N times.
   end  do
!$omp  end  do
    ... code runs Np times − once per thread.
!$omp  end  parallel
```

Since processing loops in parallel is such a common case, OpenMP allows combining the **parallel** directive with the work-sharing **do** clause for ease of use:

```
!$omp  parallel  do
   do,  i =1, N
      . . .
   end  do
!$omp  end  parallel  do
```

Because data is often shared between the forked threads, OpenMP is most suitable for shared memory systems. Communication costs may become important. On shared memory systems, data that is normally associated with a given processor may likely be in that processor's cache memory. When a different processor needs to access it, as indicated by the **shared** clause in the **parallel** directive, additional memory operations may be needed to present a coherent view. An acute case of this is when multiple processors are trying to update values in the same cache line. To avoid the case where multiple threads are simultaneously updating the same location in memory, **critical** sections are used. Only one thread is allowed to be in a critical section at a time.

What follows is a short example of a loop that is processed in parallel using OpenMP. It is what is termed a reduction operation. A set of computations is performed, and the result of each computation is summed to form the final answer.

Reduction variables are a special case of shared data. Use these for associative operations, primarily summations, where each thread needs to maintain a private copy of the reduction variable, and at the end of the parallel region, the individual results are combined to create a single shared result.

The example is taken from the field of illumination optics. A grid of rays is traced through a lens and the energy, or irradiance, is computed at a surface. The lens data – the number of lens elements, their shape, spacing, optical glass, and so forth – are contained in a derived type lens_t. The data for the ray – its coordinates and direction cosines – are contained in a second derived type ray_t. Neither of these are shown here.

```
type (lens_t) :: lens
type (ray_t), allocatable :: rays(:, :)
real (WORKING_PREC) :: irradiance, total_irradiance
integer :: i_row, j_col

    ! ... code to allocate rays.

!$omp parallel do default (none) &
!$omp shared (rays) &
!$omp private (i_row, j_col, irradiance) &
!$omp reduction (+: total_irradiance)

total_irradiance = 0.0_WORKING_PREC
row_loop: do j_col = 1, size (rays, dim = 2)
  col_loop: do i_row = 1, size (rays, dim = 1)
    call Trace_ray (lens, rays(i_row, j_col), &
        irradiance)
    total_irradiance = total_irradiance + irradiance
  end do col_loop
end do row_loop

!$omp end parallel do
```

where the interface to subroutine Trace_ray is:

```
pure subroutine Trace_ray (lens, ray, irradiance)
  type (lens_t), intent (in) :: lens
  type (ray_t), intent (in) :: ray
  real (WORKING_PREC), intent (out) :: irradiance
end subroutine Trace_ray
```

The **parallel do** directive indicates the beginning of a section of code that can be executed in parallel by a team of threads; the **end parallel do** directive terminates it. In the **parallel do** directive, the clause **default (none)** indicates that the user must explicitly state the visibility of variables within the parallel region. By default, all variables in the section can be shared by the threads, which is not recommended (see Rule 162). The **shared** (rays) clause indicates data that is shared between the threads; that is, there is only one copy of the data. The clause **private** (i_row, j_col, irradiance) indicates those not shared; each thread has a private copy. And the **reduction** (+: total_irradiance) clause indicates that this is a summation and that the variable total_irradiance will store the sum.

The compiler, when the appropriate OpenMP compilation flag is set, can generate code to compile this to execute in parallel on multiple processing units. Note that the subroutine Trace_ray is pure, indicating that no side effects will occur during its execution. This characteristic is essential for creating parallel programs that execute correctly.

162. *Use* default (none) *for all parallel regions.*

By default, most variables within a parallel region are set as shared. However, accessing, and especially updating, shared data can limit the scalability of code. At worst, unintended interactions between threads on a shared variable could even lead to incorrect results. To ensure that all variables have been properly divided into shared and private, use the **default (none)** clause. The compiler will then require that all variables be explicitly set with the desired scope.

163. *Minimize shared variable locking and usage for best scalability.*

Shared data access is fast, but if the different threads need to update the same locations in memory, some interlocking is necessary to maintain coherency in the data. The OpenMP **critical** and **end critical** directives are often used to serialize blocks of code. Consider a loop that builds a histogram, written using a critical section:

```
histogram = 0.0
!$omp parallel do default(none) &
!$omp shared(histogram, indices) &
!$omp private(i, temp)
  do, i=1, size (indices)
    temp = ...
!$omp critical
    histogram(indices(i)) = histogram(indices(i)) + temp
!$omp end critical
  end do
!$omp end parallel do
```

The loop may not scale well, as the threads would spend most of their time waiting to enter the critical section. It is slightly better to use the OpenMP **atomic** directive, which is essentially a miniature critical section just for the update of the histogram variable for a single line of code:

```
histogram = 0.0
!$omp parallel do default(none) &
!$omp shared(histogram, indices) &
!$omp private(i, temp)
  do, i=1, size (indices)
    temp = ...
!$omp atomic
    histogram(indices(i)) = histogram(indices(i)) + temp
  end do
!$omp end parallel do
```

However, the best way to solve this problem is to use private arrays to build private histograms, each containing a partial result. Then merge the final results, using a critical section to maintain coherency:

```
   histogram = 0.0
!$omp parallel default(none) &
!$omp& shared(histogram, indices) &
!$omp& private(histo_private, i, temp)

! Build a private histogram in each thread.

   histo_private = 0.0
!$omp do
do, i=1, size (indices)
   temp = ...
   histo_private(indices(i)) = &
      histo_private(indices(i)) + temp
end do
!$omp end do

! Merge the private histograms into the shared histogram.

!$omp critical
   histogram = histogram + histo_private
!$omp end critical
!$omp end parallel
```

It is often possible to arrange computations on shared data such that critical sections or other synchronization directives are not needed at all.

This example is of a **parallel do** loop that repeatedly calls an FFT library routine, Cfft1d, for each of the columns of the matrix. The FFT routine requires an initialization call to subroutine Cfft1di to set up a coefficient array for the size of the FFT. The coefficient array must be of size N+FFT_FACTOR_MAX, so it is allocatable. Each thread has its own copy of the coefficient array by making it private. The matrix data is shared, but because each iteration of the loop is operating on a different column, critical section locking is not required.

```
subroutine Compute_ffts (matrix, direction)
   use fft_mod, only: Cfft1d, Cfft1di

   complex, intent(in out) :: matrix(:,:)
   integer, intent(in)     :: direction

   complex, allocatable :: coeff_array(:)
   integer :: mat_size, j, alloc_stat

   mat_size = size (matrix, dim=1)

   !$omp parallel default(none) &
   !$omp& shared(matrix, direction, mat_size) &
   !$omp& private(coeff_array, j)
```

```
allocate (complex :: &
    coeff_array(mat_size + FFT_FACTOR_MAX), &
    stat=alloc_stat)
call Cfft1di (col_size=mat_size, coeff=coeff_array)
!$omp do
  do, j=1, size (matrix, dim=2)
    call Cfft1d (sign=direction, &
      col_size=mat_size, col_array=matrix(:,j), &
      coeff=coeff_array)
  end do
!$omp end do
!$omp end parallel
end subroutine Compute_ffts
```

12.2.3 MPI

164. Use MPI to create multiple instruction, multiple data programs that execute in parallel.

The message passing interface (MPI) is an example of multiple instruction multiple data (MIMD) computing. Copies of one or more programs are launched together by a special MPI executive program typically *mpiexec* or *mpirun*. All data in each MPI process is private, and control flow can be very different between the processes. The only way you can transfer data between the processes is via calls to special message passing library routines. The MPI library is implemented using a variety of data communication mechanisms, including specialized hardware and shared memory. Due to this flexibility, MPI may be commonly used to parallelize applications in both shared and distributed memory environments. The distinction is hidden from the caller, except possibly in communication costs.

The MPI library consists of over 100 entry points and provides many features and capabilities. The Fortran bindings were designed to be FORTRAN 77 compatible. Only a basic set of these, those needed to get started, will be described here. We will use a capitalization style identical to the MPI C bindings for clarity.

On distributed memory systems, the communication costs can be much higher than on shared memory systems. This is because the additional hardware and distance involved in the communications adds additional latency to the transfers. Where a non-cached shared memory access might cost, say, 200 nanoseconds, the same access on a distributed memory machine with very high-speed interconnects might take several microseconds. Clearly, communication is to be avoided if possible.

Here is a small "hello, world" program in which each MPI process prints its unique identity and the total number of MPI processes. Informally, we will refer to each MPI process as a processing environment, or PE, to indicate that it is a program that is running with its own processor and memory, possibly on a distinct node in a distributed memory system:

Listing 12.2: Program MPI_hello

```fortran
program MPI_hello
    use mpi, only: MPI_Init, MPI_Finalize
    use mpi, only: MPI_Comm_rank, MPI_Comm_size, &
        MPI_COMM_WORLD
    implicit none

    integer :: me, npes, mpi_error

    call MPI_Init (ierror=mpi_err)

    call MPI_Comm_rank (comm=MPI_COMM_WORLD, rank=me, &
        ierror=mpi_error)
    call MPI_Comm_size (comm=MPI_COMM_WORLD, size=npes, &
        ierror=mpi_error)
    print *, 'hello, world!'
        - from PE', me, ', NPES =', npes

    call MPI_Finalize (ierror=mpi_error)

end program MPI_hello
```

The mpi module specified in the **use** mpi statement is defined as part of the MPI-2 Standard. It defines named constants and function return types used within MPI. All versions of MPI are also required to have a FORTRAN 77-compatible include file called mpif.h, which defines the same values and types. MPI-2 also allows the mpi module to provide explicit interfaces for all of the MPI routines. This should always be used when possible to ensure that the compile-time checking is performed on argument lists. It also allows the use of keyword=value style actual arguments for clarity (see Rule 60). The examples shown here use such an implementation. If your version of MPI does not provide explicit interfaces, you will have to forego the use and benefits of these features in your program or write your own MPI module (see Rule 165).

The **MPI_Init** routine is called once at the beginning of the program, and **MPI_Finalize** is called once at the end the program. These bracket the use of MPI.

To identify the number of MPI processes and allow each process to identify itself, the **MPI_Comm_rank** and **MPI_Comm_size** calls are used. The **comm** arguments refer to the MPI concept of "communicators." A communicator refers to either all of the processes, as the MPI-defined communicator **MPI_COMM_WORLD** provides, or a user-defined communicator associated with a subset of the processes. These calls return the size (number of MPI processes) associated with the communicator – in this case **MPI_COMM_WORLD**, and each process's unique rank within it.

Almost all MPI library calls return an error code as the final argument. An error value of MPI_SUCCESS is returned upon normal completion. Error processing is omitted in our examples for brevity.

When run with four processes, the output of the program would likely be something like the following. Note that the **rank** ordinals are numbered from zero. Also note that the output is unordered and should be considered to be nondeterministic, and the order might change from run to run:

```
$ mpirun -np 4 hello
hello, world! - from PE          0 , NPES =          4
hello, world! - from PE          3 , NPES =          4
hello, world! - from PE          1 , NPES =          4
hello, world! - from PE          2 , NPES =          4
```

There are many ways to communicate data between the MPI processes. The most basic is to call the MPI routines **MPI_Send** and **MPI_Recv**. These implement a "two-sided" communications model whereby a sender explicitly sends a message to a specific receiver. A receiver then accepts the data.

The interface to the two calls are similar:

```
call MPI_Send (buf, count, datatype, &
     dest, tag, comm, ierror)
. . .
call MPI_Recv (buf, count, datatype, &
     source, tag, comm, status, ierror)
```

The first three arguments, **buf, count,** and **datatype,** make up a triplet of arguments that is used throughout MPI. The argument **buf** is a buffer of data, the argument **count** specifies the number of elements in the buffer, and the **datatype** argument specifies the data type of the elements. The data types are named constants, which are defined in the mpi module and the mpif.h include file.

The **dest** and **source** arguments specify the PE to which **MPI_Send** will send the message, and likewise, the PE from which **MPI_Recv** will receive it. The **tag** argument allows the sender to uniquely identify a message, so that if multiple messages have been sent, the receiver can choose which message it desires.

The **status** argument in **MPI_Recv** is a small integer array, of size **MPI_STATUS_SIZE**, which contains information on which sender and tag the message was received from. This is used with a "wildcard" receive capability that **MPI_Recv** supports.

Finally, the desired communicator, in this case **MPI_COMM_WORLD**, is specified, along with the ever-present error return argument.

The **MPI_Send** and **MPI_Recv** calls are known as "blocking" operations. The calls do not return to the caller until the data is safely copied out of, or into, the buffer area. The receive call in particular could wait for a very long time in the case where the sender is delayed in sending the data.

Another basic tool for synchronization is called a "barrier," represented by the **MPI_Barrier** call. A barrier is simply a point where each of the PEs wait until all of the processes arrive. Once they do, the barrier opens and the PEs continue running. Its interface is:

```
call MPI_Barrier (comm, ierror)
```

Here is an example that demonstrates simple communication and synchronization. Each PE sends a random number, representing some user-defined computation, to its next higher-ranked neighbor. Likewise, each PE receives the random number from its next lower-ranked neighbor. There is a wrap-around in communication where the highest ranked PE sends its random number to rank 0, and likewise, rank 0 receives it from the highest ranked PE. A loop is then used, with a barrier, to enable each PE to print its random number in order. (For brevity, the program does no error checking.)

<u>Listing 12.3</u>:   <u>Program Comm_random</u>

```
program Comm_random
    use iso_fortran_env , only: OUTPUT_UNIT
    use mpi , only: MPI_Init , MPI_Finalize , MPI_Barrier
    use mpi , only: MPI_Comm_rank, MPI_Comm_size
    use mpi , only: MPI_Send , MPI_Recv
    use mpi , only: MPI_COMM_WORLD, MPI_REAL , &
        MPI_STATUS_SIZE
    implicit none

    ! buf argument requires arrays.
    real :: random_mine(1) , random_neighbor(1)
    integer, allocatable :: seed_values(:)
    integer :: alloc_stat , me, npes, neighbor , mpi_error ,&
        i , seed_size , stat(MPI_STATUS_SIZE)

    call MPI_Init (ierror=mpi_error)
    call MPI_Comm_rank (comm=MPI_COMM_WORLD, rank=me, &
        ierror=mpi_error)
    call MPI_Comm_size (comm=MPI_COMM_WORLD, size=npes, &
        ierror=mpi_error)
```

```
      ! Seed different random numbers on each PE.
      call random_seed (size=seed_size)
      allocate (integer :: seed_values(seed_size), &
         stat=alloc_stat)
      seed_values = me
      call random_seed (put=random_values)


      ! Send my random number to my next higher neighbor.
      call random_number (random_mine)
      random_mine = random_mine * (me+1)

      neighbor = mod (me+1, npes)
      call MPI_Send (buf=random_mine, count=1, &
        datatype=MPI_REAL, dest=neighbor, tag=1,  &
        comm=MPI_COMM_WORLD, ierror=mpi_error)

      ! Receive from my lower neighbor.
      if (me /= 0) then
        neighbor = me - 1
      else
        neighbor = npes - 1
      end if
      call MPI_Recv (buf=random_neighbor, count=1, &
        datatype=MPI_REAL, source=neighbor, tag=1, &
        comm=MPI_COMM_WORLD, status=stat, ierror=mpi_error)

      ! Print results.
      call MPI_Barrier (comm=MPI_COMM_WORLD, &
         ierror=mpi_error)
      do, i=0, npes-1
        if (i == me) then
          write (OUTPUT_UNIT, *) 'PE', me,   &
            ': original no.:', random_mine,  &
            ', neighbors no.:', random_neighbor
          flush (OUTPUT_UNIT)
        end if
        call MPI_Barrier (comm=MPI_COMM_WORLD, &
           ierror=mpi_error)
      end do

      call MPI_Finalize (ierror=mpi_error)
      end program Comm_random
```

Here is sample output produced when running this on four PEs. Note that different compilers have different random number algorithms, so the values you get will differ. The important thing is that the proper values have been transferred to the neighbor PEs and printed in the proper order:

```
$ mpirun -np 4
 PE 0 : original no.: 0.717690945, neighbors no.: 2.87076378
 PE 1 : original no.: 1.43538189, neighbors no.: 0.717690945
 PE 2 : original no.: 2.15307283, neighbors no.: 1.43538189
 PE 3 : original no.: 2.87076378, neighbors no.: 2.15307283
```

MPI, like most parallel models, supports all-to-one reductions and one-to-many broadcasts. These are examples of "collective" communications:

```
call MPI_Reduce (sendbuf, recvbuf, count, datatype, &
    op, root, comm, ierror)
...
call MPI_Bcast (buffer, count, datatype, root, comm, &
    ierror)
```

Like most MPI routines that communicate data, the triplet argument form of buffer/count/datatype is required. **MPI_Reduce** has two buffers, a source buffer that is reduced, and a receive buffer that receives the final result. The **op** argument is used to specify which operation is performed. Generally, this is a summation, **MPI_SUM**, but other associative operators such as **MPI_PROD** and **MPI_MAX** are also available.

The **root** argument specifies the rank of the processor where the result of a reduction is placed. Likewise, it specifies the location of the value to be broadcast to the other processes. And, finally, the communicator and error return arguments are specified. As an example, we could append the following lines to our example to sum the random numbers from each PE:

```
    ...
    ! Reduce (sum) values to PE 0.
call MPI_Reduce (sendbuf=random_mine, &
    recvbuf=random_sum, count=1, datatype=MPI_REAL, &
    op=MPI_SUM, root=0, comm=MPI_COMM_WORLD, &
    ierror=mpi_error)

    ! Broadcast the sum back out to everyone.
call MPI_Bcast (buffer=random_sum, count=1, &
    datatype=MPI_REAL, root=0, comm=MPI_COMM_WORLD, &
    ierror=mpi_error)
print *, 'sum =', random_sum
```

165. Write an MPI communicator module to tailor its use to the application.

It is useful to write a module that insulates the application from "bare MPI" for several reasons: MPI was developed with FORTRAN 77 in mind. It does not know much about newer versions of Fortran. In particular, the argument lists tend to be long, confusing, and error-prone. Common cases are not simple; **optional** arguments cannot be specified. And passing objects is very cumbersome because MPI does not know about derived types. A complex set of library calls is required to define an aggregate object and use it for communication.

The MPI-2 module, when available, and when it contains all the interface blocks needed for the application, can help to enhance the readability and clarity of the code by the use of the keyword=value argument style. And as always, when explicit interfaces are available, the compiler can do a much better job of checking the arguments. However, interface blocks are difficult in standard Fortran for many of the MPI routines because the **buffer** arguments are allowed to be of any data type, with the actual type being specified in the separate **datatype** argument. (MPI calls these arguments "choice buffers.") One approach to writing the module might be to define generic procedure names and use a preprocessor to replicate specific module procedures for each type/kind/rank for every "choice" argument needed by the application (see Section 10.2).

For these reasons, it is usually best to write a communications module to isolate the actual calls to the MPI library, and to provide a friendlier, less error-prone communications interface to the rest of the application. Only the specific routines that are actually used by the application need be defined, though this is a highly reusable module that would be added to over time.

Let's define a derived type containing a default communicator, and define some type-bound procedures with it:

Listing 12.4: Module Comm_mod

```
module Comm_mod
  use mpi
  implicit none
  private

  type, public :: comm_t
    integer :: comm_w = MPI_COMM_WORLD
  contains
    procedure :: Barrier => Comm_barrier
    procedure, nopass :: Init => Comm_init, &
        Final_comm => Comm_final
    procedure :: Send => Comm_send, Recv => Comm_recv
  end type comm_t

  logical, private, save :: comm_initialized = .false.
contains

  subroutine Comm_barrier (this)
    class(comm_t), intent(in) :: this
```

```fortran
    integer :: mpi_error

    call MPI_Barrier (comm=this%comm_w, ierror=mpi_error)
  end subroutine Comm_barrier

  subroutine Comm_init (me, npes)
    integer, intent(out) :: me
    integer, intent(out) :: npes

    integer :: mpi_error

    if (.not. comm_initialized) then
      call MPI_Init (ierror=mpi_error)
      comm_initialized = .true.
    end if

    call MPI_Comm_rank (comm=MPI_COMM_WORLD, &
      rank=me, ierror=mpi_error)
    call MPI_Comm_size (comm=MPI_COMM_WORLD, &
      size=npes, ierror=mpi_error)
  end subroutine Comm_init

  subroutine Comm_recv (this, buff, i_source, i_tag)
    class(comm_t), intent(in) :: this
    real,       intent(out) :: buff(:)
    integer, intent(in) :: i_source
    integer, intent(in) :: i_tag

    integer :: mpi_status(MPI_STATUS_SIZE)
    integer :: mpi_error

    call MPI_Recv (buf=buff, count=size (buff), &
      datatype=MPI_REAL, source=i_source, tag=i_tag, &
      comm=this%comm_w, status=mpi_status, &
      ierror=mpi_error)
  end subroutine Comm_recv

  subroutine Comm_send (this, buff, i_dest, i_tag)
    class(comm_t), intent(in) :: this
    real,       intent(in) :: buff(:)
    integer, intent(in) :: i_dest
    integer, intent(in) :: i_tag

    integer :: mpi_error

    call MPI_Send (buf=buff, count=size (buff), &
      datatype=MPI_REAL, dest=i_dest, tag=i_tag, &
```

```
        comm=this%comm_w, ierror=mpi_error)
    end subroutine Comm_send

end module Comm_mod
```

Using this module, the communication calls in the random number example program simplify to:

```
program Comm_random
    use comm_mod, only: comm_t
    implicit none
    ...
    type(comm_t) :: my_comm
    ...
    call my_comm%init (me=me, npes=npes)
    ...
    call my_comm%send (buff=random_mine, i_dest=neighbor)
    ...
    call my_comm%recv (buff=random_neighbor, &
        i_source=neighbor)
    ...
    call my_comm%barrier ()
    ...
    call my_comm%final_comm ()
```

Details of the communicator and anything else that needs to be maintained can be encapsulated in the comm_t object. The sizes and types of the messages to be passed are also automatically determined by the compiler. For example, if the application also needs a 2-D integer version of the send and receive calls, it is easy to create a version of them in the module and make the name generic. Or, if a communicator other than **MPI_COMM_WORLD** needs to be used, it is a simple matter to store the alternative communicator.

166. *Minimize the use of communications and barriers.*

The time it takes to transfer data from one MPI process to another is highly dependent on the underlying hardware. Compared to a shared memory model like OpenMP, the speed could be slower by a factor of 10, 100, or more. Even when run on a shared memory system, there is overhead in the library call itself.

The cost of passing a message is broken into two components: the initial latency of starting up the transfer, and the rate of communications once the transfer has been initiated. For example, if the latency of starting up the communication is, say, five microseconds, and once started, the cost of moving each additional data item is, say, 100 nanoseconds, it is obvious that moving multiple data items in a block is far more efficient than initiating a new transfer for each item.

The same considerations apply to synchronization. Often, the only synchronization needed is taking advantage of the blocking characteristics of the receive calls. Barriers are handy for debugging. As we have seen with our deterministic I/O loop, barriers are useful to get correct ordering between processes. But otherwise, barriers should be used as sparingly as possible for best performance.

167. *Avoid conditional use of synchronization.*

The MPI library does not know the location in your code from which a barrier call was made. When the MPI processes start encountering barriers, they will dutifully wait until all the processes encounter a barrier. If the control flow through the program is different from process to process, it is very easy for the code to "deadlock," waiting forever for all the processes to call the barrier for the communicator, and this may never happen.

```
if (some_condition) then
  . . .
  call MPI_Barrier (comm=MPI_COMM_WORLD, &
    ierror=mpi_error)
  . . .
end if
```

Carefully placing barriers outside of conditional constructs helps ensure that all of the processes will eventually encounter the same barrier. The same guideline applies to loops, even though our deterministic I/O loop demonstrates a case where a barrier within the loop is essential to making the code work as intended.

12.3 Fortran 2008 Parallel Processing

168. *Use the* do concurrent *statement to write loops that execute in parallel.*

The **do concurrent** statement is an explicit way to indicate that a specific **do** loop may have its iterations performed in parallel. In this sense, it is a simplified version of the OpenMP **parallel do** directive that indicates the same task. It is most appropriate for shared memory systems when enhancing existing **do** loops, when array syntax would cause the creation of temporary arrays, or as a replacement for **forall** constructs.

Here is an example of a **do concurrent** construct. The code carries out the same task, the tracing of a grid of rays through a lens to compute the irradiance at a surface, that was described in Rule 161.

```
type (lens_t) :: lens
type (ray_t), allocatable :: rays(:, :)
real (WORKING_PREC), allocatable :: irradiance(:, :)
real (WORKING_PREC) :: total_irradiance
integer :: i_row, j_col

  ! code to allocate rays and irradiance to the
  ! same shape.
total_irradiance = 0.0_WORKING_PREC
col_loop: do concurrent j_col = 1, size (rays, dim = 2)
```

```
row_loop : do i_row = 1, size (rays, dim = 1)
    call Trace_ray (lens, rays(i_row, j_col), &
        irradiance(i_row, j_col))
    end do col_loop
    total_irradiance = total_irradiance + &
        sum (irradiance(:, j_col))
end do row_loop
```

where the interface to subroutine Trace_ray is:

```
pure subroutine Trace_ray (lens, ray, irradiance)
    type (lens_t), intent (in) :: lens
    type (ray_t), intent (in) :: ray
    real (WORKING_PREC), intent (out) :: irradiance
end subroutine Trace_ray
```

When you compare this with the code in Rule 161, you will see that the variable irradiance has been changed from a scalar to an allocatable array. Note also that the **do concurrent** loop is over the columns of the ray grid, and that after each column the interim sum is calculated using the Fortran intrinsic function **sum**.

169. Use coarrays to write programs that execute in parallel.

Coarrays are a new feature that Fortran 2008 introduces. A program that uses them is SPMD, a single program is replicated into multiple "images." An image can be thought of as what we have referred up to now as a process environment (PE). Coarrays, as will soon be explained, can best be thought of as a simplified and integrated alternative to MPI. The coarray model supports both shared memory and distributed memory hardware.

As with message passing programs, each coarray image performs local memory accesses in the usual manner. However, specific arrays may be designated as "coarrays." These are data arrays that may be accessed by any of the images. Data is accessed in the coarrays using normal Fortran expressions and assignment statements. However, when a particular image needs to reference data from another one, a special notation is used to indicate which remote process is being referred to.

Coarray data access is "one-sided" in that it simply accesses the remote data without requiring any action on the part of the remote image and its processor. This can significantly reduce overhead from synchronization of the images and allow a greater speedup of the code compared to the "two-sided" technique often used in message passing where one thread has to explicitly send data and the other thread has to explicitly receive it.

The standard specifies a format for coarray declarations, a set of statements, and a set of functions. In declarations, square brackets are used to indicate coarrays. The keyword **codimension** can be added. Here are some example declarations:

```
real ,  codimension [*]  ::  ambient_temperature
real ,  dimension ( GRID_SIZE ,  GRID_SIZE )  ::  temper_grid [*]
```

Note that the coarray dimension in square brackets is an asterisk [*]; this is similar to the specification for assumed-size regular arrays. The default lower cobound is 1, not 0 as in MPI.

The variable ambient_temperature is a scalar coarray. A single scalar value exists in each image. The array temper_grid is an array coarray. Each image has its own array of values. The statement that most closely corresponds to the **MPI_Barrier** procedure is **sync all**. Two of the more useful intrinsic functions return the total number of images and the unique identification number of a particular image: **num_images** () and **this_image** (). In addition to the standard itself (see Reference [43]), Reference [64] is a good starting point to learn more about this new feature.

The following program is a coarray version of the program Comm_random in Section 12.2.3. Here, it is called Coarray_random.

Listing 12.5: Program Coarray_random

```
program  Coarray_random
   use iso_fortran_env ,  only :  OUTPUT_UNIT
   implicit none

   integer ,  parameter  ::  RANDOM_ARRAY_SIZE = 1

   integer  ::  image_number ,  number_of_images
   integer  ::  neighbor ,  i ,  alloc_stat

     ! coarray entities: each image has it's own set of
     ! seed_values , which is an array. Use [:] for
     ! allocatable coarrays.
   integer ,  allocatable ,  codimension [:]  ::  seed_values (:)
   integer  ::  seed_size

     ! use asterisk for non—allocatable coarrays.
   real ,  codimension [*]  ::  random_mine ,  random_neighbor

     ! Verify the number of images running.
   number_of_images = Num_images ()
   if ( number_of_images <= 2) &
      stop "insufficient images"
   image_number = this_image ()
   if ( image_number == 1) &
      write (OUTPUT_UNIT ,  "(A, 10)" ) &
        "the number of images is " ,  number_of_images
```

```
   ! Set up the random number generator on each image.
   ! Initialize the seed to the image number.
   ! Wait until all the initial values have been set
   ! before proceeding.
  call random_seed (size=seed_size)

   ! asterisk must be specified.
  allocate (integer :: seed_values(seed_size)[*], &
     stat=alloc_stat)

   ! colon must be specified.
  seed_values(:) = image_number
  call random_seed (put=seed_values)
  call random_number (random_mine)
  random_mine = random_mine * image_number
  sync all

   ! Set the higher neighbor to this images random
   ! number: (2 <- 1; 3 <-2; ... 1 <- 4).
   ! This accomplishes both the send and receive of the
   !   MPI program.
  neighbor = mod (image_number, number_of_images) + 1
  random_neighbor[neighbor] = random_mine

   ! Print the results in image order after all the
   ! images have reached this point.
  sync all
  do, i = 1, number_of_images
    if (i == image_number) then
      write (OUTPUT_UNIT, "(A, I0, 2(A, G14.7))") &
        "image ", image_number, ': original no.: ', &
        random_mine, ", neighbors no.: ", &
        random_neighbor
      flush (OUTPUT_UNIT)
    end if
    sync all
  end do
end program Coarray_random
```

Here is the output using four images:

```
the number of images is 4
im1: orig. no.:  0.3920868E-06, neighbors no.:  0.1568347E-05
im2: orig. no.:  0.7841736E-06, neighbors no.:  0.3920868E-06
im3: orig. no.:  0.1176260E-05, neighbors no.:  0.7841736E-06
im4: orig. no.:  0.1568347E-05, neighbors no.:  0.1176260E-05
```

Pay attention to several particular details: Coarrays can be allocatable, as the array coarray seed_values is. In this case, however, the **codimension** is specified using the deferred-shape notation, a colon. When allocating such entities, an asterisk in brackets must be specified:

```
allocate (integer :: seed_values(seed_size)[*], &
    stat=alloc_stat)
```

Moreover, when referencing an entire array coarray, a colon in parentheses must be included as was done here in the program:

```
seed_values(:) = image_number
```

The simplicity of this notation is significant. The following single statement showing inter-image communication replaces the calls to **MPI_send** and **MPI_recv** in the MPI program:

```
random_neighbor[neighbor] = random_mine
```

13.

Numerical Types, Kinds, and Operations

The first section in this chapter explains the concept of "kinds" in Fortran. The second section presents several guidelines for using floating-point numbers in the context of performing numerical calculations using a representation that is by nature inexact. The third section presents some aspects of the floating-point exception handling that are now part of modern Fortran. Finally, in the fourth section we present some of the bit manipulation features.

13.1 The Concept of KIND

Modern Fortran characterizes the sizes and characteristics of integers, floating-point numbers and other data types as different kinds, and parameterizes them by kind type parameter values. For example, the Fortran processor will almost certainly provide a kind type parameter that corresponds to a four-byte real. For one Fortran processor, the kind type parameter value may be 4, corresponding to the number of bytes; but, for a second processor, it could be 1, corresponding to the lowest precision available. The processor may also provide kind type parameters that correspond to single-byte, two-byte, and eight-byte integers.

The standard requires the processor provide at least one integer type. Similarly, two real kinds must be available. The default real kind is the less precise of the two. Normally, the default real will correspond to "single precision," and the additional required kind to "double precision." Thus, a processor may support several sizes of integers, each with a different kind type parameter value, and likewise for reals. Because each integer and real has a different size, each has different numerical limits of the number of representable digits (in the case of integers) or the representable precision and range (in the case of real and complex floating-point numbers).

Only one character kind is required, but the standard makes a provision for an international character set. The default logical type parameter, the sole one required, corresponds to a logical that is the same length as a default real and default integer to accommodate storage association with **equivalence** and **common** blocks. Many vendors provide logical kinds that occupy less memory;

they may be efficient in terms of storage for applications that have large logical arrays.

170. *Based on application numerical requirements, and using Fortran instrinsic functions such as* selected_int_kind *and* selected_real_kind *, establish a set of integer named constants that correspond to the kind type parameters needed. Place them all in a single module, and use these constants in the definition of program data objects.*

Every application has its particular requirements for both the accuracy and the range of magnitude of floating-point numbers. It will also possess requirements for the range of magnitude of integer values. You should use these requirements to specify the particular real and integer kinds used to define program data objects.

Beginning with Fortran 90, the language has provided the programmer with intrinsic functions that return the kind type parameter value that corresponds to a required range for integers and a required range and precision for reals. The values returned by these functions can be used to set the value of integer named constants, and these constants, in turn, can be used in the declaration of program data objects.

You should use the Fortran intrinsic functions **selected_real_kind** and **selected_int_kind** to define named constants for use in your program as kind type parameters. Then place them in one module. The Fortran processor will use the kind with the least precision and the smallest range that satisfies the requested values.

For example, suppose the required floating-point accuracy is 15 decimal digits of accuracy and a range between 10^{-308} to 10^{308}. This is commonly double precision accuracy. Additionally, say there is a requirement for a set of integers whose range varies between 0 and 64,000, that is, a value up to 10^5. Furthermore, there is also a requirement for integers whose values can range from -10^9 to 10^9. The program will also have an array numbering fewer than 100 elements.

```
module App_kinds_mod
  implicit none

  integer , parameter :: WORKING_PREC = &
                         selected_real_kind (15, 307)
  integer , parameter :: COLOR_INT = selected_int_kind (5)
  integer , parameter :: PIXEL_INT = selected_int_kind (9)
  integer , parameter :: INT_100   = selected_int_kind (2)
end module App_kinds_mod
```

Here these constants are used to define program data objects:

```
module  Pixel_color_mod
  use  App_kinds_mod
  implicit  none

  enum,  bind  (C)
    enumerator  ::  NO_COLOR = 0,  RED,  GREEN,  BLUE
  end  enum

  integer  (kind  (BLUE)),parameter  ::  MAX_COLOR = BLUE
  integer  (PIXEL_INT),   parameter  ::  &
    MAX_PIXEL = 10000000
  integer  (INT_100),     parameter  ::  MAX_CONFIGS = 10

  type  pixel_t
    real  (WORKING_PREC)  ::  intensity = 0.0
    integer  (COLOR_INT)  ::  colors(MAX_COLOR) = NO_COLOR
  end  type  pixel_t

  type  (pixel_t),  parameter  ::  &
    INITIAL_PIXEL = pixel_t  (intensity = 0.0, &
        colors = NO_COLOR)

  type  color_config_t
    integer  (INT_100)  ::  configuration_number = 0
    type  (pixel_t)  ::  pixels(MAX_PIXEL) = INITIAL_PIXEL
  end  type  color_config_t

  type  (color_config_t)  ::  configurations(MAX_CONFIGS)
contains
    !  ...  module  procedures.
end  module  Pixel_color_mod
```

By stringently specifying the kind type parameter values, your program will produce consistent results, and it can be ported from one Fortran processor to another more easily (see Rule 193). In Fortran 2008, the intrinsic module **iso_fortran_env** provides constants that may assist in selecting intrinsic type kinds. For example, for type real, the constant **REAL_KINDS** is an integer array whose size equals the number of real kinds supported by the compiler and whose elements are equal to the kind values. The named constants, **REAL32**, **REAL64**, and **REAL128** are integers holding the kind values for reals of storage size 32, 64 and 128 bits. (See Reference [43].)

13.2 Floating-Point Operations

Floating-point operations are essential to almost all scientific applications. The rules in this section are intentionally general. Far more detailed information is available in texts and papers than can be presented here. An excellent introduction to floating-point arithmetic and its issues is Reference 25.

171. *Never write code depending upon floating-point equality.*

Because floating-point numbers cannot always exactly represent a value, you should not use them in relational expressions where the operator is the exact equality (==). At its simplest, this means you should not write code like this:

```fortran
real :: a, b

test_number: if ( a == b )then
    ...
end if test_number
```

Given that for any particular real kind there are a fixed number of floating-point values that can be represented exactly, the chance of two numbers having exactly the same value is small.

The test statement should be written

```fortran
if (abs (a−b) < epsilon) then
```

where epsilon is a very small, user-provided, number. The code for **function** Near0_dp in the next listing shows the use of intrinsic functions to approach zero when the user does not provide a value for epsilon. Using it, the test statement would be written:

```fortran
if (Near0_dp (abs (a−b))) then
```

This is a situation in your application where you need to determine if one floating-point value is essentially the same as another, acknowledging the fact that they most likely will not be exactly the same. You wish to know if a number is essentially zero. Instead of testing for an exact comparison, you can use the code in the function Near0_dp shown here:

Listing 13.1: Function Near0_dp

```fortran
module Kinds_mod
  implicit none

  integer, parameter :: &
      DP = selected_real_kind (15, 307)
  real (DP), parameter :: TINY_DP = tiny (1.0_DP), &
      TINY_FACTOR = 5.0
end module Kinds_mod

elemental function Near0_dp (test_number, epsilon) &
      result (return_value)
```

```
! Purpose: To test if a number is near 0.

use Kinds_mod
implicit none

real (DP), intent (in) :: test_number
real (DP), intent (in), optional :: epsilon
logical :: return_value
real (kind (epsilon) ) :: local_epsilon

local_epsilon = TINY_FACTOR * TINY_DP
if (present (epsilon) ) then
  if (abs (epsilon) >= TINY_DP) &
     local_epsilon = abs (epsilon)
end if

return_value = abs (test_number) < local_epsilon
end function Near0_dp
```

Another example of a situation where you trap a particular condition in your code is the use of a sentinel. Never use floating-point quantities as sentinel values. For example, when reading floating-point values from a file, you might think to signal the end of a set of data in the file by the number -999.999. You would then write a test like the following to exit the read operation. Use integer, character, or logical values for sentinel values.

```
integer, paramter :: NUMBER_PER_RECORD = 3
real, parameter :: STOP_SENTINEL = -999.999
real :: data_row (NUMBER_PER_RECORD)
...
do
  read (UNIT_NUMBER, data_frmt) data_row

! BAD, Do not use floating-point numbers as a sentinal.
  if (any (data_row == STOP_SENTINEL)) exit
  ! ... normal processing
end do
```

172. Write code that performs floating-point operations in a manner that reduces rounding errors.

Every time your program performs a floating-point calculation, and the result does not produce a floating-point exception, it is more than likely that the result will not represent the exact correct answer; it will be the nearest number representable for the particular type parameter being used. As a series of computations is performed, this error can accumulate and become significant; code should be written to maintain the error as small as possible.

Here is an example. A loop is established that will step by increments through a range of values and a function is called at each iteration.

```fortran
function Func_call (delta, initial_val, final_val) &
     result (ret_val)
  real, intent(in) :: delta, initial_val, final_val
  real :: ret_val

  real (kind (initial_val)) :: tmp_val
  real, allocatable :: dat_ary(:), reduct_dat(:)
  integer :: i_stp

  tmp_val = initial_val
  i_stp   = 1
  do
     if (tmp_val > final_val) then
        exit
     else
        call Calc_val (tmp_val, dat_ary, reduct_dat(i_stp))
     end if
     i_stp   = i_stp + 1
     tmp_val = tmp_val + delta
  end do
  ret_val = tmp_val
end function Func_call
```

where the interface to subroutine Calc_val is:

```fortran
interface
  subroutine Calc_val (comp_value, dat_ary, return_val)
     real, intent (in) :: comp_value
     real, intent (in out) :: dat_ary(:)
     real, intent (out) :: return_val
  end subroutine
end interface
```

The problem with this code is that the value of the variable tmp_val accumulate a rounding error as the iterations proceed. Here is code that avoids the problem by eliminating the summation:

```fortran
i_stp = 1
do
   tmp_val = initial_val + (i_stp -1) * delta
   if (tmp_val > final_val) then
      exit
   else
      call Calc_val (tmp_val, dat_ary, reduct_dat(i_stp))
   end if
   i_stp = i_stp + 1
end do
```

173. *Avoid performing floating-point operations involving numbers of widely different orders of magnitude.*

Performing operations using floating-point numbers that differ widely in their orders of magnitude can produce unexpected results. Here for example is the addition of two numbers of default type real, here assumed to be single precision, with eight digits of decimal precision.

```
real :: a, b, d

a = 1.687e8
b = 2.4e-6

d = a + b
```

This operation will produce a value for the variable d that is equal to that of variable a. The following addition is being done:

```
168700000.0
      +  0.0000024
-----------------
168700000.0000024
```

The result will be 168700000.0 because the precision of the numbers does not extend past eight significant figures, and the range of significant figures here extends over an order of magnitude of 10^{14}.

13.3 Floating-Point Exceptions

174. *Use the capabilities of intrinsic modules* IEEE_exceptions, IEEE_arithmetic, *and* IEEE_features *to trap floating-point exceptions.*

Background   The publication in 2001 of Reference [30] marked the importance of adding floating-point exception handling to Fortran. The features it specified, as well as some additional ones, are now part of the language standard.

IEEE Intrinsic Modules   Reference [33], commonly referred to as "IEEE arithmetic, exceptions, and procedures," is the international standard for binary arithmetic. The Fortran 2003 features support the standard, that is, IEEE arithmetic, but do not fully implement it. They do, however, place tools in the programmer's hands that enable the writing of robust numerical code. The compiler provides access to these tools through three intrinsic modules IEEE_features, IEEE_arithmetic, and IEEE_exceptions. IEEE_arithmetic contains a **use** statement for the last. The following paragraphs are brief descriptions of the modules.

IEEE_features The module **IEEE_features** contains only named constants. Each named constant corresponds to the inclusion of support for a particular feature of IEEE arithmetic. For example, the named constant **IEEE_HALTING** specifies support for IEEE halting for at least one kind of real and at least one exception flag.

IEEE_arithmetic The module **IEEE_arithmetic** contains named constants and functions. There are two groups of functions: The first are pure inquiry functions. You use them to determine which arithmetic features are supported. The function **IEEE_support_datatype** (x), for example, returns a logical result that indicates if the compiler supports IEEE arithmetic for the kind of real variable represented by the argument x. The second set of functions are all elemental ones. Some are inquiry functions; others perform operations. For example, the function **IEEE_is_finite** (x) returns a logical value indicating if x is or is not a finite number. As an example of a function in this module that performs an operation, the function **IEEE_rint** (x) returns the rounded integer value of x.

The named constants of this module also divide into two sets: The first are constants such as **IEEE_POSITIVE_INF**, the number that represents positive infinity. The second set describes rounding modes. The constant **IEEE_NEAREST**, for example, specifies that the exact value of a number be rounded to the nearest representable value.

IEEE_exceptions The module **IEEE_exceptions** is used to handle exceptions. For this reason, we explain its properties in more detail than we did the two others. Five exceptions are defined in the module, and each is designated by a flag. The exceptions are overflow, division by zero, an invalid operation, underflow, and an operation that produces a result that is an inexact number, meaning one that cannot be represented exactly, and, therefore, must be rounded. During program execution an exception flag can be signaling, indicating an exception has occurred, or quiet. The module contains five named constants that correspond to the exceptions. It also contains pure inquiry functions, and elemental and nonelemental subroutines that will permit you to handle them. The named constants are of derived type **IEEE_flag_type**. If you want to trap an overflow condition, for instance, you will use the constant **IEEE_OVERFLOW** as the first argument in calls to the elemental subroutine **IEEE_get_flag** (**IEEE_OVERFLOW**, flag_value) to determine if the flag is signaling that an overflow exception has occurred.

This module contains two pure inquiry functions, **IEEE_support_flag** (FLAG, [,x]) and **IEEE_support_halting** (FLAG). The former returns a value of .**true**. if the processor supports the detection of the exception FLAG for the data type kind represented by x (or for all real kinds if x is absent); otherwise, it returns . **false**.. The second function returns a value indicating if the program supports halting control for FLAG. If it does, you can, using functions in this module, control whether a program does or does not terminate if the exception represented by FLAG occurs; otherwise, you cannot control halting.

The two elemental subroutines in the module are **IEEE_get_flag** (FLAG, flag_value) and **IEEE_get_halting_mode** (FLAG, halting), which, respectively, permit you to retrieve the flag value and halting mode for FLAG.

Two of the nonelemental subroutines permit you to set flag values and halting modes: subroutine **IEEE_set_flag** (FLAG, flag_value) and **IEEE_set_halting_mode** (FLAG, halting).

Example   The elemental function Divide_dp demonstrates how you can incorporate exception handling in your code. It is an elemental function that a program can call to perform a "safe" divide. Using the floating-point exception handling capabilities now in Fortran, it traps three serious exceptions: overflow, division by zero, and invalid division, and returns a number that can be used in subsequent calculations.

First, a module is created containing some named constants. The constants are defined in comment statements in the routine.

Listing 13.2:   Function Divide_DP

```
module IEEE_params
  implicit none

  ! DP — double precision
  ! HUGE_DP — the largest representable double
          ! precision number.

  integer,    parameter :: &
     DP = selected_real_kind (15, 307)
  real (DP), parameter :: HUGE_DP = huge (1.0_DP)

! enumeration corresponding to the IEEE exception flags.
! the indices correspond to the index of the each flag
! in the named constant array IEEE_USUAL.

  enum, bind (C)
    enumerator :: OVERFLOW_INDEX = 1,   &
         DIVIDE_BY_ZERO_INDEX, INVALID_INDEX
  end enum

    ! synonyms for .true. and .false.
  logical, parameter :: QUIET  = .false., &
     SIGNAL = .true., ON = .true., OFF = .false.
end module IEEE_params
```

```
elemental function Divide_DP (numer, denom, nan_result)&
    result (return_value)
  use IEEE_params
  use, intrinsic :: IEEE_exceptions
  use, intrinsic :: IEEE_features, only : &
      IEEE_INVALID_FLAG, IEEE_DATATYPE, IEEE_HALTING
  implicit none

  ! numer  — the numerator
  ! denom  — the denominator
  ! nan_result — answer to be returned for an undefined
  !            ! operation such as 0.0/0.0
  real (DP), intent(in) :: numer, denom, nan_result
  real (DP) :: return_value

  logical :: flag_values(size (IEEE_USUAL))

    ! first attempt to divide normally
  return_value = numer / denom

  ! Now check the flags and set the result accordingly
  ! if an overflow, a divide—by—zero or an invalid
  ! operation are signaling.

  call IEEE_get_flag ( IEEE_USUAL, &
      flag_values(OVERFLOW_INDEX: INVALID_INDEX) )

  flag_test: if (any (flag_values)) then
    if (any ( flag_values(OVERFLOW_INDEX:            &
                          DIVIDE_BY_ZERO_INDEX) )) then
      return_value = HUGE_DP
    else if (flag_values(INVALID_INDEX)) then
      return_value = nan_result
    end if

      ! set the sign.
    return_value = return_value * sign ( 1.0e0_DP, &
        ( sign (1.0e0_DP, numer) *                 &
          sign (1.0e0_DP, denom) ) )
  end if flag_test
end function Divide_DP
```

At every location in the code where a precarious division needs to be done, this function can be used. In the following code, the function will return a value of HUGE_DP because of the division by 0.0.

```
real (kind=DP) :: a, b, d
b = 5.0
```

```
d = 0.0
a = Divide_DP (b, d, 0.0_DP)
```

A few comments about this function are in order: Two named constants in module **IEEE_exceptions** are used. The constant **IEEE_USUAL** is the array of three of the exceptions: [**IEEE_OVERFLOW, IEEE_DIVIDE, IEEE_INVALID**].

Similarly, the named constant **IEEE_ALL** is the array [**IEEE_OVERFLOW, IEEE_DIVIDE, IEEE_INVALID, IEEE_UNDERFLOW, IEEE_INEXACT**].

The correct functioning of this function depends on several conditions being met. It assumes that the halting mode has been turned off for all the exceptions; otherwise, the program would halt when one occurs. This could have been done when the program was started by making the following call for each exception flag using the named parameter OFF defined in the previous module IEEE_Params.

call IEEE_set_halting_mode (FLAG, OFF)

This call has to be made for each exception flag separately because this subroutine is not elemental. For a program that will be built using many different Fortran processors, which may possess varying degrees of support for floating-point exception handling, support of halting control should first be checked by calls to the following pure function:

IEEE_support_halting (FLAG)

There is a similar requirement to check if the exception is supported; this is done by calls to this aforementioned pure function:

IEEE_support_flag (FLAG[, x])

The procedure Divide_DP, as previously written, assumes all these necessary conditions exist. In this manner it can execute quickly; if the division doesn't raise an exception, the division is carried out and only the exception flags need to be checked before control is returned to the calling procedure. A more general but time-consuming procedure would include calls to **IEEE_support_datatype** (x) and, if it returns .**true**., calls to **IEEE_support_halting** (FLAG) for the three exceptions being checked. If any of these calls returned . **false** ., alternative code (not shown) would be executed to trap a potential exception before it occurs.

Note that the function **IEEE_set_flag** is not called on entry to the procedure to set the flags quiet. It is conceivable that one or more might have been signaling in the calling procedure when Divide_DP was referenced. The standard specifies that signaling flags will be set quiet on entry to all procedures. On return, the flags that were signaling on entry will be reset to signaling; any flags that began signaling an exception in the procedure will remain signaling on return.

13.4 Bit Manipulation

Fortran provides a set of intrinsic procedures to allow the manipulation of individual bits within data items. Generally, bit manipulation centers around the packing of multiple small fields of data into a larger data item, and the extraction of the fields when needed. This is often needed when interfacing with external data layouts and hardware devices that are not directly supported by the compiler in use. A programmer might even recognize bit-oriented shortcuts to use instead of more time-consuming operations. For example, certain integer division operations can be performed by using simple bit shifting, thereby avoiding the need for using a more expensive general division algorithm in time critical code.

However, by their nature, bit manipulation operations introduce portability and code clarity problems. Therefore, their use should be as isolated and well documented as possible. In particular, named constants should be used wherever possible to identify bit field sizes and positions.

175. *Use high-level bit manipulation.*

The fundamental tools for bit manipulation on integers are the "shifting and masking" instrinsic functions. These include **ishft** (end-off shift), **ishftc** (circular shift), **iand** (logical product), **ior** (logical sum or inclusive OR), **ieor** (logical difference or exclusive-OR), and **not** (bit inversion). By combining these operations in various ways, any bit manipulation may be performed. However, there are additional intrinsic functions that can simplify code. Depending on the hardware in use, some may even directly translate into more efficient machine instruction sequences.

It is important to note that specifying a positive value for the second argument in **ishft** and **ishftc**, the shift count, indicates a "left shift." Likewise, a negative value specifies a "right shift." With an end-off shift, vacated bit positions are filled with zero bits. With a circular shift, bits are "wrapped around."

The **ibits** intrinsic function extracts a field of bits without explicitly coding the shift and mask operation. This is equivalent to shifting the desired bit field to the right-hand side of the integer, and then extracting the field with an OR operation:

```
! instead of:
    my_new_bits = iand (i=ishft (i=my_data, shift=-12), &
    j=b'111111')

! use:
    integer, parameter :: FIELD_POS   = 12
```

```
integer , parameter :: FIELD_WIDTH = 6
. . .
my_new_bits = ibits ( i=my_data , pos=FIELD_POS , &
    len=FIELD_WIDTH )
```

The **mvbits** intrinsic subroutine allows insertion of bits into a bit field without explicitly coding multiple shift and mask operations.

```
! instead of:
integer , parameter :: MY_FIELD_MASK = b'111111'
. . .
! Eliminate unwanted bits
temp1 = iand ( i=my_new_bits , j=MY_FIELD_MASK )
! Rotate zeros to low order bits
temp2 = ishftc ( i=my_data , shift=−12)
! Eliminate unwanted bits
temp2 = iand ( i=temp2 , j=not (MY_FIELD_MASK ))
! Insert field and rotate back to correct position
my_data = ishftc ( i=ior ( i=temp2 , j=temp1 ) , shift=12)

! use:
integer , parameter :: FIELD_POS   = 12
integer , parameter :: FIELD_WIDTH = 6
. . .
call mvbits (from=my_new_bits , frompos=0, &
    length=FIELD_WIDTH , to=my_data , topos=FIELD_POS )
```

Likewise, the **ibset**, **ibclr**, and **ibtest** intrinsic functions allow setting, clearing, and testing of individual bits without explicitly coding multiple shift and mask operations.

176. *Avoid unwanted data conversion problems.*

The bit intrinsic functions in Fortran 2003 operate on normal signed integer variables. When widening from one integer kind to a different kind via simple integer assignment, the sign bit can become a problem. When widening to a larger kind, the sign bit will be "extended" to maintain the representation of the number. Likewise, when narrowing to a smaller kind, the sign will also be maintained, thereby eliminating a possibly desired bit. One solution is to use the **transfer** intrinsic. Another is to use **mvbits**.

```
! instead of:
integer ( kind=selected_int_kind (8)) :: bits32
integer ( kind=selected_int_kind (14)) :: result64
. . .
! Possibly bad due to sign extension
result64 = bits32
```

```
  ! use:
result64 = transfer (bits32, mold=result64)
  ! or use:
result64 = 0
call mvbits (from=bits32, frompos=0, &
    length=32, to=result64, topos=0)
```

Problems can also occur when attempting to compare bit fields. Since the usual comparison operators assume signed integers, bit fields that include the sign bit may be incorrectly compared. The exclusive-OR intrinsic, **ieor**, is often used to compare fields. It is especially useful when the bit pattern for −0 is confused with the bit pattern for +0. The Fortran standard requires that comparison be performed as if +0 and −0 are equivalent.

```
  ! instead of:
integer(kind=selected_int_kind (8)) :: bits_a, bits_b
bits_a = 0
bits_b = z'80000000'
...
  ! Possibly bad due to sign extension
if (bits_a /= bits_b) then...

  ! use:
logical :: is_same
...
do, i=bit_size (bits_a)-1, 0, -1
    if (btest (bits_a, i) .neqv. (btest (bits_b, i)) exit
end do
if (i < bit_size (bits_a)) then...
```

With Fortran 2008, the above loop may be replaced with the **ieor** intrinsic function, and then you can use the new **popcnt** intrinsic function to detect differences.

```
  ! in F2008, use:
if (popcnt (ieor (bits_a, bits_b)) /= 0) then
```

Worse problems occur when converting between integer and real data types. During conversion, the bits are rearranged and sometimes eliminated. Again, the **transfer** intrinsic *must* be used to properly copy the bits without reinterpretation.

```
  ! instead of:
real(selected_real_kind (6)) :: real_value
integer(selected_int_kind (8)) :: bits
...
  ! Bad due to data conversion
bits = real_value
```

```
! use :
bits = transfer (real_value , mold=bits)
```

As a further aid to avoid these problems, Fortran 2008 has many additional versions of the intrinsic functions. They still only accept integers, so **transfer** is still needed to perform bitwise moves between the various data types.

14.

C Interoperability

177. *Use Fortran's C interoperability capabilities to interact with C programs.*

Due to the enormous popularity of the C programming language (References [46], [38], and [28]), many Fortran programmers need to be able call routines written in C, or written to conform to C calling conventions. Likewise, it is often useful for C programmers to call routines written in Fortran. Beginning with Fortran 2003, there is a new and standard mechanism to allow easier and more portable interfacing between Fortran and C.

Here are some of the topics that must be considered when code written in Fortran accesses that written in C and vice versa:

- The mapping of built-in data types between Fortran and C.
- The mapping of pointers.
- The mapping between Fortran derived types and C structs.
- The mapping of global variables.
- The internal calling sequence mechanisms for passing actual arguments and function return values during procedure calls.
- The mapping of external names between Fortran and C and invocation of functions and procedures.

The next sections present details of these various points. The first deals with the mapping of the basic data types. Using these types, the second section presents the calling mechanism between the two, including mapping of external names; we present a short example. The sections that follow continue presenting the mapping of other types of entities, pointers, global data, and so on, also with short examples.

Two entities are key to C interoperability: the intrinsic module **iso_c_binding** , and the **bind** attribute. The first contains named constants, derived types, and module procedures that must be used; the **bind** attribute allows variables to inter-operate with C.

Mapping Intrinsic and Basic Data Types Each of the named constants defined in module **iso_c_binding** specifies a **kind** value that corresponds to a particular basic type in C. Here are two examples:

```
use iso_c_binding , only : C_FLOAT, C_INT
. . .
integer (kind=C_INT) :: fort_int_value
```

```
real (kind=C_FLOAT)  :: fort_float_value
```

Calling Sequence A calling sequence defines the internal mechanisms used to pass actual arguments from a calling procedure to a called procedure, and to return values from the latter to the former. The internal details such as the machine registers to use, and the operation of any stack-based or other memory allocation, must be compatible. Fortran 2003 addresses these issues by requiring a "companion" C compiler to be used with the Fortran compiler. Once this requirement has been met, by the compiler developers themselves, programmers typically do not need to concern themselves with these low-level issues.

Mapping External Names – Invoking C from Fortran Consider a program that runs on a POSIX-compliant system, such as Linux. At some point, the program desires to call the getpid system call, which returns the program's process ID number. The C prototype is the following:

```
#include <unistd.h>

pid_t getpid(void);
```

The type pid_t is aliased to the C basic type **int** using a **typedef** keyword:

```
typedef int pid_t;
```

To map external names, the **bind(C)** statement can be used with a procedure definition in an interface block. The statement specifies that the C language will be used, and it optionally provides a C-compatible name. Here is a Fortran program, containing the interface block for the system call, that will print the process ID:

Listing 14.1: Program Pid_printer

```
program Pid_printer
  implicit none

  interface
    function getpid () bind (C, name='getpid ')

        ! minic C typedef: rename C_INT pid_t
      use iso_c_binding , only: pid_t => C_INT
      implicit none
      integer(kind=pid_t) :: getpid
    end function getpid
  end interface
```

```
   print *, 'pid is:', getpid ()
end program Pid_printer
```

Mapping External Names – Invoking Fortran from C In a similar manner,
Fortran code is made interoperable with C. Here is a subroutine, Fortran_FFT,
that is called by C, the prototype that needs to be provided to the C program,
and the C program itself:

<u>Listing 14.2:   Subroutine Fortran_FFT</u>

```
subroutine Fortran_FFT (data_array, array_size, &
    direction) bind (C, name='Fortran_FFT ')
  use iso_c_binding, only: C_DOUBLE_COMPLEX, C_INT, &
    C_CHAR
  implicit none

    ! assumed size array (0:*) whose lower bound is 0
    ! must be used with C.
  complex (kind=C_DOUBLE_COMPLEX), intent(in out), :: &
      data_array(0:*)
  integer (kind=C_INT),      intent (in) :: array_size
  character (kind=C_CHAR), intent (in) :: direction
  ! ... compute FFT
  print *, "first element: ", data_array(1)
end subroutine Fortran_FFT

#if !defined (FORTRAN_FFT_H)
#define FORTRAN_FFT_H

void Fortran_FFT (double _Complex *data_array,
  int *array_size, char *direction);

#endif


#include "Fortran_FFT.h"
#include <complex.h>

#define N 1024

int main () {
  double _Complex my_data [N];
  int array_size = N;
  char forward = 'f';
```

```
for (int i=0; i<N; i++)
   my_data[i] = (float) i + l * (float) i/100.0f;

Fortran_FFT (my_data, &array_size, &forward);
}
```

The output for this program is:

```
first element:   (0.000000000000000,0.000000000000000)
```

Mapping Pointers Fortran pointers, which are data types, are mapped to C pointers, which are addresses, by first declaring the C pointer in the Fortran code to be of derived type **C_PTR**, which is defined in **iso_c_binding**. The pointers are then converted by calls to pointer conversion procedures, also defined in **iso_c_binding**. The C and Fortran code that follows shows an example:

```
#include <stdlib.h>
int *c_allocate(int n)
{
   int *ptr, i;
   ptr = (int *)malloc(n*sizeof(int));
   for (i=0; i<n; i++)
     ptr[i] = i;
   printf("c_allocate: n = %d\n", n);
   return ptr;
}
```

Listing 14.3: Program c_f_pointer_test

```
program c_f_pointer_test
   use, intrinsic :: iso_c_binding, &
       only : c_f_pointer, C_INT, C_PTR
   implicit none

   interface
     function c_allocate(n) bind(C, name="c_allocate")
       import :: C_PTR, C_INT
       implicit none
       type(C_PTR) :: c_allocate
       integer(C_INT), value :: n
     end function c_allocate
   end interface

   integer, parameter :: ROWS=16, COLS=24
   integer(C_INT), pointer, contiguous :: fort_ptr(:,:)
```

```
type(C_PTR)      :: cptr
integer(C_INT) :: grid_size

grid_size = ROWS * COLS
cptr = c_allocate (grid_size)

! establish pointer association.
call c_f_pointer (cptr, fort_ptr, [ROWS, COLS])
print *, " size =", size (fort_ptr, dim=1), &
    size (fort_ptr, dim=2)
print *, " second column, first row: ", fort_ptr(1, 2)
end program c_f_pointer_test
```

The output is the following:

```
c_allocate: n = 384
size = 16 24
second column, first row:   16
```

Keep in mind that with arrays of rank greater than 1, the leftmost subscript varies first (columnwise storage for rank 2) in Fortran, whereas the rightmost subscript varies first (rowwise storage for rank 2) in C (see Rule 97).

Mapping Derived Types and Structs Fortran derived types that need to be compatible with C **struct**s in the companion C compiler are defined by specifying the **bind(C)** attribute when defining the derived type. Here is an example of a C **struct** and the derived type:

```
typedef struct {
  char   plant_name[70];
  _Bool deciduous;
  char   genus[32];
} plant_t;

use iso_c_binding , only: C_CHAR, C_BOOL
...
type, bind(C) :: plant_t
  character (kind=C_CHAR) :: plant_name(70)
  logical (kind=C_BOOL)   :: deciduous
  character (kind=C_CHAR) :: genus(32)
end type plant_t
```

Mapping Global Data The **bind(C)** attribute allows the interoperability of module variables in Fortran and variables in C. Changing the value of the variable in one location changes the other. Here is an example:

```
! specify the name for all mixed-case variable names.
integer(C_INT), bind(C, name="GridSize") :: GridSize
```

```
int GridSize;
```

178. *Pass Fortran character arguments to C as length-1, character arrays with a final element of C_CHAR_NULL.*

C does not support strings of characters. Instead, it only supports arrays of single characters, the last element of which is the constant **NULL**. You can map a Fortran character data type to a C **char** data type by declaring it kind **C_CHAR**, and by placing the **C_NULL_CHAR** at the end of the string. The named constants **C_CHAR** and **C_NULL_CHAR** are available in the **iso_c_binding** module. Here is a short program showing this:

Listing 14.4: Program Char_test

```
program Char_test
  use iso_c_binding , only : C_CHAR, C_NULL_CHAR
  implicit none

  interface
    subroutine c_routine (string) &
        bind (C, name='c_routine ')
      import C_CHAR
      implicit none
      character(kind=C_CHAR), intent(in) :: string(*)
    end subroutine c_routine
  end interface

  integer :: fstring_len , alloc_stat , i_char
  character(len=:), allocatable :: fstring
  character(kind=C_CHAR, len=:), allocatable :: cstring(:)

  ! Convert a character string into an array of
  ! characters , terminated with a null sentinel
  ! character .

  fstring     = "hello C world"
  fstring_len = len_trim (fstring)
  allocate (character(kind=C_CHAR, len=1) :: &
      cstring(fstring_len + 1), stat=alloc_stat)
  forall (i_char = 1: fstring_len) &
      cstring(i_char) = fstring(i_char: i_char)
  end forall
  cstring(fstring_len + 1) = C_NULL_CHAR
```

```
  call c_routine (cstring)
end program Char_test
```

```c
#include <stdio.h>
#include <string.h>

void c_routine (char *string) {
  printf ("c_routine: length = %i\n",
          (int) strlen (string));
  printf ("c_routine: text = %s\n", string);
}
```

179. *Pass scalar arguments by value when using C interoperability.*

C supports a "call by value" calling sequence where a copy of scalar arguments is passed to the called procedure (see Rule 54). In the example in Rule 177, showing a program written in C calling a subroutine written in Fortran, the Fortran code is generating, and passing, pointers to data_array, array_size, and direction as the call-by-value arguments. On the C side, the pointers need to be dereferenced by the code. For simple scalar arguments, it may be desirable to pass the values themselves, rather than pointers. Fortran supports the **value** attribute to allow this. Here is the Fortran interface and C prototype using value arguments:

```fortran
subroutine Fortran_FFT (data_array, array_size, &
    direction) bind (C, name='Fortran_FFT')
  use iso_c_binding, only: C_DOUBLE_COMPLEX, &
    C_INT, C_CHAR
  implicit none

  ! assumed size array (*) must be used with C.
  complex (kind=C_DOUBLE_COMPLEX), intent(in out), :: &
    data_array(*)
  integer (kind=C_INT), intent(in), value :: &
    array_size
  character(kind=C_CHAR), intent(in), value :: direction
end subroutine Fortran_FFT
```

In the prototype the array_size and direction arguments would not be pointers.

```c
void Fortran_FFT (double _Complex *data_array,
  int array_size, char direction);
```

This method has two advantages: simplicity – a pointer does not need to be generated, and dereferencing is not required; safety – the called procedure operates solely on its own copy of the argument. It does not modify the caller's argument.

180. *Design out potential "buffer overrun" problems.*

With C interoperability, array arguments must be declared as assumed-size; assumed-shape arrays cannot be used. There is no built-in mechanism for passing the number of elements in the array. If the array possesses the **intent** (**out**) or the **intent** (**in out**) attribute, that is, one to whose elements values will be assigned, relying on an array that is "big enough" without knowing the exact size of the array can be problematic. The program may inadvertently write beyond the last element, an event called a "buffer overrun." To avoid this problem, always pass in a separate argument the size of the array. That way, you can write code to prevent this from taking place. Here is an interface that has the **bind(C)** attribute. The elements of the array argument buffer will be assigned in readstring . The length of buffer is passed in argument buf_len so that code that monitors the assignments to the elements of buffer can be written in readstring.

```
subroutine readstring (buffer , buf_len , at_end)  &
    bind (C, name='readstring')
  use iso_c_binding , only :: C_CHAR, C_INT, C_BOOL
  implicit none
  character(kind=C_CHAR), intent(in out) :: buffer(*)
  integer (kind=C_INT ), intent(in), value :: buf_len
  logical (kind=C_BOOL), intent(out), value :: at_end
end subroutine readstring
end interface
```

181. *Use* **extern "C"** *in C++ files to allow interoperability with Fortran.*

The C++ programming language (Reference [73]) is mostly a super-set of C. It supports many advanced features, including full object-oriented capabilities, exception handling, and templates (a method for writing generic code). Fortran only supports interoperability with the C subset of C++. With limitations, however, interoperability between C++ and Fortran is possible.

Due to the characteristics of C++, and the system by which procedures are assigned names, called "name mangling," you should use the **extern** "C" reserved word to specify that C is the style of external naming within the block of code associated with it.

A second standard feature that assists in the process is the __cplusplus macro that is built into the preprocessor. By using this macro, the C++ **extern** "C" capability may be used during C++ compilations, and ignored during C compilations. This allows one header file to serve both compilation styles:

```
#if !defined (FORTRAN_FFT_H)
#define FORTRAN_FFT_H

#if defined (__cplusplus)
```

```
extern "C" {
#endif

void Fortran_FFT (double _Complex *array, &
  int array_size, char direction);

#if defined (__cplusplus)
}
#endif
```

182. *Do not throw C++ exceptions through Fortran procedures.*

When using the C interoperability, the C++ exception handling capability should not be used. While it may be possible to use exception handling within the confines of the C++ code itself, throwing an exception that requires unwinding the call stack through a Fortran-compiled routine may cause problems. In particular, automatic and allocatable arrays may not be deallocated, and final procedures may not be invoked. (A similar situation exists with **setjmp** and **longjmp** in C code.)

15.

Updating Old Programs

Over the years, the Fortran standards committee has striven to keep each new standard backward-compatible with previous releases. Fortran is one of the oldest high-level languages; much old code is still in use. The committee has admirably succeeded, and programmers have known that they could continue to write programs that contained old features and that they could add features of the new standards whenever it was convenient, useful, or appropriate. Each new standard has marked only a few old features as "obsolescent," defined as "A feature that is considered redundant but that is still in frequent use." Those so marked in one standard may be "deleted" in a subsequent one. The standard describes a "deleted" feature as "A feature in a previous Fortran standard that is considered to have been redundant and largely unused." This chapter describes many of these old features and the new ones provided by the modern Fortran standards (meaning from Fortran 90 and on) that you can use to replace them. We note the status of the each old feature. For further details, see the appropriate language standard: Fortran 90, Reference [40]; Fortran 95: Reference [42]; Fortran 2003, Reference [39]; and Fortran 2008, Reference [43].

15.1 Statements

183. *Replace* common *blocks with modules.*

In FORTRAN 66 and FORTRAN 77, programmers stored global data in **common** blocks. A program could have one unnamed **common** block and any number of named blocks. Here is an example of the latter:

```
INTEGER NNODES
PARAMETER (NNODES = 100)
DOUBLE PRECISION DPOS(NNODES)
INTEGER NODEID(NNODES)
COMMON /NODES/ DPOS, NODEID
SAVE /NODES/
```

For ease of maintenance, the normal practice was to place such code in a separate file and then to use an **include** statement to embed it in all program units that needed access to it. Because **include** was not standardized until Fortran 90, preprocessing was commonly used for compilers that did not support it. If the previous code was in a file called NODECOM.COM, you would see statements such as this in program units:

```
INCLUDE 'NODECOM.COM'
```

Blank common was indicated by either two consecutive forward slashes (//) or by no slashes:

```
COMMON // A, B, D
  . . .
COMMON A, B, D
```

Starting with Fortran 90, all **common** blocks should be replaced with modules. The following is a module equivalent for the data in **COMMON** block NODES. You access this module in every program unit that requires access to the variables with the **use** statement.

```
module node_common_mod
  implicit none

  integer, parameter :: NNODES  = 100
  integer, parameter :: WORK_PREC = &
     selected_real_kind (15, 307)
  integer, save :: node_id (NNODES)
  real (WORK_PREC), save :: d_pos (NNODES)
end module node_common_mod
```

If you are charged with updating an old program containing common blocks, the first step is to ensure that all occurrences of each common block are the same in every program unit. To accomplish that, place each common block in a separate file, remove all cases where common blocks are explicitly entered in the code and replace all such cases with **include** statements. Recognizing that common blocks may be placed inside modules, the next step is to copy each named common block into its own module. Then **use** this module in every program unit where the common block is used and eliminate the corresponding **include** statement.

```
module node_common_mod
  implicit none

  INTEGER NNODES
  PARAMETER (NNODES = 100)
  DOUBLE PRECISION D_POS (NNODES)
  INTEGER NODE_ID (NNODES)
  COMMON /NODES/ D_POS, NODE_ID
  SAVE /NODES/
end module node_common_mod
```

The final steps are to remove the **common** and **save** statements from the module and then to rewrite the code as shown previously.

184. *Remove* block data *program units. Use initializers with module scope data.*

To initialize variables in **common** blocks, you would use **block data** program units (see Rule 183).

```
BLOCK DATA EC
    INTEGER NOCOEF
    PARAMETER (NOCOEF = 14)
    REAL ECOEFS(NOCOEF)
    COMMON /COEFS/ ECOEFS
    DATA ECOEFS /NOCOEF * 0.0/
END BLOCK DATA EC
```

When the variables are defined at module scope, normal initializers may be used, thereby making **block data** unnecessary:

```
module coefs_mod
  implicit none

  integer, parameter :: NUM_COEFFICIENTS = 14
  real :: ecoefs(NUM_COEFFICIENTS) = 0.0
end module coefs_mod
```

185. *Replace multiple* entry *point procedures with separate module procedures that can share data scope.*

The **entry** statement, as its name implies, provided an alternative entry point into a procedure. If you used two or more separate subroutines instead of one subroutine with entry points, you most likely would have needed to define data entities multiple times. With **entry** statements in a subroutine, you would define entities such as local variables and possibly dummy arguments only once. All code would have access to any entities that had the **save** attribute. Sections of code in the procedure could be shared, while others could be skipped during execution.

In this following example, you would call subroutine CALSLO if you needed to check the size of the argument NEWDAT and to call the subroutine DATCHK (not shown); otherwise, you called the entry point CALFST. The subroutine PDAT (not shown) processes the data.

Listing 15.1: SUBROUTINE CALSLO

```
SUBROUTINE CALSLO (NEWDAT, N, RETERR)
    IMPLICIT NONE

    INTEGER N
    REAL     NEWDAT(N)
```

```
        INTEGER RETERR

        INTEGER MAXDAT
        PARAMETER (MAXDAT = 200)
        LOGICAL DATOK
        REAL HISDAT(MAXDAT)
        SAVE HISDAT

        RETERR = 0

C       CHECK INPUT
        IF (N .GT. MAXDAT) THEN
          RETERR = 1
          GO TO 90
        END IF

C       CHECK AGAINST HISDAT.
        CALL DATCHK (NEWDAT, N, HISDAT, DATOK)
        IF (.NOT. DATOK) THEN
          RETERR = 2
          GO TO 90
        END IF

        GO TO 10

        ENTRY CALFST (NEWDAT, N)

C       PROCESS NEWDAT
10      CALL PDAT (NEWDAT, HISDAT)

90      CONTINUE
        END SUBROUTINE
```

To replace **entry** statements, you could create a module. Declare the variables that have the **save** attribute before the **contains** statement. This makes their scope the entire module as shown in the next example. One way to convert the code is to write two distinct module subprograms:

Listing 15.2:   Module data_mod

```
module Data_mod
  implicit none

  integer, parameter :: MAX_DAT = 200
  real, save :: hisdat(MAX_DAT)

    ! return codes.
  enum, bind(C)
```

```fortran
    enumerator  ::  CALSLO_SUCCESS = 0,  CALSLO_BAD_SIZE,  &
        CALSLO_BAD_DATA
  end enum

    ! Declare a generic interface to both routines.
  interface Calc_dat
    module procedure Calslo, Calfst
  end interface Calc_dat
contains

  subroutine Calslo (newdat, reterr)
    real,     intent (in out) :: newdat(:)
    integer,  intent (out) :: reterr

    logical :: datok

    reterr = CALSLO_SUCCESS

      ! check array size; process and report errors.
    if (size (newdat) > MAX_DAT) then
      reterr = CALSLO_BAD_SIZE
    else
      call Datchk (newdat, datok)
      if (.not. datok) then
        reterr = CALSLO_BAD_DATA
      else
        call Calfst(newdat)
      end if
    end if
  end subroutine Calslo

  subroutine Calfst (newdat)
    real, intent (in out) :: newdat(:)

    call Pdat (newdat, hisdat)
  end subroutine Calfst
end module Data_mod
```

As an alternative to breaking the procedure into two separate ones, you could use a single procedure, add a variable to its argument list, and branch to the appropriate code based on its value.

The Fortran 2008 standard degrades the **ENTRY** statement to be an obsolescent feature.

186. *Replace alternate returns with structured code.*

The alternate return feature allowed you to specify that, on return from a subroutine, program execution branch to a specific labeled statement instead of proceeding normally with the next sequential executable one. You could accomplish this by specifying labels, preceded by an asterisk, as actual arguments in the subroutine call. In the called procedure, the dummy arguments corresponding to the labels were indicated with asterisks. You specified the label of the branch desired on return using the **return** statement followed by an integer indicating the ordinal position of the alternate return, that is, the statement **return** 1 caused the program to branch to the first alternate return label, **return** 2 to the second, and so forth. As an example, here, in outline form, is a call to a subroutine with alternate return arguments:

```
        CALL INTSCT (ORIG, VECT, PLANE, INTPNT,
      +    *100, *200)
        GO TO 500


100     CONTINUE
        CALL LOGERR ("Intersect: parallel")
        GO TO 500


200     CONTINUE
        CALL LOGERR ("Intersect: no intersect")

C          CONTINUING NORMAL EXECUTION
500     CONTINUE

        SUBROUTINE INTSCT (PT, VEC, PLANE, INTER, *, *)
        REAL PT(3), VEC(3), PLANE (3, 3), INTER(3)
        INTEGER CALSTA

        CALL PARLEL (PT, VEC, PLANE, CALSTA)

C          ! RETURN AND BRANCH TO LABEL 100
        IF (CALSTA /= 0) RETURN 1

        CALL CALINT (PT, VEC, PLANE, INTER, CALSTA)
C          ! RETURN AND BRANCH TO LABEL 200
        IF (CALSTA /= 0) RETURN 2

C          ! RETURN TO NORMAL EXECUTION
        RETURN
        END SUBROUTINE
```

You can easily replace alternate returns by returning an integer variable from the called subroutine and then use a **select case** construct to execute the desired code:

```
enum, bind(C)
   enumerator :: PARAL = 1, NO_INTERSECT
end enum
```

```
call Intersect (orig, vect, plane, intpnt, return_stat)
select case (return_stat)
case (PARAL)
  call Log_error ("Intersect: parallel")
case (NO_INTERSECT)
  call Log_error ("Intersect: no intersect")
case default
  ...normal execution
end select
```

The alternate return feature was first designated an obsolescent feature in Fortran 90, and it remains one in both Fortran 2003 and Fortran 2008.

187. *Replace arithmetic* if *statements with* case *or block* if *constructs.*

The arithmetic if statement specified three different branches for the continuation of program execution. It accomplished this with three statement labels that corresponded to the location to which the program would branch if the value of a numeric expression was less than, was equal to, or was greater than 0.

```
         IF (INT (x)) 10, 20, 30
10         PRINT *, "left hemisphere"
           GO TO 40
20         PRINT *, "near axis"
           GO TO 40
30         PRINT *, "RIGHT HEMISPHERE"
40         CONTINUE
```

Use instead an if−elseif−else−endif or select case construct

```
if (abs (x) < epsilon) then
  print *, "near axis"
else if (x < 0.0) then
  print *, "left hemisphere"
else
  print *, "right hemisphere"
end if
```

The Fortran 90 standard declared the arithmetic if statement an obsolescent feature; both the Fortran 2003 and the Fortran 2008 standards continue to do so.

188. *Replace computed* GOTO *statements with* case *constructs.*

You could use the computed GOTO statement to branch to different parts of a program according to the value of an integer expression.

```
         DO 100 I = 1, NELEMS
            NCOLOR = INT ( (TEMP(I)/MAXTMP) * 3.0 ) + 1
```

```
            NCOLOR = MIN0 (MAX0 (NCOLOR, 1), 3)
            GO TO (10, 30, 50), NCOLOR
   10       COLOR( I ) = BLACK
            GO TO 100
   30       COLOR( I ) = GREEN
            GO TO 100
   50       COLOR( I ) = RED
            GO TO 100
  100 CONTINUE
```

The most logical replacement for this feature is the **select case** construct.

```
do i = 1, number_of_elements
  n_color = int ( (temp(i) / max_temp) * 3.0 ) + 1
  n_color = min (max (n_color, 1), 3)
  select case (n_color)
  case (1)
    color(i) = BLACK
  case (2)
    color(i) = GREEN
  case (3:)
    color(i) = RED
  case default
  end select
end do
```

This feature was first declared an obsolescent one in the Fortran 95 standard and continues to be so in the standard for both Fortran 2003 and Fortran 2008.

189. *Replace assigned* GOTO *with structured constructs.*

The assigned **GOTO** statement allowed you to assign a label number to an integer variable and then to branch to that label from a particular form of the **GOTO** statement.

```
      INTEGER ISTAGE, FAIL_PHASE_1, FAIL_PHASE_2,
     +   SUCCESS
      PARAMETER (FAIL_PHASE_1=20, FAIL_PHASE_2=30,
     +   SUCCESS=100)
      ASSIGN SUCCESS TO ISTAGE

      CALL PHASE1 (N, DAT, RETVAL)
      IF (RETVAL .NE. 0) THEN
        ASSIGN FAIL_PHASE_1 TO ISTAGE
        GO TO 10
      END IF

      CALL PHASE2 (N, DAT, RETVAL)
      IF (RETVAL .NE. 0) THEN
```

```
        ASSIGN FAIL_PHASE_2 TO ISTAGE
        GO TO 10
      END IF

  10 GO TO ISTAGE (FAIL_PHASE_1, FAIL_PHASE_2,
    + SUCCESS)

  20   PRINT *, "PHASE1 failed"
       PRINT *, "no recovery"
       GO TO 100

  30   PRINT *, "PHASE2 failed"
       PRINT *, "use PHAS3A"
       CALL PHAS3A (N, DAT)
       GO TO 100
 100 CONTINUE
```

As shown in the following short example, you can use a **select case** construct in place of this feature.

```
enum, bind(C)
  enumerator :: FAIL_PHASE_1 = 1, FAIL_PHASE_2
end enum
istage = 0
call Phase1 (n, dat, retval)
if (retval /= 0) then
  istage = FAIL_PHASE_1
else
  call Phase2 (n, dat, retval)
  if (retval /= 0) istage = FAIL_PHASE_2
end if

select case (istage)
case (FAIL_PHASE_1)
  print *, "Phase1 failed"
  print *, "no recovery"
case (FAIL_PHASE_2)
  print *, "Phase2 failed"
  print *, "use Phas3a"
  call Phas3a (n, dat)
case default
end select
```

In cases where the assigned **GOTO** was used to emulate internal procedures, simply use internal procedures.

The Fortran 90 standard declared this feature an obsolescent one; beginning with the Fortran 95, it has been a deleted feature.

190. *Replace statement functions with internal procedures.*

Statement functions were a single-line of code, an assignment that accepted arguments, performed a calculation, and returned a value. You needed to place them in a program unit after the specification statements, but before the executable ones.

Here, as an example, is the code to calculate the local curvature of a curve, given the first and the second derivatives of its *y*-coordinate with respect to its *x*-coordinate:

```
CURV (YP,YPP) = YPP / ((1.0 + YP * YP) *
+                      SQRT (1.0 + YP * YP) )
```

Throughout the program unit, you could refer to the function in this manner:

```
LCURV = CURV (DER1, DER2)
```

To replace a statement function, write an internal function.

```
subroutine Some_subroutine ()
   ...
   lcurv = ... curv (der1, der2)
   ...
contains
   function curv (yp, ypp) result (ret_val)
      real, intent (in) :: yp, ypp
      real :: ret_val

      ret_val = ypp / ( (1.0 + yp * yp) * &
          sqrt (1.0 + yp * yp) )
   end function curv
end subroutine Some_subroutine
```

From the Fortran 95 standard on, statement functions have been an obsolescent feature.

191. *Replace* PAUSE *statements with normal I/O and* stop *statements.*

You could use the **PAUSE** statement to suspend the execution of a program. It then waited for operator intervention in some processor-defined way.

```
PAUSE 'REMOVE TAPE 1, MOUNT TAPE 2'
```

This capability was rarely used. The standards committee declared it an obsolescent feature beginning with FORTRAN 77 and a deleted one beginning with Fortran 95. If needed, you can accomplish the same end by writing a statement to standard output and reading from standard input:

```
character (len=1) :: temp_char
write (*, "(a)", advance = "no") &
    "Terminate operation?(Y/N):"
read (*, *) temp_char
```

192. *Use the* character *(length-selector) form to declare all character variables, arrays, and named constants.*

Two old forms of declaring a variable, an array, or a named constant of intrinsic type character exist. You could specify the number of characters by appending an asterisk and the number to the keyword **CHARACTER**, or to the variable itself:

```
CHARACTER*80 FILE_LINE , ERROR_MESSAGE*40
```

Instead, declare character data objects like this:

```
character(len=80) :: file_line
character(len=40) :: error_message
```

193. *Replace* double precision *or any other type declaration that explicitly specifies the storage size, with* kind *specifications.*

The standard requires that the processor provide two distinct floating-point intrinsic data types. One corresponds to the specification **real**; the second is of greater precision, and you can use the specification **double precision** to specify it. There was also a manner in which the exponent letter D replaced the exponent letter E, to express a literal constant of the corresponding precision. An example would be 1.0D0. Typically, a **real** type occupied four eight-bit bytes of memory, and the **double precision** type twice as much (see Section 13.1).

In addition to this specification, which was, and still is, part of the standard, compiler vendors often added the capability of declaring the type of floating point, integer, and logical data objects by appending an asterisk followed by the number of bytes to the type specification. This method is not standard but is widely supported. Here are declarations for a two-byte integer, a one-byte logical, and a **double precision** real variable:

```
INTEGER*2 ICOUNT
LOGICAL*1 GOODNO
REAL*8    VELOC
```

You should not use these statements to declare data objects. Rule 170 contains the rules for establishing the precision of data objects using the intrinsic functions **selected_real_kind** and **selected_int_kind** .

194. *Do not use* real *or* double precision *do variables.*

FORTRAN 77 permitted floating-point variables to be used as the do variable in do loops.

```
REAL A, TURB, MAT(100,20)
DO 100 A = 0.0, 1.0, 0.000001
   CALL CALTUR (MAT,INP ,A,TURB)
100 CONTINUE
```

Rounding errors can cause an unintended number of iterations to be executed. This code should now be written as follows:

```
real      :: a, turb, mat(100,20)
integer :: i
do i = 0, 1000000
   a = real (i * 0.000001, kind (a))
   call CalTur (mat, inp, a, turb)
end do
```

The standards committee made the use of floating-point variables as do variables an obsolescent feature in Fortran 90.

15.2 Techniques

195. *Replace Hollerith constants with* character *data type.*

Prior to FORTRAN 77, there was no **character** data type. Numeric variables, usually integers, were used to hold fields of characters. Hollerith constants were "typeless" constants that could be used in a **DATA** statement to initialize a numeric variable with characters. Because of the differences in integer sizes on different computer systems, a numeric variable could hold anywhere from two to ten characters. This led to portability problems. The following assumes a computer with four characters per integer:

```
      INTEGER HELLO(3)
      DATA HELLO/4HHELL,4HO WO,4HRLD./
      . . .
      WRITE (6,100) HELLO
  100 FORMAT (3A4)
```

Replace this with:

```
character(12) :: hello = 'hello world.'
. . .
write (*, '(a)') hello
```

Hollerith constants were also allowed as actual arguments in procedure calls. An array was used as a dummy argument:

```
      CALL PRINTR (3, 12HHELLO WORLD.)
      . . .
      SUBROUTINE PRINTR (NWORDS, STRING)
      INTEGER NWORDS, STRING(NWORDS)
```

Replace this with:

```
call printer ('hello world')
. . .
subroutine printer (string)
   character(*), intent(in) :: string
```

The previous example illustrates that in larger programs where integer variables containing Hollerith data are being passed between procedures, such as through argument lists or **common** blocks, interfaces are being changed. Because of this, a stepwise approach must be made to code conversion. It is recommended that all procedures first be placed into modules, and **common** blocks converted to module form (see Rule 183). Then, as variables are converted to **character**, the compiler will quickly be able to find any problem areas when checking subprocedure interfaces.

196. *Replace Hollerith,* H, *edit descriptors with quoted strings.*

Prior to Fortran 77, the H edit descriptor was the only method to describe character strings. Here's an example in a **format** statement:

```
        WRITE (6, 10100) ATOM
10100 FORMAT (5X, 5HATOM:, 1X, A4, A2)
```

This technique was already declared an obsolescent feature in FORTRAN 77, and the H format descriptor has been a deleted feature starting with Fortran 95. Use either single or double apostrophes as the descriptor for character strings.

```
write (*, "(5x, 2a)") 'Atom: ', atom
```

197. *Do not branch to an* end if *statement from outside its block.*

The following code, with the branch to a labeled **end if** statement, was permitted in Fortran 77:

```
      IF (SHADE) THEN
        . . .
        IF (HIDDEN (X, Y)) GO TO 100
          GO TO 50
        END IF
 50     IF (XMIN .LE. X .AND X .LE. XMAX) THEN
          IF (YMIN .LE. Y .AND. Y .LE. YMAX)
     +      CALL SHADING (X, Y)
100     END IF
```

You can quickly replace this by adding a labeled **continue** statement immediately after the **end if** and branching to it instead (see also Rule 100).

This technique was declared obsolescent in Fortran 90, and further downgraded to a deleted feature beginning with Fortran 95.

198. *Replace nonblock* do *constructs with block versions.*

A nonblock **do** construct is a **do** construct that either shares a terminal statement with another **do** construct or terminates in an action statement instead of in a **continue** statement. Here are two examples, one of each type:

```
   DO 50 J = 1, NCOLS
     DO 50 I = 1, NCOLS
       A(I, J) = A(I, J) * B(I)
50 CONTINUE

   SUM = 0
   DO 50 I = 1, NNODES
50   SUM = SUM + A(I)
```

Since the Fortran 90 standard, this technique has been obsolescent. Use a block **do** construct, with its paired **do** and **end do** statements, in place of the nonblock form.

15.3 Nonstandard Features

This subsection describes several capabilities that were introduced by specific compiler vendors to overcome limitations in earlier versions of Fortran. They were never part of any standard. When encountered, they should be replaced with standard conforming code.

199. *Replace all* decode *and* encode *statements with* read *and* write *statements using internal files.*

The encode statement transferred data from internal, that is, binary, form to character form. The decode statement did the reverse. Here's an example of the latter:

```
   CHARACTER*8 CH
   REAL X,Y
   DATA CH/'12.513.3'/
   DECODE(8, 900, CH) X, Y
   PRINT (*, 910) 'X = ', X, ', Y = ', Y

900   FORMAT(2F4.1)
910   FORMAT(2(A, F4.1))
```

The first argument, here 8, in the DECODE statement is the number of characters in the third argument, CH. The label of the **FORMAT** statement, 900, is the second argument. The transfer is from the character variable to the two real variables as the **FORMAT** statement specifies. The variables X and Y would have the values 12.5 and 13.3 after the program executed the DECODE statement; therefore, it would print:

X = 12.5, Y = 13.3

Use the **read** statement with internal files to transfer data:

```
character (len=8) :: ch
real :: x, y
...
```

```
ch = "12.513.3"
read (ch, "(2F4.1)") x, y
```

Here is an example of the encode statement:

```
INTEGER I, J, ISAVE, JSAVE
CHARACTER*8 ICH
ENCODE (8, 900, ICH) ISAVE, ',', JSAVE
WRITE (*, 910) 'NEG. ELEMENT, ROW, COL:', ICH
```

```
900 FORMAT (I3, A1, I3)
910 FORMAT (23A, 8A)
```

The first argument for ENCODE is the number of bytes to transfer. Here it is 8 representing two four-byte integers. The second argument is the format label, and the third argument is the recipient of the data transfer. A typical line of output would appear as follows:

```
NEG. ELEMENT, ROW, COL:140,130
```

Use the **write** statements with internal files to transfer data. Here the previous code that used the encode statement is replaced by a **write** statement to an internal file.

```
integer :: i, j
character(len=4) :: ich(2)

write (ich(1), "(i3)") i
write (ich(2), "(i3)") j
write (*, "(a)") "Neg. element, row: " // &
    adjustr (ich(1)) // ", col: " // adjustr (ich(2))
```

200. *Replace the* BYTE *data declarations with the appropriate integer kind.*

The nonstandard BYTE data type could be used to define a single-byte integer. In its place use the **selected_int_kind** instrinsic function to declare a named constant for this type of data (see Rule 170):

```
! old byte data type
BYTE INT_BYTE
```

```
! use instead
integer, parameter :: &
    BYTE_INTEGER = selected_int_kind (2)
...
integer (kind=BYTE_INTEGER) :: int_byte
```

201. *Replace structures, records, unions, and maps with derived types.*

STRUCTURESs and RECORDs, along with UNIONs and MAPs, constituted a nonstandard form of data structure whereby heterogeneous data types could be referred to, and manipulated by name. Structures and records could be nested. A typical structure could look like this:

```
C         DEFINE STRUCTURE EMPLOYEE
          STRUCTURE /EMPLOYEE/
              CHARACTER*20 LASTNAME, FIRSTNAME
              INTEGER SSNUMBER
              LOGICAL SALARIED
          END STRUCTURE
          . . .
C         ARRAY OF EMPLOYEES
          RECORD /EMPLOYEE/ EMPLOYEES(1000), WORKER

C         REFER TO EMPLOYEE LAST NAME
          I = 20
          WORKER = EMPLOYEES(I)
          WRITE (*, 100) 'NO.:', I, 'NAME:', WORKER.LASTNAME
100       FORMAT (A, I5, A, A20)
```

Derived types should be used instead of structures:

```
type employee_t
  character(:), allocatable :: last_name, first_name
  integer :: ss_number
  logical :: salaried
end type employee_t
. . .
type (employee_t) :: employees(1000)
i = 20
write (*, "(A, I0, A)") "no.:, "i, "name:", &
    employees(i)%last_name
```

Unions, containing maps, created a specific area of data that could then be referred to, as indicated previously, by name. However, the map areas within the union are "overlaid" with one another to conserve storage. In this sense, unions are much like **equivalence**. For example, in the following, component REAL_1 is overlaid with INT_1, and REAL_2 is overlaid with INT_2:

```
          STRUCTURE REALINT
              UNION
                  MAP
                      REAL REAL_1, REAL_2
                  END MAP
                  MAP
                      INTEGER INT_1, INT_2
```

END MAP
  END UNION
    END STRUCTURE

There are no direct replacements for unions. One possibility when converting to standard derived types is to simply not overlay the data components. A second possiblity is to define and use extended types:

```
type realint_t
end type realint_t

type, extends(realint_t) :: realint_real_t
  real :: real_1, real_2
end type realint_real_t

type, extends(realint_t) :: realint_int_t
  integer :: integer_1, integer_2
end type realint_int_t
```

202. *Replace integer pointers with* allocatable *arrays.*

Integer pointers are a nonstandard technique for basing an array to a user-specified area of memory. The **pointer** statement incorporates two pieces of data: a "pointer" name that is used to set the base address of the array, and the "pointee" array it is associated with.

Integer pointers were generally used with nonstandard allocation procedures simply to provide a dynamic memory allocation capability. In many cases, the code can be modified to use **allocatable** arrays, along with the **allocate** statement. For example, the following uses a nonstandard allocator called "MALLOC." In the following declaration, PARRAY is the pointer and contains an integer address; the rank-1 array ARRAY is the pointee:

```
REAL ARRAY(1)
POINTER (PARRAY, ARRAY)
EXTERNAL MALLOC
INTEGER MALLOC
...
PARRAY = MALLOC (1234*4)
```

In modern Fortran, you should use Fortran **allocatable** arrays:

```
real, allocatable :: array(:)
...
allocate (array(1234))
```

When allocation mechanisms outside the Fortran standard are needed, such as the need to reference data in a shared memory area, the **c_f_pointer** intrinsic subroutine in intrinsic module **iso_c_binding** may be useful (see Rule 177).

Appendix A

Source Code

A.1 Type_bound_demo

Listing 1.1: Program Type_bound_demo

```
module Pt2d_mod

! Purpose: Module for type Pt2d_t

  implicit none
  private
  public :: operator (==)

  type, public :: pt2d_t
    private
    real :: x = 0.0, y = 0.0
  contains
    procedure :: Get_len => Comp_dist
    procedure :: Get_coord
    procedure :: Get_xy_coord_pair
    procedure :: Print_pt
    procedure :: Set => Set_coords

    generic :: Get => Get_xy_coord_pair, Get_coord
    generic :: Print => Print_pt
  end type pt2d_t

    ! *Cmnt-1: Argument parameter for calls to
    ! Get_coord.
  type, public :: coord_spec_t
    integer :: coord
  end type coord_spec_t

  type (coord_spec_t), public, parameter :: &
      X_COORD = coord_spec_t (1), &
      Y_COORD = coord_spec_t (2)

  interface operator (==)
    module procedure Coord_spec_eq
  end interface
```

```fortran
     character(*), parameter :: &
         MOD_HEAD = "Callee: Module pt2d_mod: ", FA = "(A)"
contains

   function Coord_spec_eq (this, that) result (ret_eql)
     type (coord_spec_t), intent (in) :: this, that
     logical :: ret_eql

     ret_eql = this%coord == that%coord
   end function Coord_spec_eq

   function Comp_dist (pt_1, pt_2) result (ret_val)

     ! *Cmnt-4: overridden for some instances in
     ! module pt3d_mod. See *Cmnt-5
     class (pt2d_t), intent (in) :: pt_1, pt_2
     real ( kind (pt_1%x) ) :: ret_val
     real ( kind (pt_1%x) ) :: x_dist, y_dist

     write ( *, FA) MOD_HEAD // "Comp_dist"
     x_dist = pt_1%x - pt_2%x
     y_dist = pt_1%y - pt_2%y
     ret_val = sqrt ((x_dist ** 2) + (y_dist ** 2))
   end function Comp_dist

   function Get_coord (this, mold) result (ret_val)
     class (pt2d_t),          intent (in) :: this
     type (coord_spec_t), intent (in) :: mold
     real ( kind (this%x) ) :: ret_val

     write (*, FA) MOD_HEAD // "Get_coord"

     ! *Cmnt-3 select case cannot be used with derived
     ! types. see *Cmnt-2 for alternative.
     select case (mold%coord)
     case (1)
       ret_val = this%x
     case (2)
       ret_val = this%y
     case default
       ret_val = 0.0
     end select
   end function Get_coord

   function Get_xy_coord_pair (this) result (ret_val)
     class (pt2d_t), intent (in) :: this
     real ( kind (this%x) ) :: ret_val(2)
```

```fortran
      write (*, FA) MOD_HEAD // "Get_xy_coord_pair"
      ret_val = [this%x, this%y]
    end function Get_xy_coord_pair

    subroutine Print_pt (this)
      class (pt2d_t), intent (in) :: this

      write (*, FA, advance="no") MOD_HEAD // "Print_pt:"
      write (*, "(2(A, G8.3))") " x: ", this%x, "y: ", &
          this%y
    end subroutine Print_pt

    subroutine Set_coords (this, coords)
      class (pt2d_t), intent (in out) :: this
      real (kind (this%x)), intent (in) :: coords(:)

      write (*, FA) MOD_HEAD // "Set_coords"
      this%x = coords(1)
      this%y = coords(2)
    end subroutine Set_coords

end module Pt2d_mod

module Pt3d_mod

! Purpose: Module for type pt3d_t

  use Pt2d_mod, only : coord_spec_t, pt2d_t, &
      X_COORD, Y_COORD, operator (==)
  implicit none
  private

  type, public, extends(pt2d_t) :: pt3d_t
    private
    real :: z = 0.0
  contains
    procedure :: Get_coord
    procedure :: Get_len => Comp_dist
    procedure :: Print_pt
    procedure :: Set => Set_coords
  end type pt3d_t

  type (coord_spec_t), public, parameter :: &
          Z_COORD = coord_spec_t (3)

  character(*), parameter :: &
      MOD_HEAD = "Callee: Module pt3d_mod: ", FA = "(A)"
```

```
contains

    function Comp_dist (pt_1, pt_2) result (ret_val)

        ! *Cmnt-5: overrides some cases in module
        ! Pt2d_mod.
        ! See *Cmnt-4
      class (pt3d_t), intent (in) :: pt_1
      class (pt2d_t), intent (in) :: pt_2
      real ( kind (pt_1%z) ) :: ret_val
      real ( kind (pt_1%z) ):: x_dist, y_dist, z_dist

      write (*, FA) MOD_HEAD // "Comp_dist"
      select type (pt_1)
      type is (pt3d_t)
        select type (pt_2)
        type is (pt3d_t)
          associate (pt1 => pt_1%pt2d_t, &
            pt2 => pt_2%pt2d_t)
            x_dist = pt1%Get (X_COORD) - pt2%Get (X_COORD)
            y_dist = pt1%Get (Y_COORD) - pt2%Get (Y_COORD)
            z_dist = pt_1%z - pt_2%z
          end associate
        end select
      end select
      ret_val = sqrt ((x_dist ** 2) + (y_dist ** 2) + &
        (z_dist ** 2))
    end function Comp_dist

    function Get_coord (this, mold) result (ret_val)
      class (pt3d_t), intent (in)       :: this
      type (coord_spec_t), intent (in) :: mold
      real ( kind (this%z) ) :: ret_val

      write (*, FA) MOD_HEAD // "Get_coord"
      select type (this)

        ! *Cmnt-2: alternative to select case. See *Cmnt-3
      type is (pt3d_t)
        if (mold == X_COORD .or. mold == Y_COORD) then
          associate (pt2d => this%pt2d_t)
            ret_val = pt2d%Get (mold)
          end associate
        else if (mold ==Z_COORD) then
          ret_val = this%z
        end if
      end select
```

```fortran
  end function Get_coord

  subroutine Print_pt (this)
    class (pt3d_t), intent (in) :: this

    write (*, FA) MOD_HEAD // "Print_pt"
    select type (this)
    type is (pt3d_t)
      associate (pt_2d => this%pt2d_t)
        call pt_2d%Print ()
      end associate
    end select
    write (*, FA, advance="no") MOD_HEAD // "Print_pt:"
    write (*, "(A, G8.3)") " z: ", this%z
  end subroutine Print_pt

  subroutine Set_coords (this, coords)
    class (pt3d_t), intent (in out) :: this
    real ( kind (this%z) ), intent (in) :: coords(:)

    write (*, FA) MOD_HEAD // "Set_coords"
    select type (this)
    type is (pt3d_t)
      associate (pt_2d => this%pt2d_t)
        call pt_2d%Set (coords)
        this%z = coords(3)
      end associate
    end select
  end subroutine Set_coords

end module Pt3d_mod

program Type_bound_demo

  use Pt2d_mod, only : pt2d_t, Y_COORD
  use Pt3d_mod, only : pt3d_t, Z_COORD
  implicit none

  type (pt2d_t), target      :: pt_2d
  type (pt3d_t), target      :: pt_3d
  class (pt2d_t), pointer     :: poly_pntr
  class (pt2d_t), allocatable :: poly_alloc_var

  integer :: alloc_stat
  real, allocatable :: point_pair(:)
  real :: coordinate_value
```

```fortran
    character (*), parameter :: FA = "(A)", &
        FG14_BLANK = "(A, 2G14.7, /, A)"

! Part I: Inheritance

call pt_2d%Set ( [1.0, 2.0] )
point_pair = pt_2d%Get ()
write (*, FG14_BLANK) &
    "Result: point_pair (pt_2d) x/y: ", point_pair, ""

call pt_3d%Set ( [11.0, 12.0, 13.0] )

    ! *Cmnt-8: Generic call.
point_pair = pt_3d%Get ()
write (*, FG14_BLANK) &
    "Result: point_pair (pt_2d) x/y: ", point_pair, ""

coordinate_value = pt_2d%Get (Y_COORD)
write (*, FG14_BLANK) &
    "Result: coordinate_value", coordinate_value, ""
coordinate_value = pt_2d%Get (Z_COORD)
write (*, FG14_BLANK) &
    "Result: coordinate_value", coordinate_value, ""

coordinate_value = pt_3d%Get (Y_COORD)
write (*, FG14_BLANK) &
    "Result: coordinate_value", coordinate_value, ""
coordinate_value = pt_3d%Get (Z_COORD)
write (*, FG14_BLANK) &
    "Result: coordinate_value", coordinate_value, ""
coordinate_value = pt_3d%pt2d_t%Get (Y_COORD)
write (*, FG14_BLANK) &
    "Result: coordinate_value", coordinate_value, ""

! Part II: Polymorphism

poly_pntr => pt_2d
call poly_pntr%Print
write (*, FA) ""
nullify (poly_pntr)

poly_pntr => pt_3d
call poly_pntr%Print
write (*, FA) ""
nullify (poly_pntr)

    ! *Cmnt-6: sourced allocation
```

```fortran
    allocate (poly_alloc_var, source=pt_2d, &
      stat=alloc_stat)
    if (alloc_stat /= 0) then
      stop "allocation problem"
    else
      call poly_alloc_var%Print
      write (*, FA) ""
      deallocate (poly_alloc_var, stat=alloc_stat)
      if (alloc_stat /= 0) &
        stop "deallocation problem, Demo "
    end if

    ! *Cmnt-7: sourced allocation
    allocate (poly_alloc_var, source=pt_3d, &
      stat=alloc_stat)
    if (alloc_stat /= 0) then
      stop "allocation problem"
    else
      call poly_alloc_var%Print
      write (*, FA) ""
      deallocate (poly_alloc_var, stat=alloc_stat)
      if (alloc_stat /= 0) &
        stop "deallocation problem, Demo "
    end if
end program Type_bound_demo
```

A.2 Unlimited_demo

Listing 1.2: Program Unlimited_demo

```fortran
module Base_object_mod

  ! Purpose: A module defining an abstract type that
  ! every derived type is extended from.

  implicit none
  private

  type, abstract, public :: base_object_t
  contains
    procedure (Print_type), deferred :: Print
  end type base_object_t

  abstract interface
    subroutine Print_type (this)
```

```fortran
        import :: base_object_t
        class (base_object_t), intent (in) :: this
      end subroutine Print_type
  end interface
end module Base_object_mod

module Base_node_mod
  use Base_object_mod , only : base_object_t
  implicit none
  private

  type, extends (base_object_t), public :: base_node_t

    ! *Cmnt-2: Unlimited polymorphic entity
    class (*), allocatable :: object
    type (base_node_t), pointer :: next_node => null ()
  contains
    procedure :: Get   => Get_object
    procedure :: Print => Print_object
    procedure :: Put   => Put_object
  end type base_node_t
contains

  subroutine Get_object (this , object)

    ! Purpose: Retrieve the object component.

    class (base_node_t),   intent (in)  :: this
    class (*), intent (out), allocatable :: object
    integer :: alloc_stat

    allocate (object , source=this%object , &
      stat=alloc_stat)
  end subroutine Get_object

  subroutine Print_object (this)
    use Base_object_mod , only : base_object_t

    class (base_node_t), intent (in) :: this

    ! cannot use allocatable deferred-length character
    ! because text is used for internal write
    ! (see *Cmnt-4).
    character (80) :: text
    character (*), parameter :: FA = " (A)"
    logical :: print_txt
```

```fortran
      ! obj required because this%object is a component
        ! not a variable
      ! *Cmnt-5: select both derived and intrinsic types
    print_txt = .true.
    select type (obj => this%object)
    class is (base_object_t)
      call obj%Print
      print_txt = .false.

      ! not all intrinsic types required by standard are
        ! listed
    type is (real)

        ! *Cmnt-4: Internal write to fixed-length
        ! character variable text.
      write (text, "(A, F0.8)") "real: ", obj
    type is (integer)
      write (text, "(A, I0)") "integer: ", obj
    type is (complex)
      write (text, "(A, 2(F0.8, 1x))") "complex: ", obj
    type is (character(*))
      write (text, FA) "character: " // trim (obj)
    class default
      write (text, FA) "indeterminate type"
    end select
    if (print_txt) write (*, FA) trim (text)
  end subroutine Print_object

  subroutine Put_object (this, object)
    class (base_node_t), intent (in out) :: this
    class (*), intent (in) :: object
    integer :: alloc_stat

      ! *Cmnt-3: Fortran 2008: this%object = object
    allocate (this%object, source=object, &
      stat=alloc_stat)
  end subroutine Put_object

end module Base_node_mod

module Base_stack_mod

  ! Purpose: A stack data structure.

  ! Notes
  ! ======
  ! Implemented as a single-linked list.
```

```
! Component top is the beginning of the list.
! Component bottom is the end of the list.
! Items are pushed onto and popped off the top of the
! stack.

use Base_node_mod,    only : base_node_t
use Base_object_mod,  only : base_object_t

implicit none
private
public :: BASE_OP_SUCCESS

type, public, extends (base_object_t) :: base_stack_t
  private
  integer :: number_of_nodes = 0
  character (:), allocatable   :: name
  type (base_node_t), pointer :: top => null (), &
      bottom => null ()
contains
  procedure :: Count_stack_no
  procedure :: Count_stack_str
  procedure :: Empty    => Empty_stack
  procedure :: Get      => Get_stack
  procedure :: Pop      => Pop_stack
  procedure :: Print    => Print_stack
  procedure :: Print_stack_status
  procedure :: Push     => Push_stack
  generic :: Count => Count_stack_no, Count_stack_str
  final :: Destroy
end type Base_stack_t

enum, bind(C)
  enumerator :: BASE_OP_SUCCESS = 0, BASE_OP_FAIL, &
      BASE_ALLOC_ERROR, BASE_BAD_DATA
end enum

character (*), parameter :: FA = "(A)", &
    F_TXT_BLANK = "(A, /, A)"

contains
  function Count_stack_no (this, mold)
    result (ret_no_of_nodes)
    class (base_stack_t), intent (in) :: this
    integer, intent (in) :: mold
    integer :: ret_no_of_nodes

    ret_no_of_nodes = this%number_of_nodes
```

```fortran
end function Count_stack_no

function Count_stack_str (this, mold) result (ret_str)
  class (base_stack_t), intent (in) :: this
  character, intent (in) :: mold
  character (:), allocatable :: ret_str

  character (len=80) :: local_str
  write (local_str, "(I0)") this%Count (1)
  ret_str = trim (local_str)
end function Count_stack_str

subroutine Destroy (this)

  ! *Cmnt-1: Finalizer, using recursion.

  type (base_stack_t), intent (in out) :: this

  type (base_node_t), pointer :: traverse_ptr
  integer :: call_stat

  call_stat    = BASE_OP_SUCCESS

  if (.not. this%Empty () ) then

      ! initiate recursive destruction of nodes
    traverse_ptr => this%top
    call Destroy_worker (traverse_ptr, call_stat)
  else
    write (*, F_TXT_BLANK) "Stack is empty.", ""
  end if

    ! clean up
  if (call_stat == BASE_OP_SUCCESS) then
    this%number_of_nodes = 0
    nullify (this%top)
    nullify (this%bottom)
  end if
contains

  recursive subroutine Destroy_worker (current_ptr, &
      return_stat)

      ! Note that return_stat is intent (in out) to
      ! allow retention of a failure at any call.
    type (base_node_t), intent (in out), pointer :: &
      current_ptr
```

```fortran
      integer, intent (in out) :: return_stat
      integer :: dealloc_stat
      logical :: last_node

        ! recursive calls to the bottom of the stack
      if (associated (current_ptr%next_node) ) then
        last_node = .false.
        call Destroy_worker (current_ptr%next_node, &
            return_stat)
      else

          ! deallocate the bottom
        last_node = .true.
        deallocate (current_ptr, stat=dealloc_stat)
        if (dealloc_stat /= 0) then
          return_stat = BASE_ALLOC_ERROR
        else
          return_stat = BASE_OP_SUCCESS
        end if
      end if

          ! deallocate backing out of recursive calls
      if (.not. last_node) then
        deallocate (current_ptr, stat=dealloc_stat)
        if (dealloc_stat /= 0) then
          return_stat = BASE_ALLOC_ERROR
        else
          return_stat = BASE_OP_SUCCESS
        end if
      end if
    end subroutine Destroy_worker
  end subroutine Destroy

  function Empty_stack (this) result (return_value)
    class (base_stack_t), intent (in) :: this
    logical :: return_value

    return_value = .not. associated (this%top)
  end function Empty_stack

  subroutine Get_stack (this, object)

    ! Purpose: Return the first item (not node) in the
    ! list without removing it.

    class (base_stack_t), intent (in) :: this
    class (*), intent (out), allocatable :: object
```

```fortran
      if (.not. this%Empty () ) then
        call this%top%Get (object)
      else
        write (*, F_TXT_BLANK) "Stack is empty", ""
      end if
end subroutine Get_stack

subroutine Pop_stack (this, return_object, &
    return_stat)

    ! Purpose: Get the top of the stack and remove it.

    class (base_stack_t), intent (in out) :: this
    class (*), intent (out), allocatable :: &
      return_object
    integer, intent (out) :: return_stat

    integer :: alloc_stat
    type (base_node_t), pointer :: node_ptr

    return_stat = BASE_OP_SUCCESS
    stack_status: if (.not. this%Empty ()) then

        ! Get the object. Reassociate top pointer and
          ! deallocate. Decrement node count.
        call this%top%Get (return_object)
        node_ptr => this%top%next_node
        deallocate (this%top, stat=alloc_stat)
        if (alloc_stat == 0) then
          this%top => node_ptr
          this%number_of_nodes = this%number_of_nodes - 1
        else
          return_stat=BASE_ALLOC_ERROR
        end if
      else stack_status
        write (*, F_TXT_BLANK) "Stack is empty.", ""
      end if stack_status
end subroutine Pop_stack

subroutine Print_stack (this)
    class (Base_stack_t), intent (in) :: this
    type (base_node_t), pointer :: traverse_ptr

    integer, parameter :: NODE_CHAR_WID = 15

    character (len=NODE_CHAR_WID) :: node_num
```

```fortran
    integer :: i_nod

    call this%Print_stack_status
    stack_status: if (.not. this%Empty () ) then
      traverse_ptr => this%top
      i_nod = 0
      do
        i_nod = i_nod + 1
        write (node_num, "(A, I0, A)") "Node ", i_nod, &
          " :"
        write (*, FA) trim (node_num) // " "
        call traverse_ptr%Print
        traverse_ptr => traverse_ptr%next_node
        if (associated (traverse_ptr , this%bottom)) then
          write (node_num, "(A, I0, A)") "Node ", &
            i_nod + 1, " :"
          write (*, FA) trim (node_num) // " "
          call traverse_ptr%Print
          exit
        end if
      end do
    else stack_status
      write (*, F_TXT_BLANK) "Stack is empty", ""
    end if stack_status

end subroutine Print_stack

subroutine Print_stack_status (this)
  class (base_stack_t), intent (in) :: this
  character (80) :: text

  write (*, F_TXT_BLANK) "Stack status", &
    "============= "
  if (this%Empty ()) then
    write (text , FA) "Stack is empty"
  else
    write (text , "(A)") " The stack has " // &
      this%Count ('a') // " nodes."
  end if
  write (*, F_TXT_BLANK) trim (text), ""
end subroutine Print_stack_status

subroutine Push_stack (this , object , return_stat)
  class (base_stack_t), intent (in out) :: this
  class (*), intent (in) :: object
  integer, intent (out) :: return_stat
```

```fortran
      integer :: alloc_stat , call_stat
      type ( base_node_t ), pointer :: node_ptr

      call_stat    = 0
      return_stat = BASE_OP_SUCCESS
      stack_status : if ( this%Empty ()) then

          ! Empty stack , use top.
        allocate ( base_node_t :: this%top , &
          stat=alloc_stat )
        if ( alloc_stat == 0) then
          this%bottom => this%top
          nullify ( this%bottom%next_node )
          call this%top%Put ( object )
          call this%top%Print ()
        else
          return_stat = BASE_ALLOC_ERROR
        end if
      else stack_status

          ! use temporary storage node.
        allocate ( base_node_t :: node_ptr , &
          stat=alloc_stat )
        if ( alloc_stat == 0) then
          call node_ptr%Put ( object )
          node_ptr%next_node => this%top
          this%top => node_ptr
          nullify ( this%bottom%next_node )
          call this%top%Print ()
        else
          return_stat = BASE_ALLOC_ERROR
        end if
      end if stack_status

        ! Increment number of nodes.
      if ( return_stat == BASE_OP_SUCCESS ) &
          this%number_of_nodes = this%number_of_nodes + 1
    end subroutine Push_stack

end module Base_stack_mod

module Key_mod
  use Base_object_mod , only : base_object_t
  implicit none
  private

  type , public , extends ( base_object_t ) :: key_t
```

```
      integer  ::  key = 0
      character(:),  allocatable  ::  key_name
   contains
      procedure  ::  Print => Print_key_t
   end type key_t

   character  (*),  parameter  ::  FA = "(A)" , &
        F_TEXT_BLANK = "(A, /, A)"

contains

   subroutine Print_key_t (this)
      class (key_t),  intent (in)  ::  this
      character(80)  ::  text

      write (*, F_TEXT_BLANK) "key_t", "====="
      write (*, "(A, 10)") "key: ", this%key
      if (allocated (this%key_name) ) then
         write (text, FA) "key_name: " // &
             trim (this%key_name)
      else
         write (text, FA) "key_name: unassigned"
      end if
      write (*, F_TEXT_BLANK) trim (text), ""
   end subroutine Print_key_t
end module Key_mod

module Simple_mod
   use Base_object_mod ,  only : base_object_t
   implicit none
   private

   type,  public,  extends (base_object_t)  ::  simple_t
      real     ::  real_comp    = 0.0
      integer  ::  integer_comp = 0
   contains
      procedure  ::  Print => Print_simple_t
   end type simple_t

   character  (*),  parameter  ::  FA = "(A)" , &
        F_TEXT_BLANK = "(A, /, A)"

contains
   subroutine Print_simple_t (this)
      class (simple_t),  intent (in)  ::  this
      character(80)  ::  text
```

```fortran
      write (*, F_TEXT_BLANK) "simple_t", "==========="
      write (text, "(A, T16, F0.8)") "real_comp: ", &
         this%real_comp
      write (*, FA) trim (text)
      write (text, "(A, T16, I0)") "integer_comp: ", &
         this%integer_comp
      write (*, F_TEXT_BLANK) trim (text), ""
   end subroutine Print_simple_t
end module Simple_mod

! Main program

program Unlimited_demo
   use Base_object_mod , only : base_object_t
   use Base_stack_mod , only : base_stack_t
   use Key_mod , only : key_t
   use Simple_mod , only : simple_t
   implicit none

   type (simple_t) :: simple
   type (key_t) :: key
   type (base_stack_t) :: stack
   integer :: call_stat , i_node , integer_value
   real :: real_value
   complex :: cmplx_val
   class (*), allocatable :: object
   character (80) :: text
   character (len=:), allocatable :: char_string

   integer_value = 23
   real_value    = 14.5
   cmplx_val     = cmplx (10.5 , -8.1)
   char_string   = "hello world"
   call stack%Push (simple , call_stat )
   call stack%Push (integer_value , call_stat )
   call stack%Push (key , call_stat )
   call stack%Push (real_value , call_stat )
   call stack%Push (char_string , call_stat )
   call stack%Push (cmplx_val , call_stat )
   call stack%Print

  do i_node = 1, stack%Count (1)
    call stack%Pop (object , call_stat )
    call Print_obj (object )
  end do
  call stack%Print_stack_status
contains
```

```
   subroutine Print_obj (obj)
     class (*), intent (in), allocatable :: obj

     character (*), parameter :: FA = "(A)", &
         F_TXT_BLANK = "(A, /, A)"
     logical :: print_txt

     print_txt = .true.
     select type (obj)
     class is (base_object_t)
       call obj%Print
       print_txt = .false.
     type is (real)
       write (text, "(A, F0.8)") "real: ", obj
     type is (integer)
       write (text, "(A, I0)") "integer: ", obj
     type is (complex)
       write (text, "(A, 2(F0.8, 1x))") "complex: ", obj
     type is (character(*))
       write (text, FA) "character: " // trim (obj)
     class default
       write (text, FA) "Indeterminate type"
     end select
     if (print_txt) write (*, F_TXT_BLANK) trim (text), &
       ""
   end subroutine Print_obj
end program Unlimited_demo
```

The following is the output of the program:

```
simple_t
========
real_comp:     .00000000
integer_comp:  0

integer: 23
key_t
=====
key: 0
key_name: unassigned

real: 14.50000000
character: hello world
complex: 10.50000000 -8.10000038
Stack status
============
```

```
   The stack has 6 nodes.

Node 1:
complex: 10.50000000 -8.10000038
Node 2:
character: hello world
Node 3:
real: 14.50000000
Node 4:
key_t
=====
key: 0
key_name: unassigned

Node 5:
integer: 23
Node 6:
simple_t
========
real_comp:      .00000000
integer_comp:   0

complex: 10.50000000 -8.10000038

character: hello world

real: 14.50000000

key_t
=====
key: 0
key_name: unassigned

integer: 23

simple_t
========
real_comp:      .00000000
integer_comp:   0

Stack status
===========
Stack is empty
```

Appendix B

Rule List

This appendix provides the user with a complete list of all the guidelines contained in the book. They are listed in the order of their appearance and grouped by chapter. The page on which each rule can be found in parentheses following the rule.

Chapter 2. General Principles

1. *Write programs that are clear to both the reader and the compiler.* (3)

2. *Write programs that can be efficiently tested.* (4)

3. *Write programs that will scale to different problem sizes.* (5)

4. *Write code that can be reused.* (6)

5. *Document all code changes, keeping a history of all code revisions.* (6)

Chapter 3. Formatting Conventions

6. *Always use free source form.* (9)

7. *Adopt and use a consistent set of rules for case.* (10)
   7.1 *Use lowercase throughout.* (11)
   7.2 *Capitalize the names of all user-written procedures.* (11)
   7.3 *Write all named constants using uppercase letters.* (12)
   7.4 *Begin the name of all data entities using a lowercase letter.* (12)

8. *Use a consistent number of spaces when indenting code.* (13)

9. *Increase the indentation of the source code every time the data scope changes.* (13)

10. *Indent the block of code statements within all control constructs.* (14)

11. *Indent all the code after a named construct so the name stands out.* (15)

12. *Consider using one indentation for block constructs and a different one for statement continuation.* (15)

13. *Left-justify major documentation blocks; indent short comments the same as the code it describes or one additional indentation level.* (16)

14. *Use all optional white space in keywords.* (17)

15. *Align similar code.* (17)

16. *Consider using white space to differentiate between the use of parentheses to enclose the argument list in calls to subprograms and their use to enclose the index list of arrays.* (19)

17. *Place a space after all commas.* (19)

18. *Do not use "hard" tabs.* (20)

19. *Consider using leading ampersands* (&) *to mark continuation lines.* (20)

20. *Place each program statement on its own line.* (21)

21. *In general, avoid putting comments at the end of lines containing source code.* (21)

22. *Use the symbolic relational operators,* <, <=, /=, ==, >=, >. (22)

23. *Use the square bracket notation,* [ ], *introduced in Fortran 2003, for array constructors.* (22)

24. *Write at least one digit on each side of the decimal point of floating-point literal constants.* (23)

Chapter 4. Naming Conventions

25. *Use detailed names for data objects whose scope is global, less detailed names for those whose scope is a module, and simple but clear names for those whose scope is a single procedure.* (24)

26. *Name user-written procedures using verbs.* (24)

27. *Use a consistent set of verbs throughout to name common procedures.* (25)

   27.1 *Name accessor procedures using either the verb "Set" or "Put" and the verb "Get" followed by the component name.* (25)

   27.2 *Name procedures that traverse data structures using the verbs that are commonly used – "Next, Previous, Pop, Push," and so on.* (26)

   27.3 *Use the same verb for all final procedures followed by the name of the derived type.* (26)

27.4 *Name functions that return a logical result using verbs such as "Is," or "Has." (26)*

28. *Add an identifying tag to all module names. (27)*

29. *Add an identifying tag to all derived type names. (28)*

30. *Consider adding an identifying tag to all pointers. (29)*

31. *Use plural nouns to differentiate arrays from scalars. (30)*

32. *In modules in which a derived type is defined, use either the name "this" or the name "self" for the* pass *argument a in all type-bound procedures and procedure pointer components and for the dummy argument of the type in all module procedures. (30)*

33. *Establish pairs of logical named constants to replace the values of* .true. *and* .false. *in cases where this will clarify the code. (31)*

34. *Consider using a unique name or a limited number of names throughout a program as the names of the value returned by a function. (32)*

35. *Use common names for variables that represent accepted mathematic, scientific, and engineering terms. Spell out the names of quantities whose symbol is not part of the Fortran character set. (33)*

36. *Consider beginning the names of all do, index, and subscript variables using the letters "i" through "n." (33)*

37. *Name all executable construct blocks with a name describing the purpose of the construct. (34)*

38. *Always use optional names on end statements. (35)*

39. *Make liberal use of the* associate *construct. (35)*

Chapter 5. Documentation Conventions

40. *Write self-documenting code. (38)*

41. *Add comments to your code to allow other programmers to understand its purpose. It is especially important to explain what cannot be read from the source text itself. (39)*

42. *Always synchronize the documentation with the code. (41)*

43. *Write a documentation block for every program unit. (41)*

Chapter 6. Programming Principles

44. *Always write standard-conforming code.* (44)

45. *Do not rely on compiler switches that change code semantics.* (44)

46. *Order the statements in modules in a fixed and consistent manner.* (44)

47. *Place data objects that require global accessibility in modules.* (46)

48. *Include a default* private *statement in the specification section of all modules. Provide either public or read-only access to module entities on an as-needed basis.* (47)

49. *Use the* only *option in* use *statements.* (49)

50. *Indicate the intent of all dummy arguments.* (50)

51. *In functions, specify the intent of all dummy arguments as* intent (in). (53)

52. *Whenever possible, write procedures such that they can be prefixed by the* pure *prefix.* (56)

53. *Use caution when specifying derived-type dummy arguments with the* intent (out) *attribute.* (57)

54. *When appropriate, assign the* value *attribute to dummy arguments to allow their values to change without affecting the value of the actual argument.* (60)

55. *Be attentive to the particular standard specifications regarding arguments possessing either the* pointer *or the* target *attribute.* (62)

56. *Be attentive to the particular standard specifications regarding arguments possessing the* target *attribute; do not rely on pointers that become associated with dummy arguments possessing this attribute to retain their value or their association status.* (69)

57. *Consistently place subprogram arguments in the following order:* pass *arguments,* intent (in out) *arguments,* intent (in) *arguments,* intent (out) *arguments,* optional *arguments.* (74)

58. *Assign a default value to all dummy arguments possessing the* optional *attribute.* (77)

59. *Reduce long argument lists by placing arguments in derived types.* (78)

60. *In all calls to subprograms, use the form* dummy-argument-name = actual-argument-name *with all optional arguments.* (79)

Chapter 7. Programming Conventions

79. *Wherever possible, use allocatable variables rather than data pointers.* (103)

80. *Use allocatable deferred-length character strings wherever possible.* (111)

81. *Create simple data structures using derived types with allocatable components.* (113)

82. *Use pointers to create dynamic data structures.* (115)

83. *Use pointers to access array sections and to form arrays of components of nested derived types.* (115)

84. *Use pointers to arrays as dummy arguments when it is necessary to maintain the array bounds of the actual argument.* (116)

85. *When needed, create an array of pointers by defining a supplemental derived type with a single component.* (117)

86. *Avoid assigning an* intent (out) *attribute to a dummy argument that is a derived type containing pointer components.* (117)

87. *Do not use defined assignments for pointer assignment.* (119)

88. *In a hierarchy of derived types containing allocatable components, begin allocation with the component of the parent type and proceed through the hierarchy; deallocate in the reverse order.* (120)

89. *Establish a convention for tracking the owner of a pointer target.* (123)

90. *Use procedure pointers to invoke different subprograms possessing identical interfaces.* (125)

91. *Where possible and appropriate, use the intrinsic function* kind *in conjuction with the instrinsic conversion functions* int, real, *and* cmplx *when converting types.* (128)

92. *Use the Fortran intrinsic functions* lbound *and* ubound *to determine both the lower and upper limits of iterations performed using the* do *construct and both the lower and upper limits of array assignments accomplished using both the* forall *and* where *statements and the* forall *and the* where *constructs.* (131)

93. *Use the intrinsic functions* shape *and* reshape *when initializing arrays of rank 2 or larger.* (132)

94. *When specifying the kind of both subprogram dummy arguments and function results, take advantage of the fact that Fortran knows the kind of a data type.* (132)

95. *Always include the* stat= *option in all* allocate *and* deallocate *statements; always check its value.* (133)

96. *Check the status of allocatable entities using the* allocated *intrinsic function before allocating or deallocating them.* (134)

97. *Write all loops that index arrays of rank 2 or greater such that the innermost (first) rank varies first, then the next most inner loop, and so on.* (134)

98. *Where possible, assign the contiguous attribute to assumed-shape arrays and array pointers to improve performance.* (135)

99. *Code all logical tests that make up the scalar logical expressions of an* if *construct such that they can always be successfully executed.* (136)

100. *Use a single-pass loop to avoid deeply nested constructs.* (136)

101. *For portability, use the lexical comparison functions* llt *,* lle *,* lge *, and* lgt *to compare character strings.* (138)

Chapter 8. Input and Output

102. *Use the named constants in the intrinsic module* iso_fortran_env *.* (140)

103. *Manage unit numbers as a resource.* (141)

104. *Use the optional* iostat= *specifier in all input/output statements to verify that the operation was successful and to control the program flow.* (143)

105. *Use* open *and* close *statements for all data files.* (144)

106. *Use the* inquire *statement for computing direct-access record length.* (145)

107. *When reading or writing arrays, use implied loops only when the storage order needs to be changed from the default.* (146)

108. *Use the same formats and I/O lists when writing, and reading back, a data file.* (146)

109. *Read and write only a single data record in each data transfer statement.* (147)

110. *When writing I/O routines for each derived type, consider using defined derived-type I/O.* (148)

111. *Consider using asynchronous I/O to increase the speed of data transfer.* (150)

112. *Use formatted I/O for human-readable files.* (155)

113. *Use named character constants for frequently used format specifications.* (156)

114. *For infrequently used format specifications, use character literals directly in I/O statements.* (157)

115. *Use internal* read *and* write *statement for converting between character strings and numeric items.* (157)

116. *Use format reversion where possible to simplify format statements.* (159)

117. *Use unformatted I/O when full numerical accuracy needs to be maintained.* (160)

118. *Issue meaningful error messages.* (163)

119. *Use meaningful* stop *statements for error termination.* (163)

Chapter 9. Packaging Conventions

120. *Place each program unit in a separate file.* (165)

121. *Whenever possible, use the module name, the type name, the subprogram name, or the program name as the file name.* (165)

122. *Group the interface blocks for all user-defined external procedures in one or more modules. Use these modules in all procedures where these external procedures are referenced.* (165)

123. *Place the declaration of the dummy arguments of external procedures in a separate file and then include it using an* include *line in the file containing the procedure and every file containing its interface block.* (167)

124. *Use submodules to separate the interfaces of module procedures from their implementations. Specify the interface in the parent module only.* (168)

Chapter 10. Generic Programming

125. *Use parameterized derived types to create generic code.* (172)

126. *Create generic names for related specific procedures.* (173)

127. *Use* optional *arguments to avoid replication.* (176)

128. *Use* elemental *procedures to create rank-insensitive code.* (177)

129. *Use the* result *clause for function return values.* (178)

130. *Use the generic form of intrinsic functions.* (179)

131. *Use a preprocessor to automate generation of generic code via CoCo.* (180)

132. *Use a preprocessor to automate generation of generic code via the C language preprocessor.* (180)

Chapter 11. Object Orientation

133. *Define every derived type in its own module, along with its type-specific procedures.* (184)

134. *Use a unique name for every derived type.* (185)

135. *Declare any data component of a derived type that is not required for computation-intensive calculations to be* private. *Provide access to its components so declared using type-bound accessor procedures.* (186)

136. *Whenever possible, initialize the components of derived types in their definition. Always initialize pointer components to* null *().* (189)

137. *Initialize all derived-type parameters in the definition of parameterized derived types.* (190)

138. *Always use keywords in structure constructors.* (191)

139. *Always use keywords to specify the values of type parameters when declaring parameterized derived types and when initializing them using structure constructors.* (193)

140. *For derived types requiring extensive initialization, consider using user-defined structure constructors.* (193)

141. *For derived types requiring extensive initialization, consider using a defined assignment.* (195)

142. *Write type-bound procedures to implement inheritance and polymorphism.* (197)

143. *Create generic specifications for type-bound bindings that perform similar tasks but have distinct dummy arguments.* (200)

144. *Use procedure pointer components to invoke different subprograms possessing identical interfaces.* (201)

145. *For debugging purposes, for every derived type, write a type-bound procedure that prints its components.* (204)

146. *Write type-bound subroutines for defined assignments.* (204)

147. *Provide a final subroutine for all derived types that have pointer components or that require special handling when they cease to exist.* (205)

148. *Be aware of the situations where finalization occurs.* (207)

149. *Use type inclusion for Has-A relationships and type extension for Is-A relationships.* (208)

150. *Provide an abstract base object type for the application.* (210)

151. *Provide a concrete base object type for the application.* (211)

152. *Do not confuse the meaning of a derived data type, keyword* type, *with the meaning of a polymorphic variable, keyword* class. (213)

153. *Use sourced allocation to allocate polymorphic variables.* (213)

154. *Exploit inheritance and polymorphic dummy arguments to write generic code.* (214)

155. *Use the* select *type construct to dynamically dispatch polymorphic data objects to the appropriate type-bound procedure.* (214)

156. *Use unlimited polymorphic variables to create data structures containing heterogeneous data types.* (215)

Chapter 12. Parallel Processing

157. *Tune programs to run correctly and as quickly and efficiently as possible as a single thread program running on a single processor before rewriting them for parallel processing.* (217)

158. *Estimate the performance improvement that can be realized using parallel programming methods.* (217)

159. *Determine the hardware configuration on which the application will run.* (219)

160. *Use built-in Fortran data parallelism to replace simple loops that can execute in parallel.* (221)

161. *Use the OpenMP API to create sections of code that execute in parallel.* (228)

162. *Use* default (none) *for all parallel regions.* (231)

163. *Minimize shared variable locking and usage for best scalability.* (231)

164. *Use MPI to create multiple instruction, multiple data programs that execute in parallel.* (233)

165. *Write an MPI communicator module to tailor its use to the application.* (238)

166. *Minimize the use of communications and barriers.* (241)

167. *Avoid conditional use of synchronization.* (242)

168. *Use the* do concurrent *statement to write loops that execute in parallel.* (242)

169. *Use coarrays to write programs that execute in parallel.* (243)

Chapter 13. Data Types, Numerical Operations, and Floating-Point Numbers

170. *Based on application numerical requirements, and using Fortran instrinsic functions such as* selected_int_kind *and* selected_real_kind, *establish a set of integer-named constants that correspond to the kind type parameters needed. Place them all in a single module, and use these constants in the definition of program data objects.* (248)

171. *Never write code depending upon floating-point equality.* (250)

172. *Write code that performs floating-point operations in a manner that reduces rounding errors.* (251)

173. *Avoid performing floating-point operations involving numbers of widely different orders of magnitude.* (253)

174. *Use the capabilities of intrinsic modules* IEEE_exceptions, IEEE_arithmetic, *and* IEEE_features *to trap floating-point exceptions.* (253)

175. *Use high-level bit manipulation.* (258)

176. *Avoid unwanted data conversion problems.* (259)

Chapter 14. C Interoperability

177. *Use Fortran's C interoperability capabilities to interact with C programs.* (262)

178. *Pass Fortran character arguments to C as length-1, character arrays with a final element of C_CHAR_NULL.* (267)

179. *Pass scalar arguments by value when using C interoperability.* (268)

180. *Design out potential "buffer overrun" problems.* (269)

181. *Use* extern *"*C *" in* C++ *files to allow interoperability with Fortran.* (269)

182. *Do not throw* C++ *exceptions through Fortran procedures.* (270)

Chapter 15. Updating Old Programs

183. *Replace* common *blocks with modules.* (271)

184. *Remove* block data *program units. Use initializers with module scope data.* (273)

185. *Replace multiple* entry *point procedures with separate module procedures that can share data scope.* (273)

186. *Replace alternate returns with structured code.* (275)

187. *Replace arithmetic* if *statements with* case *or* block if *constructs.* (277)

188. *Replace computed* GOTO *statements with* case *constructs.* (277)

189. *Replace assigned* GOTO *with structured constructs.* (278)

190. *Replace statement functions with internal procedures.* (280)

191. *Replace* PAUSE *statements with normal I/O and* stop *statements.* (280)

192. *Use the* character (*length-selector*) *form to declare all character variables, arrays, and named constants.* (281)

193. *Replace* double precision *or any other type declaration that explicitly specifies the storage size, with* kind *specifications.* (281)

194. *Do not use* real *or* double precision *do variables.* (281)

195. *Replace Hollerith constants with* character *data type.* (282)

196. *Replace Hollerith,* H, *edit descriptors with quoted strings.* (283)

197. *Do not branch to an* end if *statement from outside its block.* (283)

198. *Replace nonblock* do *constructs with block versions.* (283)

199. *Replace all* decode *and* encode *statements with* read *and* write *statements using internal files.* (284)

200. *Replace the* BYTE *data declarations with the appropriate integer kind.* (285)

201. *Replace structures, records, unions, and maps with derived types.* (286)

202. *Replace integer pointers with* allocatable *arrays.* (287)

Bibliography

[1] Adams, Jeanne C., Walter S. Brainerd, Richard A. Hendrickson, Richard E. Maine, Jeanne T. Martin, and Brian T. Smith. *The Fortran 2003 Handbook: The Complete Syntax, Features and Procedures*. Springer, 2009.

[2] Adams, Jeanne C., Walter S. Brainerd, Jeanne T. Martin, Brian T. Smith, and Jerrold L. Wagener. *Fortran 95 Handbook: Complete ISO/ANSI Reference*. Cambridge, MA: The MIT Press, 1997.

[3] Adams, Jeanne C., Walter S. Brainerd, Jeanne T. Martin, Brian T. Smith, and Jerrold L. Wagener. *Fortran 90 Handbook: Complete ISO/ANSI Reference*. New York: Intertext Publications, The McGraw Hill Book Company, 1992.

[4] Akin, Ed. *Object-Oriented Programming via Fortran 90/95*. Cambridge, United Kingdom: Cambridge University Press, 2003.

[5] Anderson, E., Z. Bai, C. Bischof, J. Demmel, J. Dongarra, J. Du Croz, A. Greenbaum, S. Hammarling, A. McKenney, S. Ostrouchov, and D. Sorensen. *LAPACK User's Guide*. 2nd ed. Philadelphia: Society for Industrial and Applied Mathematics, 1995.

[6] Amdahl, Gene. "Validity of the Single Processor Approach to Achieving Large-Scale Computing Capabilities." AFIPS Conference Proceedings, no. 30 (1967): 483–485.

[7] Blelloch, Guy E. *Vector Models for Data-Parallel Computing*. Cambridge, MA: MIT Press, 1990.

[8] Budd, Timothy. *An Introduction to Object-Oriented Programming*. 3rd ed. Boston: Pearson Education, Inc., 2002.

[9] Baldwin, Kenneth, Andrew Gray, and Trevor Misfeldt. *The Elements of C# Style*. New York: Cambridge University Press, 2006.

[10] Brainerd, Walter S., Charles H. Goldberg, and Jeanne C. Adams. *Programmer's Guide to Fortran 90*. 3rd ed. New York: Springer-Verlag, 1996.

[11] Chandra, Rohit, Dagum Leonardo, Dave Kohr, Dror Maydan, Jeff McDonald, and Ramesh Menon. *Parallel Programming in OpenMP*. San Diego, CA: Academic Press, 2001.

[12] Chapman, Stephen J. *Fortran 95/2003 for Scientists and Engineers*. 3rd ed. New York: McGraw-Hill, 2008.

[13] Chapman, Barbara, Gabriele Jost, and Ruud Van Der Pas. *Using OpenMP: Portable Shared Memory Parallel Programming.* Cambridge, MA: MIT Press, 2008.

[14] Clerman, Norman S. "Fortran 90 'Gotcha!' (variation on a theme)." Fortran Forum, Association for Computing Machinery, 18, no. 3, December 1999.

[15] Clerman, Norman S. "Notes on creating an array of procedure pointers." Fortran Forum, Association for Computing Machinery, 28, no. 1, April 2009.

[16] Concurrent Versions System, http://www.nongnu.org/cvs.

[17] Decyk, Victor K., Charles D. Norton, and Boleslaw K. Szymanski. "Fortran 90 'Gotchas' (Part 1)." Fortran Forum, Association for Computing Machinery, 18, no. 2, August 1999.

[18] Decyk, Victor K., and Charles D. Norton. "Fortran 90 'Gotchas' (Part 3)." Fortran Forum, Association for Computing Machinery, 19, no. 1, April 2000.

[19] Program coco, Purple Sage Computing, Inc., http://users.erols.com/dnagle/coco.html.

[20] Dongarra, J. J., C. B. Moler, J. R. Bunch, and G. W. Stewart. *LINPACK: Users' Guide.* Philadelphia, PA: Society for Industrial and Applied Mathematics, 1979.

[21] Dorn, William S., and Daniel D. McCracken. *Numerical Methods with Fortran IV Case Studies.* New York: John Wiley & Sons, Inc., 1972.

[22] Dowd, Kevin, and Charles Severance. *High Performance Computing.* 2nd ed. Sebastopol, CA: O'Reilly & Associates, Inc., 1998.

[23] Earth System Modeling Framework, http://www.earthsystemmodeling.org. ESMF_KeywordEnforcer arguments were based on a suggestion by Alan Wallcraft of the Noval Research Laboratories.

[24] Ellis, T. M. R., and Ivor R. Philips. *Programming in F.* Harlow, England: Addison Wesley Longman, Limited, 1998.

[25] Goldberg, David. "What Every Computer Scientist Should Know About Floating Point Arithmetic." ACM Computing Surveys, 23, no. 1 (1991): 5–48.

[26] Gropp, William, Ewing Lusk, and Rajeev Thakur. *Using MPI-2: Portable Parallel Programming with the Message-Passing Interface.* Cambridge, MA: MIT Press, 1999.

[27] Gropp, William, Ewing Lusk, and Anthony Skjellum. *Using MPI-2: Portable Parallel Programming with the Message-Passing Interface.* 2nd ed. Cambridge, MA: MIT Press, 1999.

[28] Harbison, Samuel P., and Guy L. Steele Jr. *C – A Reference Manual.* 5th ed. Upper Saddle River, NJ: Prentice Hall, 2002.

[29] Hughes, Charles E., Charles P. Pfleeger, and Lawrence L. Rose. *Advanced Programming Techniques: A Second Course in Programming Using FORTRAN*. New York: John Wiley & Sons, 1978.

[30] *ISO/IEC TR 15580:2001(E), Information technology – Programming languages – Fortran – Floating-point exception handling*. ISO/IEC JTC 1/SC 22/WG 5, 2001.

[31] *ISO/IEC/JTC/SC 22 SO/IEC TR 15581:1999(E), Information technology – Programming languages – Fortran – Enhanced data type facilities*. 2nd ed. 2000.

[32] *ISO/IEC/JTC/SC 22 SO/IEC TR 19767:2005, Information technology – Programming languages – Fortran – Enhanced Module Facilities*. 2005.

[33] *Binary floating-point arithmetic for microprocessor systems*. IEC 60669 (1989-01).

[34] *ISO/IEC 7942-1: Information technology – Computer graphics and image processing – Graphical Kernal System (GKS) – Part 1: Functional Description*. 2nd ed. 1994.

[35] *ISO 8651-1 Information processing systems – Computer graphics – Graphical Kernal System (GKS) language bindings – Part 1: FORTRAN*. 1988.

[36] *ISO/IEC 8651-4 Information technology – Computer graphics – Graphical Kernal System (GKS) language bindings – Part 4: C*. 2nd ed. 1995.

[37] *ISO 9241 – Ergonomics of Human System Interaction*. Geneva, Switzerland: International Standards Organization.

[38] *ISO/IEC 9899:1999 (C99)*. Geneva, Swizerland: International Standards Organization.

[39] *ISO/IEC 1539-1:2004 Information technology – Programming languages – Fortran – Part 1: Base language*. 2nd ed. 2004.

[40] *ISO/IEC 1539:1991 Information technology – Programming languages – Fortran*. 2nd ed. 1991.

[41] f90gl, Fortran bindings for OpenGL. http://math.nist.gov/f90gl.

[42] *ISO/IEC 1539-1:1997 Information technology – Programming languages – Fortran – Part 1: Base language*. 1997.

[43] *ISO/IEC JTC1/SC22/WG5/N1723 J3/08-007r2* March 2008.

[44] Hatton, Les. Fortran, C, or C++ for geophysical development. *Journal of Seismic Exploration*, January 1992.

[45] Kernigan, B., and P. Plauger. *The Elements of Programming Style*. 2nd ed. New York: McGraw-Hill, 1978.

[46] Kernighan, Brian W., and Dennis M. Ritchie. *The C Programming Language*. 2nd ed. Englewood Cliffs, NJ: Prentice-Hall, 1988.

[47] Kit, Edward. *Software Testing in the Real World: Improving the Process*. ACM Press, 1995.

[48] Koelbel, Charles H., David B. Loveman, Robert S. Schreiber, Guy L. Steele Jr., and Mary E. Zosel. *The High Performance Fortran Handbook*. Cambridge, MA: MIT Press, 1994.

[49] McVoy, Larry, and Carl Staelin. http://www.bitmover.com/lmbench.

[50] LAM/MPI parallel computing. http://www.lam-mpi.org/.

[51] Mattson, Timothy G., Beverly A. Sanders, and Berna L. Massingill. *Patterns for Parallel Programming*. Boston, MA: Pearson Education, Inc., 2005.

[52] McConnell, Steve. *Code Complete*. Redmond, WA: Microsoft Press, 1993.

[53] McConnell, Steve. *Code Complete*. 2nd ed. Redmond, WA: Microsoft Press, 2004.

[54] Metcalf, Michael, and John Reid. *The F Programming Language*. New York: Oxford University Press, 1996.

[55] Metcalf, Michael, John Reid, and Malcolm Cohen. *Fortran 95/2003 Explained*. Oxford, United Kingdom: Oxford University Press, 2004.

[56] Metcalf, Michael. *Effective FORTRAN 77*. Oxford, United Kingdom: Oxford University Press, Reprint with corrections, 1986.

[57] Misfeldt, Trevor, Gregory Bumgardner, and Andrew Gray. *The Elements of C++ Style*. New York: Cambridge University Press, 2004.

[58] MPICH – a portable implementation of MPI. http://www-unix.mcs.anl.gov/mpi/mpich.

[59] netcdf, A Network Common Data Format. http://www.unidata.ucar.edu/software/netcdf.

[60] Netlib Repository at UTK and ORNL. http://www.netlib.org.

[61] Oliveira, Suely, and David Stewart. *Writing Scientific Software: A Guide to Good Style*. New York: Cambridge University Press, 2006.

[62] OpenMP: Simple, portable, scalable SMP programming. http://www.openmp.org.

[63] *IEEE Std 1003.9-1992 IEEE Standard for Information technology – POSIX FORTRAN 77 Language Interfaces – Part 1: Binding for System Application Interface [API]*. Institute of Electrical and Electronics Engineers, Inc., 1992.

[64] Reid, John. *Coarrays in the next Fortran Standard*. ISO/IEC JTC1/SC22/WG5 N1747, October 31, 2008.

[65] Roark, Raymond J., and Warren C. Young. *Formulas for Stress and Strain*. 5th ed. New York: McGraw-Hill, 1975.

[66] Roberts, Eric. *Thinking Recursively*. New York: John Wiley & Sons, 1984.

[67] Sale, A. H. J. The Classification of FORTRAN Statements. *The Computer Journal* 14, no. 1.

[68] United States Public Law 107–204, *Sarbanes-Oxley Act of 2002.*

[69] Shonkwiler, Ronald W., and Lew Lefton. *An Introduction to Parallel and Vector Scientific Computing.* New York: Cambridge University Press, 2006.

[70] Siever, Ellen, Stephen Figgins, and Aaron Weber. *Linux in a Nutshell: A Desktop Quick Reference.* 4th ed. Sabastopol, CA: O'Reilly Press & Associated, Inc., 2003.

[71] Smith, Alan Jay. *Cache Memories.* ACM Computing Surveys, September 1982.

[72] Steele Jr., Guy L., and W. Daniel Hillis. *Data Parallel Algorithms.* Communications of the ACM, December 1986.

[73] Stroustrup, Bjarne. *The C++ Programming Language.* 3rd ed. Upper Saddle River, NJ: Addison-Wesley, 1997.

[74] Apache Subversion, http://subversion.apache.org/.

[75] Vermeulen, Allan, Scott W. Ambler, Greg Bumgardner, Eldon Metz, Trevor Misfeldt, Jim Shur, and Patrick Thompson. *The Elements of Java Style.* New York: Cambridge University Press, 2000.

[76] von Hagen, William. *The Definitive Guide to GCC.* 2nd ed. Berkeley, CA: Apress, 2006.

[77] Vowels, R. A. *Algorithms and Data Structures in F and Fortran.* Tucson, AZ: Unicomp, 1998.

[78] Zwillinger, Daniel. *Standard Mathematical Tables and Formulae.* 31st ed. Boca Raton, FL: Chapman and Hall/CRC Press LLC, 2003.

Index

Printed in the United States
By Bookmasters